Whistlin' Dixie

A Dictionary of Southern Expressions

Whistlin' Dixie

A DICTIONARY OF SOUTHERN EXPRESSIONS

Robert Hendrickson

Volume I:
Facts On File
Dictionary of
American Regional Expressions

Facts On File
New York

Whistlin' Dixie: A Dictionary of Southern Expressions

Copyright © 1993   by Robert Hendrickson

Facts On File, Inc.
460 Park Avenue South
New York NY 10016
USA

Library of Congress Cataloging-in-Publication Data
Hendrickson, Robert, 1933–
    Whistlin' Dixie : a dictionary of southern expressions / Robert Hendrickson.
        p.   cm. — (Facts On File dictionary of American regional expressions ; v. 1)
    ISBN 0-8160-2110-4 (alk. paper)
    1. English language—Southern States—Terms and phrases.
2. English language—Southern States—Dictionaries.   3. Southern States—Popular culture—Dictionaries.   4. Americanisms—Southern States—Dictionaries.   I. Title.   II. Series.
PE2926.H46   1992
427'975'03—dc20   91-47861

A British CIP catalogue record for this book is available from the British Library.

Facts On File books are available at special discounts when purchased in bulk quantities for businesses, associations, institutions or sales promotions. Please call our Special Sales Department in New York at 212/683-2244 (dial 800/322-8755 except in NY, AK or HI) or in Oxford at 865/728399.

Text and Jacket design by Catherine Hyman
Composition and manufacturing by the Maple-Vail Book Manufacturing Group
Printed in the United States of America

10 9 8 7 6 5 4 3 2 1

This book is printed on acid-free paper.

*For my grandson Andrew
and his mother, Becky,
who is quickest on the drawl.*

On journeys through the States we start . . .
We willing learners of all . . .

Walt Whitman

Acknowledgments ─────────────

I would like to thank here, in addition to the numerous sources mentioned in the introduction and text, a few of the many people, laymen and specialists, who helped me over a period that approaches seven years in researching and writing this book. Words cannot express my debt to my wife Marilyn for her usual help and understanding, which know no bounds. Especially appreciated are the valuable suggestions of my editors Susan Schwartz and Gerry Helferich and those of copy editor Joan Atwood. I am grateful to Bill and Margarite Menard for their hospitality when I visited Marjorie Kinnan Rawlings' Cross Creek country in Florida. My friend Joseph Hallstein provided many of the Gullah expressions recorded here from his researches in the Sea Islands, and I owe special thanks to author Erwin Lewis for material he sent me, as well as to historian Harmon L. Remmel of Fayetteville, Arkansas. I'd also like to single out Lauren Walsh, Heidi Rosenbaum, Becky Hendrickson, Ed Lowman and Tony Kafeiti. Yet so many Southern folk with so many varied Southern voices helped me in my travels from Baltimore to Key West, from Charleston to Houston, that I can really offer only a blanket thank you to y'all, adding that all the accolades about Southern hospitality are true.

Introduction ————————————

*W*histlin' Dixie is the first in a series of Facts On File books on American regional expressions and is to my best knowledge the only extensive collection of Southern regional expressions published (possibly the only full-length book on the subject), though I am equally sure that it is far from complete and I welcome contributions for future editions. In trying to write a book for the general reader that is fun to read yet reliable, I am indebted to numerous general scholarly works, including, among many others, John Russell Bartlett's *Dictionary of Americanisms,* the *American Dialect Dictionary,* John Farmer's *Americanisms, The Oxford English Dictionary, Webster's Third New International Dictionary, The Random House Dictionary of the English Language,* H. L. Mencken's *The American Language,* the *Dictionary of American Regional English* (only a small part of which has been published at this writing) and Mitford M. Mathews' *A Dictionary of Americanisms on Historical Principles,* which was invaluable for checking the many Southern historical expressions I have included where I thought they were edifying or entertaining, even if obsolete today. Other important sources include newspapers and magazines, such as *Dialect Notes* and *American Speech,* past and present, Southern correspondents kind enough to supply me with material, and personal experience of colorful words and expressions while my wife Marilyn and I traveled in the South. To save space these sources are noted after individual entries when necessary. The same applies to the many quotations from Southern writers, ranging from Thomas Jefferson, Joel Chandler Harris, Sidney Lanier and Jonathan Daniels to excellent recent books by Pat Conroy, Calder Willingham, Larry Brown, Pete Dexter and Peter Matthiessen, author of *Killing Mr. Watson* (1990), though Mr. Matthiessen, despite his skill with the dialect, is not a writer born to the South. My greatest pleasure in writing this book has in fact been the opportunity to read again the complete works of Mark Twain, George Washington Cable, William Faulkner, Flannery O'Connor, Erskine Caldwell, Robert Penn Warren, Eudora Welty and so many other great Southern writers, not only for the Southernisms I've found but for the little known masterpieces (such as Erskine Caldwell's never anthologized "Joe Craddock's Old Woman") I've stumbled upon and the great passages I've come to understand better on close rereading. I recommend the experience to everyone.

I should add that in addition to the current and historical Southern-fried expressions collected here, I've included a good number of unique Southern pronunciations, though, as Mr. Mason may have told Mr. Dixon, a line has to be drawn somewhere and I've had to hold these to a minimum for want of time and space. As important, humorous or unusual as such pronunciations may be, they would require at least another volume to do justice to them. ("You-all," for example, took a full page to attempt to explain.) I think I can safely say that I've turned up a number of Southernisms that haven't been published before in book form, not to mention a great number of stories real and apocryphal about the origins of Southern expressions. Finally, I must advise that I did not appoint myself a censor to eliminate terms that are in "bad taste" in a work that ranges from the days of slavery to modern times.

Southerners were proud of their accents and distinctive verbal expressions even before that fiery statesman John Randolph of Virginia, known for his sharp, biting soprano tongue on the floors of the House and Senate, actually fought a duel over the pronunciation of a word. But then Randolph of Roanoke was widely known for his eccentricity, which deteriorated to dementia in his later years. Better for an alien without the slightest trace of a Southern accent to contend at the outset that "South Mouth," despite all the fun made of it, is the most charming of American dialects. It is, in the words of the late Anatole Broyard, "an attempt, at least in part, to find and keep the music in the American language, in some cases almost to sing it"— even if there's a lot of unintentional humor in it, too.

There surely is a royal sound to Southern speech at its most eloquent, perhaps because, as one nameless South Georgian says, "It's the closest thang on God's green earth to the King's natchul English." Linguist Lee A. Pederson of Atlanta's Emory University, who specializes in Southern dialects, agrees that there is truth in the anonymous claim. "The North," he says, "was largely settled by immigrants who learned English as a second language and were heavily dependent on the *written* word. Southerners, on the other hand, have always relied on the *spoken* word. In that respect, Southern speech is closer to the native speech of England, and often to Elizabethan England. It is a much more sensitive and effective medium of communication than Northern speech, for the most part, because it is so rooted in the spoken word."

Quite possibly the Southern accent's close links with the King's English made it possible for British actors Vivien Leigh and Leslie Howard to affect such authentic Southern accents in *Gone With the Wind*. In any case, only American mountain, or hill, dialect preserves old English so well as Southern talk, and, though it is treated as a separate dialect in this series, the so-called Ozark accent is often considered a variety of Southern dialect, deriving as it doubtlessly does from the dialect of the southern Appalachians, which, in turn, was brought there from Pennsylvania by Scotch-Irish immigrants.

Southern dialect is extremely varied, and many linguists divide it into smaller dialects. Some experts call these divisions the *Mountain* (or *Hill*), *Plains* and *Coastal* dialects, but others opt for the *Mountain* dialect plus the three classifications below:

- Virginia Tidewater, a pleasing soft dialect with little nasalization that is spoken by the most aristocratic of Southerners and prevails along the coast from the Delaware-Maryland-Virginia peninsula to South Carolina, with speakers found in Charlottesville and Richmond, Virginia, as well as in some northern sections of the Shenandoah Valley.
- South Carolina Low Country, spoken in an area extending from northeastern South Carolina's Pee Dee River to northeastern Florida but found along the river valleys of the Deep South as far inland as Columbia, South Carolina and Augusta, Georgia.
- General Southern Lowland, spoken by more than 60 million people in the Southern lowland (outside the mountains, South Carolina and the Tidewater) and including at least parts of 16 states: Maryland, West Virginia, Delaware, Kentucky, Tennessee, Alabama, Georgia, Florida, Louisiana, Arkansas, Missouri, Mississippi, southern Illinois, southern Ohio, southern Indiana and all but southeast Texas.

In addition, there are the *East Texas* dialect, local dialects with Charleston, Baltimore and New Orleans as focal points and, especially, Southern dialects like *Cajun, Creole, Gumbo, Conch* and *Gullah*, from all of which there are abundant examples here.

Local dialect subspecies thrive in the South. In the *Linguistic Atlas of the Gulf States,* to be published in four or five volumes when completed, some 13 separate Southern dialects are treated. Elsewhere it has been noted that former President Carter's accent isn't merely Southern but Gulf Coastal Plain. What's more, it appears that his home state, Georgia, includes not only the Gulf Coastal Plain dialect but smaller dialects called Carolina Mountain, Alabama-Tennessee Low Country, Northern and Southern Piedmont, Atlantic Coastal Plain and Thomaston-Valdosta.

Charlestonians are particularly proud of their distinctive accent, which they describe as possessing "a smattering of Old English, a sea-island lilt and soft Southern tones." Older Charlestonians are sometimes taken for Britains or Scots. Lord Ashley Cooper, the pen name of Frank Gilbreth, author of *Cheaper by the Dozen* and a columnist for *The News and Courier,* has compiled a pamphlet called *A Dictionary of Charlestonese* "to assist sloppy talkers from other sections of the country to understand Charlestonians." He defines *cholmondely* (pronounced *chumley*) as "the brick thing on a roof that lets out smoke," *ho, ho, ho* as "three ladies of the evening," *poet* as "pour it," *version* as "the kind of queen Elizabeth I was" and *tin sin stow* as "the foive and doyme." When I visited Charleston recently, I heard the name of his newspaper pronounced as *The Newsand Korea!*

The *Cajun* and *Creole* dialects constitute two French dialects spoken in Louisiana *(Loozeeanna)*. The third, *Gumbo,* is also a dialect of the French language rather than English; it was the pidgin French of the blacks who came as slaves to New Orleans from Senegal in colonial times and is spoken by relatively few people today.

Cajun takes its name from *Acadia,* the former French province centered on Nova Scotia, from which the British expelled the Acadians, or Cajuns, in 1755, deporting those who did not pledge allegiance to Britain, about 4,000 of whom settled in the region around St. Martinville in southwestern Louisiana. Deportees were officially designated French, but they were usually called *Acadians,* this word pronounced *Cadian* by 1868 and finally *Cajun.* The sufferings of the expulsion are of course described by Longfellow in *Evangeline* (1847), familiar to generations of American schoolchildren. But the Cajuns endured and soon were maintaining a separate folk culture, including their own dialect, which has been declining in use since the end of World War I, although it is still heard in the area. The Cajuns' name for the dialect they speak is *Bougalie* (bogue talk). *Bogue* and, of course, *bayou* come ultimately from the Choctaw word *bayuk* (creek), which the Creoles and Cajuns got from the local Indians.

The picturesque Cajun dialect retains archaic French forms, and the Cajuns use a great number of French words in their speech, including the common and very useful *oui* (yes), *mais* (but), *mais non!* (no!), *bien* (good), *grand* (tall), *m'sieu* (mister), *demoiselle* (miss), *comment?* (how?), *pardon* (pardon me), *adieu* (goodbye) and *cherie* (dear). Common French phrases heard among these people include *c'est vrai* (it's true), *comme ça* (like that), *la bas* (down there), *il est bon heur* (it is early), *il dit* (he said) and *qu'est-ce c'est?* (what is it?). To such words and phrases are added English, Spanish, German, Indian and American black expressions and inflections accumulated over the years in Cajun country, which primarily includes the Louisiana parishes of Acadia, Evangeline, Allen, Beauregard, Calcasieu, Cameron, Iberia, Jefferson Davis, Lafayette, St. Landry, St. Martin and St. Mary—though Cajun is also spoken in a number of other parish towns from New Orleans to the French Settlement east of the Mississippi in Livingston Parish.

Cajun music and food have a nationwide following today. The music derives from Celtic and country tunes and is very popular on the "crawfish circuit" from New Orleans to Houston. Cajun cooking features dishes like *jambalaya,* the word deriving from the Spanish *jamón* (ham) since this dish was originally made with ham. *Gumbo, crawfish étouffée* and other peppery delights are also part of the cuisine, which has been quite popular in Eastern cities recently.

The original Cajuns were isolated in the south Louisiana bayous, fishing and hunting in their *bateaux,* shallow craft well suited to navigate such backwaters. There the Cajun language developed, from a mixture of old Breton French, English, Spanish and Native American words and at least to some extent from the language of freed black slaves and black Caribbean immigrants who came to work in the area as laborers and sharecroppers.

American black pronunciation is notable in Cajun speech in such words as *aks* (ask), *sho'n-nuf* (sure enough), *ehf* (if), *jis* (just), *haw* (horror), *git* (get), *yoh* (your), *uh* (of) *ayg* (egg) and *uh mehs uh* (a mess of). In this respect Cajun differs from Creole speech, which shows little black influence. The Creoles, descendants of the French who first colonized New Orleans, did not at first associate with blacks and Indians as the more democratic Cajuns did. The word *Creole* comes from the French *creole,* meaning "a native." By the end of the 18th century, however, Creole began to be applied to black slaves of the Creoles as well as to themselves, was next applied to a black person with any French or Spanish blood, then came to mean a native-born black as opposed to a black born in Africa, and by the middle of the 19th century described any Louisianan, with the state of Louisiana dubbed the "Creole State." The word is a confusing one that can be defined only in the context in which it is being used, for creole also means a pidgin language spoken by a second generation of speakers, and in Alaska of the late 1860s it even meant a native of mixed Russian and Indian blood!

Cajun French words are often more colorful than their French counterparts. The French, for example, call the hummingbird an *oiseaumouche* (bird-fly). Good enough, but hardly comparable to the poetic Cajun *susfleur* (upon flower). The French have no name for the white perch, a fish not known in France; the Cajuns call it by the descriptive name *sac-a-lait* (bag of milk).

Cajuns sometimes take American words and make them into something new, imitating the sound of *bacon* with the French *bequine,* for example. A Saturday-night dance in Cajun country is called *fais-dodas,* a rough approximation of one of the French calls in a square dance.

Cajun speakers tend to repeat proper names in sentences, as in "He bring Paul, but Paul, Paul he drown, Paul." What a standard English speaker might call "grammatical errors" also enhance Cajun speech, probably giving it its peculiar flavor more than any other single feature, as these common expressions show:

- For why you ask me?
- He been try make me mad.
- You see ma cow down by bayou, you push him home, yes.
- What for she call?
- He be gone tree day now—yesterday, today and tomorrow.
- I don't got but ten cents, me.

- His horse more better as that.
- She the bestest child.
- Us, we can go.
- I don't see those girl.
- I ain't got noplace to go.
- He don't got no more better boat.

Creole speakers traditionally had more education than Cajuns, and Creole doesn't contain as many grammatical "errors" as Cajun, though there is a tendency in Creole speech to omit auxiliary verbs, as in "She going fall soon" ("She is going to fall soon"), to use the present tense instead of the past ("Who tell you that?") and to use plural for singular verbs ("Those man are coming"), among other peculiarities. Generally, Creole vowel and consonant differences approximate those of Cajun, with several important differences (such as the soft pronunciation of *r*), and the French words and phrases Creole uses are very similar to those used in Cajun. The French accent is heard among some Creole speakers, especially in New Orleans, but Southern-type speakers in Louisiana are mostly free of French influence.

Cajun appears to have given us the local pronunciation of many Louisiana town names, as well as the word *shivaree* for an elaborate noisy celebration, *shivaree* being an alteration of the French *charivari*—a word Cajuns brought to America. The French word means a mock celebration with pots, pans and other noisemakers and originated in medieval times, when it was used to express disapproval of widows who didn't wait long enough to remarry. Creole has also contributed several words to the English vocabulary, including *lagniappe* (pronounced lan-yap), meaning a gift or bonus, the word borrowed from the Spanish *la napa* (gift) and used by New Orleans' Creole merchants for the gifts they gave to customers.

Today, very few young people speak Cajun fluently, and many speak none at all. Traditionally a spoken language and not a written one, it has in recent years become a language of the old, causing a steady erosion of Cajun culture and language. A Cajun textbook published in 1977 by James Donald Faulk of Abbeville, Louisiana, set out to correct this situation. Its good sales have indicated that there is widespread interest among Cajuns to preserve their language and way of life, which has so long resisted assimilation.

Monsignor Jules Daigle, an 85-year-old Roman Catholic priest from Welsh, Louisiana, in late 1984 published the first Cajun dictionary, a 650-page volume that reflects a lifetime of studying the language in the Cajun community he serves. He insists that Cajun is not a poor linguistic relation of French and "is no more a broken language because it contains so much English" than the Roman languages, which combined Latin and other tongues. He appears to believe it his mission to revive the Cajun dialect or language, and while this may not be possible, he will at least have preserved a great part of it that might have been lost. "In my day, when everybody spoke Cajun, you made a mistake and were corrected," he says. "But when people became ashamed to speak Cajun and it was forbidden in the schools, there were fewer and fewer people able to do the correcting . . . It would be a crime against history to let a language [dic] that has existed for 220 years, that has been spoken by millions of Cajuns . . . The Cajun people fused beautifully with the American culture. Because we were so cooperative, our language is almost gone."

The Conchs (pronounced *Conks*) of the Florida Keys speak a Southern American subdialect called *Conch* that is notably different from the rest of the speech of the South and even differs from the dialect of south Floridians, who were called *fly-up-the-creeks* in the mid-19th century (after the popular nickname of the small green heron, *Butoridis virescens,* native to Florida).

Conchs are so named because as the first English fishermen to settle in the Keys they depended on the conch (*Strombus altus,* a spiral-shelled gastropod) for food and even used its giant shell as a trumpet to communicate from shore to ship and from key to key. The descendants of a band of Cockney Englishmen called the Eleutherian Adventurers who migrated from London to Bermuda in about 1649 in search of religious and political freedom, they came to the Florida Keys early in the 19th century from Eleutheria in the Bahamas. Once in the Keys, they made their living from fishing, wrecking and gathering sponges. From the beginning, the Conchs built homes on both sides of Key West and tried to keep separate from other settlers, their close family ties binding them together. Their aloofness helped the Conch dialect last as long as it has. Influenced by Bahamian English, Cuban Spanish and Cockney as well as Southern American and General American dialects, their speech contains words and expressions found nowhere else in the area. A dishcloth, for example, is called a *natural sponge* by the Conchs. Their umbrella is a *bumhershoot,* and a closet in their homes is a *locker.* A Conch stove is a *grits box,* and they regard the pantry as the *kitchen safe.* Conchs call any native of Nassau a *saw.*

In Conch speech, as in Cockney speech, the *w* and *v* are confused, a *vest* becoming a *west* and *visit* becoming *wisit.* An *a* before *g* is pronounced like short *i,* so that *rag* is transformed into *rig* and *bag* into *big.*

The Conchs treat the *h* in the Cockney way, saying *orse* instead of *horse* and pronouncing *hell* as the letter *l.* Other special characteristics are the frequent use of *ain't* instead of *haven't* or *won't* and the omission of *ed* from verb past-tense forms ("The orse jump the fence yesterday").

Spanish idioms tend to be translated literally by the Conchs; *"Cuántos años tiene?"* for example, becomes "How many years you got?", not "How old are you?" They pronounce *i* in the Spanish manner, particularly in the names of people—Olivia becomes *Oleevia* when addressed by a Conch.

Conchs use the *a* of *father* for *ar* in words such as *cigar, park* and *car,* just as Southerners characteristically do but which is also a characteristic of British speech. There are a number of other similarities to Southern talk, just as there are to British and General American dialect features.

Conch talk lives on in the Florida Keys but appears to be slowly disappearing, as is the case with other island languages, including the Ocracoke dialect of the Outer Banks of North Carolina. Recent studies have shown that among younger people, Conch is giving way to Southern and General American English.

Gullah, still another language of the South, is spoken in its purest form by blacks on the Sea Islands off the Georgia-South Carolina coast. Gullah is an example of a kind of Plantation Creole that has survived until today. The Plantation Creole languages of the South were invented by black slaves from the languages of their homelands, the pidgin English used in the slave trade and the varying English dialects of the owners and overseers on their plantations. A good number of Americanisms—including *goober, okra, chiggers, poor Joe* (a heron), *banjo, jazz, voodoo, mumbo jumbo, zombie, cooter* and *yam*—derive from these languages, and less certain claims have been made for many others, including *massa* (master), *dig* (to understand), *hip, jukebox, tote, sweet talk, speak softly and carry a big stick* and even the universally known *OK,* the most American of all words.

The word *Gullah* itself takes its name from either *Ngola* (Angola) or the West African *Gola* tribe. For several centuries the Sea Islands have harbored this language, a tongue foreign to most Americans and one of whose very existence most are still unaware. Because of its geographical isolation, Gullah has escaped much of the eroding influence of American English that has afflicted the mainland communities where it is spoken. Although it was once the prevalent black language of the South's great cotton and rice plantations, the language has contracted and thrives only on these few islands that originally provided optimum conditions for its birth and incubation. Possibly arriving in the Sea Islands directly, instead of from Barbados through the Caribbean route, the slaves who first came there had, at any rate, little acquaintance with English. The heat, dampness and inevitable malaria of the islands discouraged white settlement, so the black population always sharply exceeded the white, and black overseers were commonplace. Unfortunately, today's islands are under siege by those two most formidable foes of tradition—tourist trade and real-estate development. But though Gullah may be doomed to the notebooks and recordings of philologists, it is still spoken to some extent by more than 250,000 people along the southeastern coast from South Carolina to the Florida border, and its vitality echoes from the rhythmic chanting of the flower sellers at Charleston's Four Corners to the rappin' of ghetto youths on the streets of New York. In fact, there are also about 1,000 pure Gullah speakers in New York City, most of them living in Brooklyn's Bedford-Stuyvesant section.

In the past, Gullah (more usually called *Geechee* among its speakers) was for some a source of derision and shame, but for others it has always been and continues to be one of ethnic pride. Beyond all else today, Gullah stands as the living testimony of a people's determination to survive and preserve the linguistic bulwark that had shielded them from the most divisive and dehumanizing conditions.

Though we might question the medical wisdom of "Mumps ain't nuttin' if you can get sardine grease to grease em wid," we have little difficulty understanding what is being said. Gullah appears at first glance to be simply a case of "broken," "poor" or "childish" English. Early scholars, misled by the superficial similarities between the languages and perhaps reluctant to credit blacks with any cultural contribution, conceived of Gullah as a corruption of English. One theory described the language as a simplified form of English that arose by necessity when masters had to communicate with their slaves. Relying on sentences shorn of all but uninflected words in the simplest word order and accompanied by extensive gestures, the master would make known his wishes, and the slaves would accede to his language as well as his commands. This "baby talk" theory gained wide acceptance because it was plausible and because it made the white man, who had lost his political sovereignty after the Civil War, still the linguistic master of any black. Another theory that would have wholly excluded African influence posited a complex system of geographical references according to which every idiosyncrasy of the language was traced to dialects and localisms within England, Wales or Scotland.

Not until midway in our own century did scholars recognize the contribution of African languages to Gullah, for the first speakers of Gullah were also its originators. Born speakers of Bantu, Wolof, Fante, Mandingo, Ewe, Twi, Ibo, Yoruba or another of the hundreds of distinct tongues of West Africa, they forged from this diverse linguistic heritage a unique language. The pioneering studies of the black scholar Lorenzo D. Turner revealed in their comparisons of Gullah and West African languages that the grammatical peculiarities of Gullah are not corruptions of English but an amalgam of forms indigenous to a number of West African dialects. Gullah is not an infant's rendering of English or a random sampling of British dialects but a language whose structure is the outcome of a historical experience in which select aspects of West African dialects adaptable to an English environment merged to form a common grammar and syntax.

Chief among the 28 or so African languages that influenced the development of Gullah are Wolof, spoken on the coastline closest to the United States; Mandingo, spoken by the largest percentage of first-generation blacks to arrive here; Akan, the language of what was formerly known as the Gold Coast; and Hausa, the geographically extensive language of West Africa's interior and a tongue spoken as a second language by many of the smaller tribes.

Turner, in his *Africanisms in the Gullah Dialect* (1949), compiled the first extensive list of African words that were directly loaned to Gullah. Most of these 6,000 or so words were personal names, and many were descriptive of the African zoological or botanical experience. Mandingo gave its word for turtle, *cooter,* and Wolof yielded *banana.* Turner's etymological investigations of the personal names and nicknames of Gullah (such as *Angku,* "boy born on Saturday," or *Betsibi,* "mischievous") revealed more than 4,000 traceable to African personal or proper names. Other African words used in Gullah include common terms like *dafa* (fat) and *bong* (tooth). Many such terms are convergences, words introduced from Africa that merge with similar-sounding English words, as has been previously noted in the case of *massa* and the slang *dig* (to understand). The vocabulary of Gullah at its inception may have reflected more clearly the pervasive influence of Africa, but as the language expanded, it borrowed most of its vocabulary from English. Recent scholarship has enlarged considerably Turner's list of Africanisms in Gullah, but except for names, the vocabulary of Gullah is nevertheless derived predominantly from English. It is rather the grammar of Gullah that best reflects the defining influence of Africa.

All the distinctive aspects of Gullah's grammatical structure have been identified with West African dialects, though the language is not a pale reflection of one or several of these tongues. In the slave camps awaiting shipment to the New World and during those endless months aboard the slave ships on which death-in-life prevailed, the slaves, bereft of family and friends, were by necessity forced to find some means of communicating their most basic needs to their masters as well as to one another, just as their masters needed to communicate with them. From the mutually unintelligible but linguistically related languages of West Africa and the language of their oppressors, the slaves and their captors developed their own pidgin, a simple language capable of serving only the most essential needs in very restricted linguistic contexts. Finally, on the plantations of the South, this pidgin evolved into a language suited to the slaves' complete needs.

Gullah had to accommodate itself to English, which it did in large part by accepting English vocabulary and certain grammatical categories while retaining those African terms and syntactic rules that were uniquely descriptive of its past. It was never overwhelmed by English. In the segregation of their slave cabins and long halls, in the fields of rice and cotton, slaves reinforced and expanded the uses of their by-now native tongue.

The syntactic structure, or underlying grammar, of Gullah is relatively simple and extraordinarily economical, making it quickly and readily accessible to new learners—an important feature for a language that in its infancy would be exposed to a highly developed, socially preferred and legally enforced tongue. If Gullah had not been so easy to learn, it would doubtless not have survived even a generation.

One could devote a book to Gullah's grammar. Indeed, the world's foremost Gullah authority, Professor William A. Stewart of the City University of New York, plans to do just that; he believes nothing less than a four-volume work on Gullah is needed, one volume each on grammar, vocabulary, evolution and historic background. He hopes such a work "will affect attitudes toward black children, who are too often thought to be backward when they are instead products of a different though no less complex linguistic and cultural background." Professor Stewart loves the rapid, melodic, almost calypso cadence of drawlless Gullah. "You can't help but fall in love with this language," he says. "When kids speak it, it sounds like a bird song."

Several of Gullah's syntactical peculiarities are found in today's urban-based Black English dialect, just as they have influenced black speech in general. An example of the latter is what has been described as "the behind proposition," the use of *at* at the end of sentences (Where you stay at?). As for Gullah's vocabulary, it not only used African words such as *okra, cushie* (a cornmeal cake), *yam, cooter, goober, tote, banana* and *buckra;* it passed these words on to speakers of English. African words used by Gullah speakers that *didn't* pass into general usage include *nyam* (to eat), *ki!* (an exclamation) and *plat-eye* (for an evil spirit). Expressions long common to Gullah include:

- To study on (think about) it
- First fowl crow (early morning)
- 'Posit your word (take an oath)
- All two (both)
- Tiel (stole—'E tiel um, He stole it).
- Evening (afternoon)
- Peruse (to stroll)
- Wha' fuh ya is fuh ya (whatever is for you is for you, *que serà, serà*)
- Up all the windows (open the windows)
- Great God in Zion, man! (an exclamation)

The Gullah expression *love come down* refers to the arousal of passion, an intentional stimulation of sexual desire. A woman might have this irresistible power by virtue of the way she walks or talks or sings or smiles, the object of this arousal sometimes reduced to abject pleading: "Ah ain't drunk, Sedalia. Mah love jes come down fer yu, Sugah. Ah'm yu man. Now loose up."

A leg party is an expression used by Gullah speakers on Daufuskie Island off South Carolina, the island so named because it was *da* (the) *fust* (first) *key* (island) north of the Savannah River. An elderly Daufuskian explained the leg party to the late Alex Haley:

Sometime dancin' be after what we call a leg party. All the mens, ol' an' young, in a room with big table full of treatin' plates, a apple, a pigfoot, an' a slice of cake cost fifteen cent. Now the next room be full of womens, separated from us at the door by a long, thick curtain, maybe a blanket. Now, the rules was three, four womens at the time stick out one leg an' foot below that curtain, with all 'em wearin' the same color ol' thick cotton stockin's. An' every man got to bend down, lookin' an' guessin' hard as he can, 'cause pretty young gals back in there, same as plenty they mamas an' them ol' gran'mas, too. Oh, Lord, how you hopin' you can guess a leg of somethin' nice an' fine 'stead of somebody's gran'ma. But all you can do finally is decide which one them three, four ankles just to go 'head an' grab an' squeeze—an' then, Lordy, whoever's hooked onto that ankle, well, out she come, walkin' before everybody! An', buddy, you grabbed somebody's ninety-year-ol' ankle? That's jus' what you got. An' everybody includin' her is fallin' out laughin.' An' rules say you got to buy her one of them fifteen-cent apple an' cake an' pig-foot plates.

Eben do a wak tru de daak walley ob de shada ob det, a yent scayd, cuz oona da stay 'long me is a translation of the fourth verse of the 23d Psalm into Gullah. Many Gullah words and expressions are related to religion. No cultural institution underwent so complete a transformation by the black slave community as the Christian Church. The doctrine may have remained orthodox but little else did. The African tradition of emotional ritual dances and songs became the regulated swaying body movements, the controlled vocal chanting and the dramatic emotional conversions of the black church. Regarding the latter, prospective converts are said to be *seeking*, which is "a distinct, passionate, fervid desire to lose oneself in the community of Christ as represented by His church." Those who enjoy the process of conversion are *coming through* and are often struck with mystic visions, which with simple unadorned eloquence they share with the faithful. As a former slave interviewed for the *Slave Narratives* put it:

> "When I been converted I went to Hebben in de sperit an' see wid de eye of fait!"
> "How did you feel when you were there?"
> "Oh, I 'joicing! I 'joicing! Nebber de lak befor', an' angel cord, an' de moon jes a ball ob blood, but I ain't know how it hold up, an' de sun on de rim ob all dese goin' round an' round, an' Christ settin' in a rocking chair obber de sun. Gabriel an' Michael was wid 'em, one on dis side an' on de odder holding de laws. I see eberyt'ing jes lak I say. Sweet Jesus I hope I reach dat place I see."

Two of the most cherished of African linguistic traditions, proverbs and child-naming, were preserved in Gullah. The African proverb, with its indirect construction, ambiguous speech and poetical language, survives in its combination with English vocabulary. The form of these proverbs was rigidly fixed. They were conditionals, rhetorical questions of simple propositions, but the language was anything but rigid. It was ambiguous, allusive and fashioned with poetical devices ranging from alliteration, repetition and rhyme to personification and parallelism. Some proverbs defined metaphysical notions: *Hell, det one ditch you cannot jump;* others offered advice: *Work while it is day;* still others reflected a fatalistic view: *Trouble goin' fall.* In continuing the African tradition of proverbs, Gullah provided for the cultural initiation of the young into a world of beliefs, superstitions, hopes and fears that was beyond their own degrading American experience. They identified with a culture and its language that were not shackled by the constraints of plantation life.

An example of a practical Gullah proverb that passed into general American use is *Likker'll make you not know your mamma,* which dates back at least to the 18th century and probably before this, possibly being adapted from an African proverb brought to America by South Carolina slaves.

The African practice of naming had an almost mystical importance to Gullah speakers. Naming afforded an opportunity of sharing personal and historical experiences, attitudes toward life and a system of values. Slaves would often have two names: one that the master gave, such as Brutus, and a unique name, such as Sabe, that would be the individual's within the community that really mattered to him, his own. In accordance with African tradition, children were often named after the English equivalents of the days of the week. Sometimes, African names themselves ("Sango," "Mingo," "Sambo") or homonyms of African names (such as "Joe," for "Cadjo") were chosen. Finally, the tradition of naming according to prevalent ideas was carried on in the new tongue, so that children were named for the weather: "Bright" or "Rainy"; their appearance: "Curly" or "Noisy"; or their parent's attitude toward their birth: "Welcome." In all, Gullah strove to strengthen the naming traditions, which gave the family a sense of power over their masters and their children a sense of heritage and pride. The black child was not defenselessly incorporated into the white man's slave society at birth but entered the inhumane system protected by a sense of self and history—the parents had given the child, and would continue to give the child, everything that it was possible to give.

Southern dialect—no matter how many subdialects such as Gullah, Conch and Cajun it is composed of—is generally heard south and east of an imaginary line traced along the Maryland-Virginia northern boundary, along West Virginia's southern boundary, then along the Ohio River and past the Mississippi (including southern Missouri) and finally down through southeastern Oklahoma and East Texas. Here South Mouth prevails and indeed has held out better than any major dialect against the encroachment of the General-American Middle Western speech that has been the darling of radio and television announcers for the past half century. Although large migrations from the North in recent times threaten to homogenize the South, especially in growing urban areas like Atlanta, it appears certain that there will remain large pockets of resistance where the Southern dialect will prevail for many years. It will also certainly be heard in the works of our best writers, so many of whose voices have always been framed in the inflections of the South. Just reading Larry Brown's excellent novel *Joe* (1991) recently, I came upon, among many other Southern expressions, the terms "She like to have a goddamned hissy [fit]"; "I used to couldn't see that. I see it now"; "as rich as six feet up a bull's ass"; "Reckon [I wonder] who hit him in the eye?"; "Bad as I hate to do it"; "Go put him up [Put the dog away]"; and (in reply to "I saw you laughing at me"): "I wasn't done it."

Southern talk, like that of New England, began as a type of speech basically southeastern English in nature. More than half of the colonists in the Virginia colony, for example, hailed from the southern part of England. Puritans, royalists, soldiers, indentured servants and transported criminals (like Defoe's fictional Moll Flanders, "twelve year a whore . . . twelve year a thief, eight year a transported felon in Virginia") all formed part of this largely uneducated group, whose speech among the religious often had a whine added, possibly to connote a superior piety. Some speech patterns were established early on; for example, the scholar Schele de Vere claimed that Southern disregard for the letter *r* should be charged to "the guilty forefathers, many of whom came from Suffolk and the districts belonging to the East Anglians."

"Proper" London English of the 18th century influenced Tidewater Southern speech more than most American regions for the obvious reason that these Southerners (like Bostonians and New Yorkers) were from earliest times in closer contact with England than were other parts of the country. This contact led the wealthy gentry in the region to ape fashionable Londoners down to their way of talking, a habit that remained long after their days of glory and one that, in turn, was copied from them by the plainer folk. But while Southern seaport and plantation owner speech was largely modeled on London English, inland speech had little chance of blending into a broad regional usage because of cultural isolation, thus resulting in the great diversity of local usages in the area. Nevertheless, the aristocrats of the South made their own (and made a large part of the region's) such upper-class English speech as *jin* (join), *pisen* (poison), *varmint* (vermin), *gwine* (going), *starling* (sterling), *widder* (widow), *piller* (pillow), *winder (window) and varsity* (university).

Other Southern linguistic ties with England included the Scotch-Irish Presbyterian ministers of North Carolina and western Virginia, who were sent back to Scotland for religious training by their congregations and were responsible for *hae* being used for "have," *gin* for "if" and *wha* for "who" over the course of several generations. Scotch-Irish schoolteachers, who were often indentured servants, also "had no inconsiderable influence . . . upon our pronunciation and language," according to John Pickering, writing in the *American Quarterly Review* of September 1828.

Some critics contend that the Southern accent is distinctive solely because the region was settled from England's Southwest country, but this seems unlikely. Although Southwest country dialect has many similarities, Southern speech doesn't possess its most conspicuous features, neither is there any strong evidence that the South was settled by people from England's Southwest. It does appear likely that distinctive features of black speech, different from any English dialect, must have influenced the Southern speech to some extent, given the enormous population of blacks in the area and the closeness of blacks and whites on plantations, especially children, who often played together (some black children were indeed designated "play children" for the whites). On the other hand, white speech probably influenced black speech in the area even more.

In general, Southern dialect is best characterized by a slower enunciation than is common in most of the country combined with the gliding or diphthongization of stressed vowels. This so-called Southern drawl results in pronunciations like *yea-yis* for "yes," *ti-ahm* for "time" *I-ah* for "I," *fi-ahn* for "fine," *a-out* for "out," *tyune* for "tune" and *nyu* for "new." The final consonants (particularly *d, l, r* and *t*) following such slow drawling vowel sounds are often weakened, resulting in such characteristic Southern pronunciations as *hep* for "help," *mo* for "more," *yo* for "your," *po* for "poor," *flo* for "floor," *kep* for "kept," *nex* for "next," *bes* for "best," *sof* for "soft" and *las* for "last." Southern speech is also noted for being more melodious and various than other dialects because the vowels are long-embraced, like a lovely woman.

If fully 72 human muscles are required in speaking one word, as physiologists say, it certainly seems that Southerners often employ considerably fewer in tawkin so dif'runt. The Southern drawl, which makes it possible to deliver a sentence in twice as much time as in any other dialect, is most noticeable at the end of a sentence or before a pause and has been ridiculed on the stage and screen in such phrases as *nice white rice* with the undiphthongized vowel in all positions—something no elegant Southerner would do.

By no means is the Southern drawl found only in the South. Even today it can be heard in parts of New England, of all places, where the "y glide" of the *u* sound after *d, n,* and *t* results in Yankee pronunciations like *dyu* for "due" and *nyu* for "new." The drawl, in fact, first came to the attention of Americans when Noah Webster enjoined the New England "yeomen" to improve their "drawling nasal way of speaking" in his *Dissertations on the English Language* (1789). Webster believed the New England drawl was the result of a people unaccustomed to commanding slaves and servants and "not possessing that pride and consciousness of superiority" that he thought enabled people to speak in a decisive way. Certainly he did not take into account the drawling Southern slaveowner. In any case, Americans South and North were proud of their drawls. When the gallant Captain Frederick Marryat, British novelist and adventurer, asked an American lady why she drawled, the linguistically patriotic lady replied, "Well, I'd drawl all the way from Maine to Georgia rather than clip my words as you English people do." Nevertheless, Marryat held to his opinion that Americans dwelt upon their words when they spoke "from their cautious calculating habits."

Southern expressions color the works of our best Southern novelists, ranging from *a rubber-nosed woodpecker in a petrified forest* (an incompetent) to *as mad as a rooster in an empty henhouse* and *don't get crosslegged* (don't lose your temper). Most of these haven't become nationally known despite their charm, often, one guesses, because they are basically too countrified and relaxed for our increasingly urbanized frenetic republic.

Southern expressions, like Southern drawls, are often longer and more relaxed than most of the nation's, the dialect indeed filled with what linguists classify as phatic speech, sentences that do little more than make what Anatole Broyard called "a friendly noise." Certainly as Mr. Broyard further noted, this is no reason to condemn "You-all" accents, as too-proper people often do—better phatic than frenetic. Southerners do tend to make the "essay response" when speaking, as Mary Hood has pointed out in *Harper's* magazine.

> Suppose a man is walking across a field. To the question 'Who is that?' a Southerner would reply: 'Wasn't his granddaddy the one whose dog and him got struck by lightning on the steel bridge? Mama's third cousin—dead before my time—found his railroad watch in that eight-pound catfish's stomach the next summer just above the dam. The way he married for that new blue Cadillac automobile, reckon how come he's walking like he has on Sunday shoes, if that's who it is, and for sure it is.' A Northerner would reply to the same question, 'That's Joe Smith.' To which the Southerner might think (but be much too polite to say aloud), 'They didn't ask his name—they asked who he is!'

Though it is hard to generalize about Southern grammatical peculiarities, which vary with a Southerner's education and regional heritage, there are differences from General American that are frequently heard. The familiar and still fashionable use of such verb phrases, or double modals, as *might could* and *used to could* by educated Southerners is practically unique in America. *American Speech* editor Ronald R. Butters has noted a linguistic feature "by which you can always detect a Southerner if you wait long enough" because he or she invariably inserts the word *to* shortly after *have* when asking questions like "Shall I have him to call you?" Many other peculiarities are noted throughout this book.

Southerners have always been able to joke about their drawls and other peculiar linguistic institutions, as former Vice-President Alben Barkley did in this limerick:

In New Orleans dwelled a young Creole
Who, when asked if her hair was all reole,
   Replied with a shrug,
   "Just give it a tug
And decide by the way that I squeole."

Millions of Southerners do say *squeole* (instead of *squeal*) like Barkley's Creole. Millions also say *scat* instead of *gesundheit* or *God bless you* after someone sneezes. (People in Arkansas, it is said, prefer *scat* six to one.) A woman who refuses a proposal of marriage from a man *turns him in the cold* or *puts him on the funny side* in Kentucky, *gives him the go-by* in South Carolina and *rings him off* in Georgia. A South Carolinian will say *outten the light* for turn off the light, but *cut off the light* is more generally heard throughout the South. A fussbudget is generally a *fussbox* south of the Mason-Dixon Line, and Mom is usually *Mamma*. Older Southerners sometimes say *everwhat* for "whatever" and *everwho* for "whoever," while their *a gracious plenty* means "enough." Southerners have their groceries packed in a *sack* or *poke* instead of a bag, call a small stream or brook a *creek* or *run* and call *laurel* what Northerners generally know as rhododendron. In West Virginia a big party is a *belling*. Southerners call a jalopy a *rattletrap* and tend to say they are *wore out* or *about to give out* when tired. They often use the conjunctive *which* in a confusing way, according to Ronald Butters, who cites: "The President was not happy with the results of the election, which I couldn't be happier about that."

Southerners also like to say *drug* for "dragged." William Faulkner had some fun with this usage in *The Town* (1957):

Ratliff looked at me a while. "For ten years now . . . I been . . . trying to . . . teach myself words right. And, just when I call myself about to learn and I begin to feel a little good over it, here you come . . . correcting me back to what I been trying for ten years to forget."

"I'm sorry," I said. "I didn't mean it that way. It's because I like the way you say it. When you say it, 'taken' sounds a heap more took than just 'took.' just like 'drug' sounds a heap more dragged than just 'dragged.' "

"And not just you neither," Ratliff said. "Your uncle too: me saying 'dragged' and him saying 'drug' and me saying 'dragged' and him saying 'drug' again, until at last he would say, 'In a free country like this, why ain't I got as much right to use your *drug* for my *dragged* as you got to use my *dragged* for say drug?' "

"All right," I said. "Even if he drug her back."

"—even if he drug, dragged, drung—You see?" he said. "Now you done got me so mixed up until even I don't know which one I don't want to say.' "

One persistent old joke has *The War to Suppress Yankee Arrogance,* one of the 20 or so Southern names for the Civil War recorded in these pages, caused by a dialect difference. It seems that three high-ranking Northern generals stomped into a Washington, D.C. bar and shouted, "We want a bottle right away!" A Southern spy overheard them and breathlessly reported to General P. G. T. Beauregard: "Top Union generals want a bottle right away!" Chivalrous Beauregard obliged, leaving the evening's quadrille in Montgomery and proceeding to Charleston, South Carolina, where he gave them the *bottle* (or battle) of Fort Sumter.

In a more serious vein, it is interesting to note that Southerners sometimes don't understand their own compatriots. It is said that on September 19, 1902, in Birmingham, Alabama the cry of "fight!" was mistaken for "fire!" and 78 blacks were killed in the resulting panic.

One is *afeared* to list dialectical words peculiar only to a single region because there is so much traffic between regions today, but *shut my mouth* if *sigogglin, spizzerinctum, catawampus* and *snollygoster* don't qualify for South Mouth. *Sigogglin* (sy-gog-lin) means "crooked, askew or out of plumb," as in "You sawed that board off a little sigogglin," and has the variant forms *antigodlin, antigogglin* and *slantigodlin,* all of which may have their origin in the thought that something crooked goes against God's plan for an orderly world. *Spizzerinctum* is a Southern rural term for energy or enthusiasm ("I wish I had his spizzerinctum"), and a *snollygoster* is usually a man "who wants office, regardless of party, platform or principles," though President Truman, from Missouri and famous for his use of such terms, defined it as "a man born out of wedlock." *Catawampus* is heard throughout the South for cater-cornered (four cornered) and is often used in such expressions as "He walked catawampus across the street," or "You might call a rhombus a catawampus square."

A real Southerner will drawl and say *sho' nuff, honeychile* and *y'all,* and he or she will also tend to accent only the first syllable of each word, giving us pronunciations like *po*-lice, *At*-lanta and *in*-come. Despite their *ain'ts,* however, educated Southern speakers often take great care in *not* talking like their compatriots, especially regarding exaggerated speech characteristics that have become the butt of Southern jokes. No *honeychiles* or *sho-nuffs* for them, unless he or she is putting you on.

Another Southern peculiarity is the use of *ain't* among cultured speakers. Raven I. McDavid Jr. pointed out in *American Speech* that during *Linguistic Atlas* interviews "nearly every cultured informant . . . in South Carolina and Georgia used *ain't* at some time during the interview. In fact, one of the touchstones often used by Southerners to distinguish the genuine cultured speaker from the pretenders is that the latter are too socially insecure to know the proper occasions for using ain't, the double negative and other such folk forms, and hence avoid them altogether." Then again some educated people in other regions use *Ain't I?* in place of *Am I not?*, or use the *Aren't I?* acceptable in England.

Southerners are often a genteel breed much given to euphemisms about sexual matters. Aristocratic Southerners could indeed be quite contemptuous about sex, giving more lip service to chivalrous love. When a fellow congressman chided the fiery John Randolph about his impotence, he shot back in his shrill voice: "Sir, you boast of an ability in which any slave is your equal and every jackass your superior."

Two redundancies often heard that illustrate the Southerner's predilection for extravagant language are *in a manner* ("She acts like she's rarin' in a manner to go") and *standin' in need of* ("I'm standin' in need of a stiff drink"). There are hundreds more usages often heard in the South and never or rarely heard in other parts of the country. A *used-to-be* is Southern for a "has-been," *dinner* can be the Southern noon (not nightly) meal, *airish* means "drafty" and *bad to* means "inclined to" ("When he gets drunk, he's bad to get in trouble").

Problems can arise from word use variations in the South (although the Southerner might see the problem as variations in the rest of the country). "What in other parts of America is called a sidewalk was and still may be called a *pavement* in my native section of Maryland," wrote Thomas Pyles in *Words and Ways of American English* (1952), "and what is elsewhere called a pavement was in our usage the *street* if in town and the *road* if in the country. Whether the road was paved or not, it would never have been called a pavement; pavements were in towns and cities and were for the use of pedestrians only. Consequently, I step from the pavement to the street; speakers from other sections step from the sidewalk to the pavement. No serious injury has thus far resulted from the ambiguity."

Like all dialects, South Mouth differs widely within the region. The Southern dialect for *son-of-a-bitch*, for example, can range from *sommuma-bitch* to *sum bitch*, with infinite variations. A very distinct pronunciation heard nowhere else in the South is heard (if rarely now) among older citizens of Memphis, Tennessee, who will tell you they are from *Mimphis, Tinnissee*. The differences are not only geographic and can even extend to Southern nationality groups. In his book *A Highly Ramified Tree*, Robert Canzoneri wrote of how his family mixed the lingua franca of Sicily with a Southern accent on settling in Mississippi. This resulted in an invented tongue sometimes all their own with almost incomprehensible rhythms like *July gots?* ("Do you like apricots?") and *Jugo Marilla tax?* ("Did you go by way of Amarillo, Texas?")

Vocabulary is also strikingly different in various parts of the South. Nowhere but in the Deep South is the Indian-derived *bobbasheely*, which William Faulkner employed in *The Reivers*, used for "a very close friend," and only in Northern Maryland does *manniporchia* (from the Latin *mania a potu*, "craziness from drink") mean the D.T.'s (delirium tremens). Small tomatoes would be called *tommytoes* in the mountains, (*tōmytoes* in East Texas, *salad tomatoes* in the plains area and *cherry tomatoes* along the coast. Depending upon where you are in the South a *large porch* can be a *veranda, piazza* or *gallery;* a *burlap bag* can be a *tow sack, crocus sack* or *grass sack; pancakes* can be *flittercakes, fritters, corncakes* or *battercakes;* a *harmonica* can be a *mouth organ* or *French harp;* a *closet* can be a *closet* or a *locker;* and a *wishbone* can be a *wishbone* or *pulley bone.* There are hundreds of synonyms for a cling peach (*green peach, pickle peach,* etc.), kindling wood (*lightning wood, lighted knots)* and a rural resident (*snuff chewer, kicker, yahoo).*

Notable differences occur in grammar too. In some Southern dialect areas, for example, uneducated speakers will say *clum* for the past tense of climb, while in Virginia many uneducated speakers say *clome* ("He clome the tree"). In this case many Southerners are closer in speech to uneducated speakers in Midland dialect areas, who also use *clum,* than they are to their fellow Southerners in Virginia.

In parts of the Deep South, people pronounce bird *boid,* girl *goil,* word, *woid,* earth *oith,* oil *earl* (*all* is an alternate pronunciation in some Southern parts) and murder *moider*—just as they do in Brooklyn. The *r*-colored vowel of these words and others is followed by a short *i* sound (which is somewhat inaccurately but traditionally represented as *oi* in dialect writing) and the pronunciation is not considered substandard where it is used.

Of all the major American dialects, South Mouth is the most consistently difficult to translate. Among the most amusing examples is the expression *a fade barn* that the editors of the *Dictionary of American Regional English* tried to track down for a couple of years. The editors knew that the expression existed because field interviews had recorded it in North Carolina without establishing its meaning. When a Raleigh newspaper joined in the search, the answer was quickly apparent. Dozens of correspondents chided the editors for not knowing, in the words of one North Carolinian, that "a fade barn is whar you stow fade (feed) for the livestock."

The experts still can't solve some Southern expressions. Up until the early 19th century, surveyors in Bourbon County, Kentucky (which does, incidentally, give its name to bourbon whiskey but was itself named for the Bourbons of France), used a species of a common tree called the *bettywood* to establish property boundaries. The elusive tree should not have disappeared in little over a century and is probably known by another name today, yet no one has identified it despite extensive etymological, historical and botanical detective work. The *bettywood* appears doomed to obscurity possibly because the original name was garbled beyond belief into another name bearing not the faintest resemblance to it. (I venture a wild guess: Could the *bettywood* possibly be the mispronounced *buttonwood* of the North, which is called the sycamore in the South?)

Some pure South Mouth is becoming widespread. I've often heard the expression *He's three bricks shy of a load* and variations on it for someone not too bright. The term to *fall out* is principally a Southern expression meaning "to faint" but today is also heard in communities as far north as northern Wisconsin, northern Indiana and southeastern Pennsylvania. Similarly, *to tote* is a Southernism now heard in all other regions, as is *to carry* in the sense of *to transport* or *escort* (a guest being carried out to lunch or dinner instead of taken out).

A Southern pronunciation becoming more national every year is *vee-hick-el* for *vee-uh-cul,* as most Americans pronounce "vehicle." I first heard this pronunciation more than 40 years ago in the Army, where it was said to be used to make the word clearer when transmitted over a field radio, but probably the fact that so many noncommissioned officers were Southerners had more to do with this Southern pronunciation. In any case, one agrees with *New York Times* columnist William Safire that the Southern pronunciation makes the word "sound punchier and more authoritative than the vowel-joined VEE-uh-cul."

Despite the increased mobility of Americans and the homogenization of speech by television, it doesn't appear likely that Southern speech will be quietly erased from the American tape, for it is too widespread and deeply rooted in the past. There may be fewer and fewer Senator Claghorns as time goes by, but the sweet sound of the extended *ou* diphthong will be with us for a long time. Southerners who employ one syllable where three or four could be used will be suspect throughout Dixie for many years to come. Who knows, perhaps the lazy or relaxed rhythms of Southern speech will even become the national mode within the next century or so, if temperatures go up due to the greenhouse effect and the whole country gets as hot as Mississippi, in which case the thousands of entries that follow *raht cheer* (right here) may well become essential for survival.

R. H.
Peconic, New York

A

a   In Southern speech *a* often replaces the indefinite article *an,* as in "I'll be there in a hour."

Aaron's rod   A tall smooth-stemmed herb with yellow flowers *(Thermopsis caroliniana)* found from North Carolina to Georgia and named after the Biblical Aaron's rod, which miraculously blossomed and produced almonds.

A-B-Abs   The simple ABCs of the Southern schoolroom; the basics or the most elementary knowledge of anything, as in "He don't know a letter of his A-B-Abs" [he's stupid]. The expression is also used in New England. Synonyms are *abb and ebb, B-A-Bas* and *abiselfa.*

aback   Behind, as in "His house is aback the others"; also used to mean ago: "It happened ten years aback."

aback of   A variant of ABACK also meaning "behind," as in "His house is aback of the others."

abanded   Abandoned, as in "That building was abanded." The word derives from the obsolete *aband,* a contraction of *abandon* that also means "to forsake or banish." First recorded in 1559, it was later used by the English poet Edmund Spenser.

abasicky   (pronounced *a-bah-sicky)* A children's expression of unknown origin roughly meaning "Naughty! Naughty! Shame on you!" Children frequently taunt others with it, repeating the word while rubbing their right index finger over the left index finger in the old "Shame, shame!" gesture.

abb and ebb   See A-B-ABS.

ABC store   A liquor store run by the Alcoholic Beverage Control agency in several Southern states.

abcess of the bowels   An old Southern name for appendicitis that is still heard, though infrequently.

Abe Lincoln bug   Anti-Lincoln feelings died hard in the South after the Civil War, as the name of this little bug shows. Because of its extremely bad odor and destructive habits, Southerners, especially Georgians, called the harlequin cabbage bug *(Murgantia histrionica)* after their hated adversary, President Lincoln. According to one old dictionary, the bug gets both its more common name and its Latin nomenclature from "the gay, theatrical, harlequin-like manner in which its black and orange-yellow colors are arranged upon its body."

1

abide To endure, stand or tolerate, usually in the negative sense, as in "I can't abide him." Mark Twain used this expression, which is now common nationally and has been considered standard American English since at least 1930.

able Wealthy; powerful, influential. Once a fairly common expression, *able* in this sense is rarely heard even in the mountains of the South today. The word dates back at least to 1578, where it appears in a Scottish song. In his famous diary, Samuel Pepys writes of "the child of a very able citizen in Gracious Street."

abouten A form of about. "How abouten them bootses?" writes Marjorie Kinnan Rawlings in her novella *Jacob's Ladder* (1931), set in Florida's hummock country. John Faulkner uses the expression in *Men Working* (1941), set in Mississippi.

abouts Nearby. "I found it along abouts here."

about to die Someone about to die is a person taken suddenly or seriously ill or who feels very ill, as in "He thought he was about to die the other day."

about to give out Very tired. "I'm afraid I'm about to give out." A common variation is *about give out*.

above one's bend Used in the South and West, this expression meaning "beyond one's ability, limit or capacity" has its origins in a phrase Shakespeare used in *Hamlet:* "To the top

of one's bent." The "bent," according to the *Oxford English Dictionary,* refers to the "extent to which a bow may be bent or a spring wound up, degree of tension; hence degree of endurance, capacity for taking in or receiving . . ."

an Abraham Lincoln; an Abe; an Abe's picture A five-dollar bill, because of Lincoln's portrait on the front.

abroad Heard especially among old-fashioned speakers in the South, a trip abroad is often not a journey overseas but a trip or visit in the community, even a stroll down to the store. It can, however, mean "at or to a distance of 50 miles or more," as in the common newspaper expression "[Mr. Jones] has returned from his trip abroad." An *abroad* or *broad* means a trip, as in "Mrs. Brown is back from her abroad."

abscond To hide or conceal, as in the first recorded use of the expression in 1721: "The poor man fled from place to place absconding himself." Originating in England, *abscond* in this sense was very common in the American South up until the 20th century.

absolute auction A property auction in which the owner is required by law to sell his property to the highest bidder. The law and expression have been in effect in Kentucky for over a century.

absquatulate An old expression, obsolete except in a historical sense, that may have originated in Kentucky in the early 19th century and means to depart, especially in a clandestine, surreptitious or hurried manner. "The vagabond had absquatulated with the whole of the joint stock funds," George W. Perrie noted in *Buckskin Mose* (1873). *Absquatulate* is a fanciful classical formation based on *ab* and *squat,* meaning the reverse of to squat. Variants are *absquatilate* and *absquotulate.*

account of   Because. "He ain't full weight right now, account of his stomach bein' shrunk up." [Marjorie Kinnan Rawlings, *The Yearling,* 1938] The expression can also be *on account of;* in fact, Rawlings also used it that way in her short story "Cocks Must Crow" (1939): "I almost lost him on account of I had changed."

ackempucky   Any food mixture of unknown ingredients or a food of jellylike consistency such as gelatin; possibly from an Algonquin word meaning "to bake or roast on hot ashes."

acknowledge the corn   Much used in the 19th century as a synonym for the contemporary "copping a plea," this phrase is said to have arisen when a man was arrested and charged with stealing four horses and the corn (grain) to feed them. "I acknowledge [admit to] the corn," he declared. The expression might, however, come from corn liquor, in which case it probably originally meant to admit being drunk. Not used much anymore in the South, where it probably originated, or anywhere else, it is

sometimes heard as *acknowledge the coin* and *own the corn.*

acorn duck   Another name in the South for the common wood duck, which feeds upon acorns.

acorn tree   A synonym for the oak tree.

across-the-track   Poor or low-quality, as in "They're across-the-track [or tracks] people." It is probably based on *the wrong side of the tracks,* a common American expression used in the early 19th century when railroad tracks, which sometimes split a town in two, provided a clear social demarcation: well-to-do people living on the "right" side of the tracks and the poor living on the "wrong" side, in the slums or seedy area of town.

act like you're somebody   Show some respect for yourself, act like you're worth something.

Adam apple   Sometimes used in the South instead of the standard Adam's apple.

Adam's housecat   The Southern expression "I wouldn't know him from Adam's housecat" is an attempt to improve upon "I wouldn't know him from Adam's off ox" (referring to the "off" ox in the yoke farthest away from the driver), which in turn is a variation of "I wouldn't know him from Adam." Maybe it's better than both of its predecessors, since hardly anyone drives oxen these days and, as more than one humorist has observed, Adam had no navel, wore only a fig leaf at most and would have been fairly easy to identify.

Adam's pet monkey A variation on ADAM'S HOUSECAT.

adays An archaic expression meaning in the daytime or by day as opposed to *anights*. "We don't go there adays."

addled Dizzy; confused. " 'You're addled,' she said. 'Just plain addled.' " [Marjorie Kinnan Rawlings, *The Yearling,* 1938]

adieu Goodbye; a French word often used in southern Louisiana-French dialects.

Admiral Dewey Another unusual Southern name reported or invented by William Faulkner. See also WALLSTREET PANIC.

afeared Afraid, as in, "Hounds won't never tree a bear—they're afeared to close in." The expression, now chiefly Southern when heard at all in America, is used in dialects of Scotland, Ireland and England and was once widespread in the United States.

affidavy An affidavit. This is an example of folk etymology, where a more or less learned term is changed into a familiar or partly familiar one (davy), often by substituting, adding, or omitting a sound or two. Marjorie Kinnan Rawlings used *affidavy* in her novella *Jacob's Ladder* (1931).

afflicted Mentally or physically defective, feebleminded, deformed. "One of her boys is afflicted."

Affrishy town An expression once used to describe a place where blacks or Africans lived, more commonly called by the offensive name "nigger town," which is an expression not confined to the South.

a-fleetin' an' a-flyin' Moving rapidly in a grand style or succeeding very well at something.

afore Before, as in "He was dead afore anybody knowed it," from Jesse Stuart's short story "The Last Round-up"; once commonly used throughout the United States but now heard mostly in the South.

African-American The term *African-American* for a black person born in Africa was first used in the American South: " 'I'd buy all de . . . colored African-American citizens'." [Frederick Converse, *Old Cremona Songster,* 1836]

African Negro An obsolete Southern term, dating back to the 1830s, for a black person born in Africa, as opposed to a black person born in America.

African refugee A derogatory term used by whites for blacks. " 'You meddling African refugee!' Judge Rainey said in an angry voice. 'If I never do anything else, I'm going to court and get a writ of deportation served on you. That'll send you so deep in Africa you'll never see the sun rise again as long as you live.' " [Erskine Caldwell, *Jenny By Nature,* 1961]

Africky Temper, fighting spirit, as in the expression "to get one's Africky up." "To get one's Irish up," meaning the same, is more common countrywide, as is "to get one's dander up." "To get one's Dutch up" is seldom heard.

Afromobile Confined to Florida, this expression referred to an early 1900s Palm Beach vehicle consisting of a two-seated wicker chair in the front and a bicycle in the back pedaled by a black man. For many years, this taxi for rich white patrons was the only vehicle permitted in the city.

afternight The time after nightfall, evening or dusk. It is heard in the South but has a wider usage and was employed by D. H. Lawrence in one of his novels.

aftersupper A synonym for dessert, this expression is similar to the British dialect *afters,* meaning the same.

aftertimes Later, afterward. "The house was built in 1850, but that wing was put on aftertimes."

afterwhile After a while, later on, as in "Afterwhile I'll send for you-all, if you're of a mind to come where I am." This ellipsis is also heard in other parts of the country.

ageable Old or getting on in years. "I'm afraid she's gettin' too ageable to marry."

agent An old-fashioned term for a traveling salesman or a door-to-door salesman.

ager bumps Gooseflesh, the *ager* here meaning "ague."

aggie forti(e)s Anything very strong to drink, including medicine or liquor. As one old-timer put it: ". . . this man's whiskey ain't Red Eye, it ain't Chain Lightnin' either, it's regular Aggie-forty [sic], and there isn't a man living can stand a glass and keep his senses." Also pronounced *acker fortis* and *ackie fortis,* the expression derives from *aqua fortis* (strong water), the Latin name for nitric acid.

aggrafret Slang meaning "to aggravate or fret."

aggravoke William Faulkner used this Southern slang that means "to incite or provoke," a combination of *aggra*vate and pro*voke.*

agin Still heard in the South, though infrequently, *agin* (again) can mean "by the time that," as in "I'll have it ready agin you come." Other meanings are "by," "before" and "when."

a-going Going. "I'm a-going home, boys."

agoment Annoyance, frustration, aggravation; probably based on *agony* or *aggravation.* Says a William Faulkner character in *The Town* (1957): " 'I bear the worry and the risk and the agoment for years and years, and I get sixty dollars a head for them [mules].' "

agony No one knows why the pan used to hold fermenting fruit during the making of wine at home is called an *agony* or *agony pan,* but the expression is still used in the South. Possibly it has something to do with all the fruit's juices being squeezed out of it.

a good riddance Good riddance of someone or something. " 'And a good riddance,' Father said. 'I hope he stays there.' " [William Faulkner, "That Evening Sun," 1931]

aig A common pronunciation of *egg* in the South.

ailded Sickened, made ill. " 'I don't figger there was nothin' ailded me but green brierberries.' " [Marjorie Kinnan Rawlings, *The Yearling,* 1938]

ailish Sick, slightly ill. "Hit makes us all feel ailish." [John Faulkner, *Men Working,* 1941]

ain't *Ain't* is of course used throughout America, but see the Introduction for a special Southern preference for the word.

ain't fittin' to roll with a pig Worthless. "Folks say he ain't fittin' to roll with a pig."

ain't got a grain of sense Said of an exceedingly stupid person. "That old boy ain't got a grain of sense." A variation is *ain't got a lick of sense.*

ain't got but Have only, as in "I ain't got but a dime."

ain't got enough sense to bell a cat Hopelessly stupid; can't do the simplest things. Variations are *ain't got enough sense to bell a buzzard (buzzer, bull, cow* or *goose).*

ain't got no A common Southern double negative meaning "has no," as in "He ain't got no call badmouthing me" (he has no reason for calling me names).

ain't got no call Has no reason, as in "He ain't got no call accusing me."

ain't much Ill, not well. "John's baby, she ain't much."

ain't no place in heaven, ain't no place in hell Nowhere for one to go. From a folk song quoted in William Faulkner's *Sanctuary* (1931): " 'One day mo! Ain't no place fer you in heaven! Ain't no place fer you in hell! Ain't no place fer you in white folks' jail! Nigger, whar you gwine to? Whar you gwine to, nigger?' "

ain't only No more than. A character in William Faulkner's *The Mansion* (1959) says: " 'I'd like to hold the bank offen you myself, but I ain't only vice-president of it, and I can't do nothing with Manfred de Spain.' "

air (1) A common pronunciation of *are.* " 'Milly,' he said. 'Air you hungry?' " [William Faulkner, "Wash," 1934] (2) Rarely, *air (are)* can also be used in the sense of have, as in " 'They mought [might] have kilt us, but they ain't whupped us yit, air they?' " [William Faulkner, *Absalom, Absalom!,* 1936]

air; air up To fill up with air, as in "Let's air the tires" or "I aired up the tires."

airish (1) Drafty. "It's plenty airish in here." (2) Cool or chilly. "Today's a bit airish." (3) One who puts on airs or acts superior to others. "She's real airish, ain't she?"

A.K. An "ass kisser," one who curries favor; possibly originated in the South but widely used in this sense for over 50 years in the New York City area, among other places.

aknown To be known, acquainted; the expression is not widely used anymore.

Alabama The Cotton State, our 22d, took the name *Alabama* when admitted to the Union in 1819. *Alabama* is from the Choctaw *alba ayamule*, which means "I open the thicket," that is, "I am the one who works the land, harvests food from it." Often called *Alaham, Alabamy.*

Alabama egg An egg made by cutting a round center out of a piece of bread, putting the bread in a hot greased pan, dropping the egg into the center without breaking the yolk and frying the whole until done (sometimes turning it over). Also called a *hobo egg.*

alarm duty An obsolete term, used before and during the Civil War, for the duty of being prepared to respond to an alarm for military service. "There is a detachment of citizen soldiery . . . always on what is called alarm duty." [*The Southern Literary Magazine,* volume 3, 1837]

Aleck A name for the black or roof rat, perhaps because it is among the smartest of rats, a "smart Aleck," or possibly because it is also called the Alexandrine rat.

Alexander Hamilton Infrequently used in the South as a term for one's signature, similar to the use of "John Hancock."

alive Bread or fruit that is freshly made or retains its freshness well.

all (1) Often used after the interrogative pronouns what and who. "What all did you do last night?" "Who all was there?" See also YOU-ALL. (2) Only. "This here is all the shirt I have."

all ahoo Awry, lopsided; derives from the English dialect *ahuh,* meaning "awry."

all alligator An obsolete term meaning a person of superior strength, skill, etc. "The Mississippi navigator . . . afirmed himself to be all alligator . . ." [*Analectic Magazine,* volume 4, 1814] See also ALLIGATOR.

all around Close to, near, as in the words of a character in Marjorie Kinnan Rawlings' *The Yearling* (1938): " 'I come all around courtin' her, 'fore I married your Ma.' "

all dressed up like a country bride Dressed in one's best.

alley bat slang for a promiscuous or immoral woman.

alley cat Slang for an illegitimate child.

all-fired Extremely, very. "She's so all-fired lazy no one wants to hire her."

all fired up and full of git Ready to go, full of energy.

all fogged up Confused. "You just went out and got yourself all fogged up with rules and regulations. That's our trouble. We done invented ourselves so many alphabets and rules and recipes that we can't see anything else . . ." [William Faulkner, "The Tall Men," 1941]

all git out To an extreme degree, as in "He makes me mad as all git out."

all heeled Well-heeled; well provided for.

alligator An old nickname for a Mississippi keelboatman. "The other [man] replied, 'I am an alligator, half man, half horse; can whip anybody on the Mississippi, by G-d.' " [Christian Schultz Jr., *Travels on an Inland Voyage,* 1807] *Alligator* was formerly the nickname of any member of the Virginia House of Delegates and the nickname for a Floridian. See also ALL ALLIGATOR.

alligator bait Unpalatable food; also a derogatory term for a black person.

alligator cooter "The alligator cooter is the most highly prized of all inland turtle meats. He is very dangerous, a virulent fighter encased in a ridged, scaly shell from which he takes his name, with a fierce hawked beak at the end of his head and long neck that can make mincemeat of an enemy." [Marjorie Kinnan Rawlings, *Cross Creek,* 1942]

alligator tag A game of tag played in the water where the "alligator" tries to catch the other players, who, when captured, assist him in catching the rest.

all kinds of times A very good time, as in "I had all kinds of times last night."

all my lone Alone; all by my lonesome. "I was here all my lone."

all my whole life All my life; for as long as I can remember. "It's been like this all my whole life."

all oak and iron bound In the best of health and spirits. "Before we went down to Dallas I was feeling all oak and iron bound."

all of a green All of one shade of green, as in "rows of young corn, all of a size, all of a green."

all of a size All the same size. See example at ALL OF A GREEN.

all one's born days All the time passed since one's birth. "I never saw the like of it in all my born days."

all over hell and half of Georgia Covering a wide range. "We drove all over hell and half of Georgia."

all-overs (1) The shivers; nervousness; apprehension. "It gives me the all-overs to just think of it." Something close to the expression is first recorded in an 1820 song entitled "Oh, What a Row": "I'm seized with an all-overness, I faint, I die." (2) Underwear. "She washed his all-overs till they turned white."

allow (1) To suppose. "It was allowed to be somewhat dangerous." (2) To remark or declare. "He allowed I couldn't do it." (3) To plan or intend. "I don't allow to go." Often shortened to '*low.*

alls (1) All one owns. "We packed up our alls and moved out." (2) Sometimes used instead of "all." "Alls I know is how I feel."

all she wrote That's the end of it, it's finished. *That's all she wrote* is first recorded in 1948 as college slang but probably dates back before World War II and is now common countrywide, especially in the South and West. It may have derived from the "Dear John" letters breaking up relationships that some soldiers received from wives and sweethearts while away from home. This appears to be indicated by its use in James Jones' novel *From Here to Eternity* (1951), which takes place just before World War II: "All she'd have to do, if she got caught with you, would be to holler rape and it would be Dear John, that's all she wrote."

all the far As far as; the farthest. "That's all the far I can run."

all the fast As fast as; the fastest. "That's all the fast I can do it."

all the high As high as; the highest. "That's all the high I can jump."

all the longer As long as; the longest. "Is that all the longer you're staying here in West Virginia?"

all the more As much as; the most; all. "That's all the more I know."

all the smaller As small as; the smallest. "He's all the smaller of the two."

all the time Always. "He was all the time so good to us."

all tore up about it Very disturbed, emotionally upset. "His son got in a bad accident, and he's all tore up about it."

all two Both. "I'll tear down all two of you," says a character in Marjorie Kinnan Rawlings' *The Yearling* (1938).

allus Always. See also HONGRY.

all vine and no taters. Someone who is all talk and no action; a person of no substance. "He's all vine and no taters."

all wool and a yard wide Dating back at least to the late 19th century, this expression, used in the South and other regions, may have originated during the Civil War, when shoddy cloth made from reprocessed wool and supplied to the Union Army often literally unraveled on a wearer's back. The phrase has come to mean something or someone of high quality or reliability, as in "He's all wool and a yard wide."

am Sometimes omitted in Southern speech, as in "I goin' right now."

ambeer A Southern term, dating back to about 1755, that first meant tobacco juice and, later, spittle containing tobacco juice. The word may derive from the amber color of tobacco juice plus its resemblance to beer's color and foaminess. Also called *ambacker, ambarker juice, amber* and *amber juice*. "He spat ambeer all over the floor."

ambition "In North Carolina this word is used instead of the word grudge. 'I had an ambition against that man.' I am credibly informed that [this expression] is even used in this manner by educated men." [John Bartlett, *Dictionary of Americanisms,* 1877].

amen corner A group of fervent believers is called an *amen corner,* after the similarly named place near the pulpit in churches that is occupied by those who lead the responsive "amens" to the preacher's prayers. The term may come from the Amen Corner of London's Paternoster Row. See ANXIOUS BENCH.

American snake tree See CHITTAM-WOOD.

ammonia Coke A popular headache cure or nerve tonic consisting of Coke (q.v.) and a dash of ammonia.

Amy Dardin case; Amy's case An obsolete Southern term for procrastination. Virginia widow Amy Dardin of Mecklenburg County submitted to Congress her claim to be compensated by the federal government for a horse impressed during the American Revolution, sending a bill every year from 1796 to at least 1815; some sources say she kept dunning Congress for 50 years before the procrastinating government paid.

Ancient Dominion See OLD DOMINION STATE.

and that's a fact There's no doubt about that, it's a certainty. " 'I never was one to dig much,' Pluto said. 'And that's a fact.' " [Erskine Caldwell, *God's Little Acre,* 1933]

angel flying by (or past) Said when one gets a sudden chill.

Anglo-African A historical term describing someone with a mixed speech or character of English and African. "He speaks fluently, and with grammatical correctness but in the Anglo-African dialect." [Albert D. Richardson, *The Secret Service . . . ,* 1865]

Anglo-Confederate See ANGLO-REBEL.

Anglo-Rebel A historical term used during the Civil War to describe British supporters of the Confederacy. "The Anglo-Rebel navy . . . was fitting out in England." [*Boston Sun Herald,* April 26, 1863] *Anglo-Confederate* is a similar term.

anigh Nearby, near, close to. "Don't go anigh him."

anights See ADAYS.

ankle-biter A small child who is unusually rough and unruly; disobedient.

ankle express Going by foot, walking. "The car broke down and we got back to town by ankle express."

anoint An old, little-used, humorous term for "to flog or to beat severely"; often pronounced *noint* or *ninted.* "He nointed him real good."

another-guess A term, probably obsolete, meaning "different, of a different sort." "He is another-guess man."

an't A common pronunciation of AIN'T.

ant cow A term used in the South and elsewhere for the aphid or plant louse, which lives on ants who carry it from plant to plant.

antigoglin Out of plumb, askew. "The rope was straight till he kicked it antigoglin." Also heard as *antigodlin, antigoslin* and *antigadlin.*

ant killer An old humorous term for the foot, especially a big foot. " 'Bill Jones, quit a smashin' that ar cat's tail!' 'Well then let hir keep hir tail clar of my ant killers!' " [*Quarter Race Kentucky,* 1846]

ant mashers Big feet. See also ANT KILLERS.

antses Sometimes used as the plural for *ant,* instead of *ants.* "There was black antses all over the food."

anxious bench Also used figuratively, this is a term for a seat in the front of a church or at revival meetings reserved for people especially concerned about their spiritual welfare. See AMEN CORNER.

anxioused up A seldom-used term meaning "excited." "He was all anxioused up."

any day and time Any time at all. "I'm there for her any day and time."

anymore Now, nowadays, presently. As Jesse Stuart wrote in *Beyond the Dark Hills* (1938): "They tell me this Armco plant only hires the best of men any more . . . Eyes not as good as they used to be. Got to take the lantern any more . . . You know, Jesse, any more I don't worry a great lot."

any much Very much. "We never done it any much."

anyways Anyway, anyhow, in any case. "Anyways I've got my opinion." [Mark Twain, "The Celebrated Jumping Frog of Calveras County," 1865] It can also mean to any degree at all: "Is he anyways hurt?"; or at any time: "Come visit anyways from May to October."

apast Past, beyond, by. "I don't put that shouting apast him." It can also mean finished, completed. "Winter is something apast."

ape A derogatory term for an African-American; mainly a Southern expression but used in other areas as well.

ape oil Liquor, probably because of the insulting premise, to apes, that too much drink makes men act like apes.

aplenty Plenty, an abundance. "I've had aplenty to eat."

appearanced Having a certain appearance. "She is very good appearanced."

appearment Appearance. "His general appearment was good."

Arab A street urchin; a huckster or street peddler; a roving bookmaker.

ara thing Anything. " 'Twarn't nothing,' he said gently. He knelt and touched her hot forehead clumsily. 'Do you want ara thing?' " [William Faulkner, "Wash," 1934]

arction A common pronunciation of auction. " 'The day that Texas feller arctioned off them wild Snopes ponies, I was out there.' " [William Faulkner, *The Town,* 1957]

are (1) Often dropped as a verb in Cajun speech: "You whistle 'cause you 'fraid," or "You welcome." (2) Frequently used in Cajun speech as a singular verb. "She are not right."

argufy To argue, dispute, debate. "No use argufying the matter."

Arkansas Originally spelled Arkansaw, our 25th state, nicknamed "the Wonder State," was admitted to the Union in 1925. "Arkansas" is the Sioux word for "and of the south wind people."

Arkansas asphalt A road made of logs laid side by side.

Arkansas chicken Salt pork. "We were so poor all we could afford was Arkansas chicken." Also called *Arkansas T-bone.*

Arkansas fire extinguisher A chamberpot.

Arkansas lizard Any insect louse.

Arkansas T-bone Salt pork. See example at ARKANSAS CHICKEN.

Arkansas toothpick A bowie knife or other knife with a long blade. One writer defines the bowie knife as "the principal instrument of nonsurgical phlebotomy in the American Southwest." This lethal instrument was probably first made for the legendary Colonel James Bowie (1799–1836), friend of Davy Crockett and hero at the Alamo. According to testimony by a daughter of Rezin Pleasant Bowie, the colonel's older brother, it was *her* father who invented the knife in about 1827, though she admitted that Jim Bowie did make it famous during a fight that year at Natchez, Mississippi in which six men were killed and 15 wounded. However, most historians believe the common long-bladed hunting knife was originally made for Jim Bowie by Arkansas blacksmith James Black, who they credit as the knife's inventor. After he killed one man with it in the Natchez duel, Colonel Bowie is said to have sent his knife to a Philadelphia blacksmith, who marketed copies of it under Bowie's name. Its double-edged blade was 10 to 15 inches long and curved to a point. Called an *Arkansas toothpick,* it was even carried by some congressmen and for a time gave Arkansas the nickname the Bowie, or Toothpick, State.

Arkansas travels   The runs, diarrhea.

Arkansas wedding cake   Corn bread.

Arkansawyer   A nickname for a native of Arkansas often used by Arkansas residents themselves.

artermatic   A Southern pronunciation of automatic. " '. . . I be dawg if he didn't flench off like it was a moccasin and him barefoot, and whupped out that little artermatic pistol and shot it dead as a doornail.' " [William Faulkner, *Sanctuary,* 1931]

ary   Any. "Wolves was about the worst destroyed of ary of them creeturs." [Marjorie Kinnan Rawlings, *The Yearling,* 1938]

as   Sometimes omitted in Southern speech: "You greedy as he is."

as crooked as a barrel of snakes   Someone so dishonest he can't be trusted in the slightest matters.

ash-barrel baby   An illegitimate child.

ashcake   A loaf of corn bread baked in hot ashes.

ash-cat   Any dirty, disheveled child.

ashy   Angry; ill-tempered, ill-humored. "He argued awhile and then got right ashy about it."

as mad as a pig on ice with his tail froze in   Very mad; used especially in Texas.

as mad as a rooster in an empty henhouse   Very mad indeed.

as much chance as a one-legged man-at an ass-kissing contest   Close to no chance at all.

aspersed   Slandered; though this is of course not a Southern invention, Faulkner puts it in the mouth of a poor Mississippi farmer: " 'The Snopes name. Can't you understand that? That ain't never been aspersed yet by no living man.' " [William Faulkner, *The Hamlet,* 1940]

as rich as six feet up a bull's ass   Very rich, fertile, like bull dung. "That soil is as rich as six feet up a bull's ass."

ass in a sling   To be or appear to be sad, rejected or defeated. Originating in the South perhaps a century ago, the now-national expression was probably suggested by someone with his arm in a sling, that image being greatly and humorously exaggerated. One good story claims that the ass is really a donkey, that the expression comes from a practice of blacksmiths rigging slings for donkeys, or asses, because the creatures can't stand on their feet while being shod. But the good story isn't a true story, donkeys *can* stand on their feet and, so far as is known, no blacksmith ever shod a donkey in a sling.

ass licker A sycophant, toady; the expression is now heard throughout the United States.

ass-ripper A dive into the water buttocks first. "He took a real ass-ripper into the old swimming hole."

assurance Insurance; used chiefly by blacks.

as sure as God made little chickens With no doubt, definitely. " '. . . or as sure as God made little chickens I'll take off my belt and give you a whipping [Daddy said].' " [Calder Willingham, *Rambling Rose,* 1972]

as sure as God made little green apples Very certain; used in the rural South as well as other parts of the country. " 'The lode is there [Ty Ty said] sure as God made little green apples.' " [Erskine Caldwell, *God's Little Acre,* 1933]

asthma dog A chihuahua or other hairless dog, from the belief that sleeping with one is a cure for asthma.

at all Of all. "They had the greatest time at all."

atamasco lily The Indian name for the Virginia daffodil *(Zephyranthes atamasco)*.

ate supper before saying grace Said of a pre-marital pregnancy. "They ate supper before saying grace."

at oneself To be at one's physical or mental best. "When he's at himself, he's a clever man."

Aunt Hagar's children African-Americans; used especially among Southern black speakers; after the Biblical Hagar, concubine of Abraham.

Auntie An old black woman; common since the 19th century and once regarded as a term of respect and affection by white people but regarded by blacks today as a derogatory term. "If I knew their names I at once forgot them, contenting myself with 'Sally,' or 'Jim,' or if they were old, perhaps, 'Uncle' or 'Auntie'—generic terms we were wont to use for Negroes whose names we did not know." [Katherine Lumpkin, *The Making of a Southerner,* 1947] See UNCLE.

avaytor A pronunciation of aviator. "It's Major de Spain's boy . . . The av-aytor." [William Faulkner, "Shall Not Perish," 1943]

awfullest Worst. "You're the awfullest card player I ever seen."

AWOL This nationally used abbreviation meaning "absent without leave" originated in the South, according to H. L. Mencken (*The American Language,* supplement I, 1945): "[In the Confederate Army] unwarranted absences of short duration were often unpunished and in other cases offenders received such trivial sentences as reprimand by a company officer, digging a stump, carrying a rail for a hour or two, wearing a placard inscribed with the letters AWOL."

awork with Filled or covered with. "The net was awork with fish."

ay gonnies A euphemism for "By God."

B

baaad Bad, when slowly pronounced *baaad,* has long been black slang, with some general use in the South and elsewhere, for something or someone good. The variation is so old that it is found in the American Creole language Gullah of three centuries ago, when *baaad* was used by slaves as an expression of admiration for another slave who successfully flaunted "Ole Maussa's" rules.

Babe The most famous example of *Babe* as a pet name for a boy in the South is baseball great Babe (George Herman) Ruth, born in Maryland in 1895. The nickname is often used in the South as a familiar name for a boy or man, especially the youngest of a family. *Babe* as a sometimes disparaging and insulting term for an attractive woman is a national usage.

B-A-Bas See A-B-ABS.

Baboon See ILLINOIS BABOON.

baby-batter Sperm. ". . . it looked like I wasn't going to be pumping any red-hot baby-batter into my own favorite womb any time soon." [Larry Brown, "Waiting for the Ladies," 1990]

baby-catcher A midwife or an obstetrician. "There was no doctor around there, and she was baby-catcher for the whole town."

baby-waker A firecracker. "Baby-wakers are small firecrackers, but they make a lot of noise."

back (1) To address an envelope, from the days before envelopes when letters were folded and addressed on the back. "Let me back this letter so you can mail it for me." (2) Held back; saved for later use. See usage example at EAT ONESELF FULL.

back back A command to make a horse, mule or other animal back up.

backed up Constipated. "He was all backed up from all those nuts he et."

backfin Prime crabmeat from the rear bony chambers of the Maryland blue crab, not fin meat.

back in the saddle again Back at work, back in one's regular routine; also slang for menstruating that has been used in Florida and other parts of the South since at least the 1950s. "I'm back in the saddle again."

backset A reversal of fortune, setback. "I thought I was getting well, but I took a backset."

backwards and forwards Back and forth. "I went backwards and forwards from my house to town all day long."

backy A century-old term for an outhouse or privy.

bacon and collards A traditional Southern dish, with *collards* generally referring to the cooked leafy portion of the plant. "In the South . . . 'bacon and collards' are a universal dish." [John Bartlett, *Dictionary of Americanisms*, 1877]

bacon and greens A popular dish in the South since before the 18th century consisting of bacon and cooked greens (such as turnip, mustard or collard greens). "Several gentlemen came . . . and dined and I ate bacon and greens." [William Byrd, *Secret Diary*, 1740]

bacon and rice aristocracy A Southern nickname for those who made great fortunes raising these commodities or selling them. "Thomas Smith bought his brother's lot and remained [in Charleston, S.C.] to build up the 'bacon and rice' aristocracy." [Mathew Poyas, *A Peep Into the Past*, 1853]

bad as I hate to do it As much as I hate to do it.

badmouth To speak ill of someone. Probably originating among African-American speakers and possibly deriving from a Vai or Mandingo expression, to badmouth was at first used mostly by Southern blacks but is now used nationwide. Its first recorded use in this sense came in 1941 when James Thurber used it in a *Saturday Evening Post* story: "He badmouthed everybody."

bad pay Someone who doesn't pay his bills; a bad credit risk. "He's bad pay. Don't lend him nothing."

the bad place Hell. "I thought when I come to that I was in the bad place. I sure thought I had been knocked all the way down to there." [Erskine Caldwell, *Georgia Boy*, 1943]

bad place (spot) in the road A very small, seedy town or group of houses so small it can hardly be considered a town.

bad sick Very ill. "He was bad sick, and I didn't think he'd make it."

bad time; bad time of the month Menstruation. "It's my bad time of the month."

bad to Inclined to. "When he gets drunk, he's bad to be in trouble."

bag A historical term for a large bag of cotton packed and ready to be shipped. "We had one hundred bags of cotton ready for the steamship."

bagasse Crushed sugar cane or the beet refuse from sugar-making that is used as animal feed. The word is borrowed from the Spanish word *bagazo*.

bait (1) A large armful of wood. " 'I'll fetch water and Jody, you go split a good bait o' wood.' " [Marjorie Kinnan Rawlings, *The Yearling*, 1938] (2) A pronunciation of *bite*. "She ate three baits of turnips." (3) Food; a meal; one serving of food.

baited for widow Said of a man dressed to kill, to impress women.

bait tree The catalpa, because its branches provide abundant caterpillars to use as bait for fishing. Also called the *fishbait tree*.

bake beans Baked beans. "How to make . . . dumplins of all kinds, bakebeans and so forth." [*New Orleans Picayune*, January 2, 1841]

bald A bare or treeless mountain top. "At length, after considerable fatigue, we came to the top of the near Bald . . ." [*Southern Literary Messenger*, volume 4, 1838]

bald face The white-crowned American widgeon (*Mareca americana*), a freshwater duck hunted in the South from early times. "Went a ducking between breakfast and dinner & killed 2 mallards & 5 bald faces." [Entry from George Washington's diary, quoted in Paul Haworth, *George Washington, Farmer*, 1915]

bald face whiskey An old term for raw, unaged whiskey just out of the still. "The loudest lungs were at a premium, and so was 'bald face' whiskey." [*Southern Literary Messen-*ger, volume 12, 1846] Also called *baldface* or *ballface whiskey*.

bale A term for a compact mass of cotton, its weight now about 500 pounds.

baler A historical term for a planter producing bales of cotton. "Every farmer in the South is a planter, from the 'thousand baler' to the rough, unshaved squatter." [H. C. Lewis, *Louisiana Swamp Doctor*, 1850]

Balize pilot Balize was the historic settlement of houses built on stilts at Pass à la Outre near New Orleans in the Mississippi River and designed to take on or discharge riverboat pilots. It fell into decay at the time of the Civil War and has since disappeared.

ball naked Stark naked, completely naked; derives from *ballocks* shortened to *balls* (testicles) and may have originally been *naked to the ballocks* or *balls*.

ball the jack To move or work swiftly. "When he saw his father coming he balled the jack." It was originally a railroad term: "That train is sure balling the jack."

balks Youngsters who have fits of stubborness are said to be given to the *balks*.

Baltimore; Baltimore oriole; Baltimore clipper An early dictionary states that the *Baltimore oriole* is "so called from the colors of Or (orange) and Sable in the coat of arms belonging to Lord Baltimore." This oriole is not closely related to the orioles of Europe but belongs to the blackbird and meadowlark rather than the crow family. But whatever its true species, the *Baltimore oriole* definitely takes its name from the Baltimore family, founders of Maryland, the bright colors of the male bird corresponding to the orange and black in their heraldic arms. The city of *Baltimore, Maryland* also honors the barons Baltimore, as does the early 19th century *Baltimore clipper,* more indirectly, the famous ships having been built in the city.

'Bam; 'Bama; 'Bammy Often used for Alabama.

bambache A drinking spree or a party at which there is a lot of drinking; a Cajun term from the French *bambouche* (spree).

banana The seed of a once-prized but now obsolete variety of cotton; also called *banana seed.*

banana ring Another name for a *banana split* in Louisiana and other Southern states.

banana seed See BANANA

bandy-shanked Bandy-legged, crooked legs or shanks.

banjo The name for this musical instrument was born in the South. Of the two theories about its origin, one holds that *banjo* derives from a black mispronunciation of *bandore,* an English word of Spanish origin denoting a musical instrument similar to the banjo; the other theory cites the Angoloa Kimbinde word *mbanza,* which also means a banjo-like instrument. It would be hard to prove or disprove either supposition.

banker A North Carolina seacoast inhabitant. "This term of 'Banker' applies to a scattering population of wreckers and fishermen, who dwell on the long, low, narrow beaches . . . from Cape Fear to near Cape Henry." [James Fenimore Cooper, *The Sea Lions,* 1849]

banquette A raised sidewalk or a footpath; derives from the French word meaning the same. The term is mainly confined to Louisiana and East Texas.

banter A dare, as in "I took up his banter." The word is pronounced "banner."

barbecued pigskins A popular Southern snack. "I get beer, barbecued pigskins, Slim Jims to munch on while writing." [Larry Brown, "92 Days," 1990.]

bard Can be the pronunciation of bard (poet), borrowed, or bird, as in "The bard bard mah canary bard."

barefoot bread Another name for Southern CORN PONE.

barking dogs Tired or sore feet. "Let me rest these barking dogs of mine."

Barlow knife Russell Barlow, who has been called "the patron saint of whittlers," invented the *barlow knife* over two centuries ago, and it has been known to Southerners under this name ever since. The *barlow*, a single-bladed pocket, pen or jacknife, was the pride and joy and bartering power of many an American boy and was mentioned in the works of Mark Twain, Joel Chandler Harris and many others.

barnburner A gusher, an oil strike that lights up the sky; used by wildcat oil men for a big well. The expression may have originated in the South.

barnlot A barnyard. "The cow's in the barnlot." *Stable-lot* and *bull-lot* are also common in the South, as is the widely used barnyard.

barnyard pipe Another name for a corncob pipe.

barnyard preacher An unordained lay preacher; a part-time preacher.

baron A name given in colonial times to any very rich Carolinian in charge of a "barony" as described in John Locke's *The Fundamental Constitution for the Government of Carolina (1669)*.

Bars The flag of the Confederacy, now usually called the Stars and Bars. "Down your Black-a-moor Stripes and Stars! We'll up instead the Confederate Bars!" [Anonymous old rhyme]

bar thorn fence A small, sharp-thorned hedge fence.

baseborn child An illegitimate child. In its earliest form this appears to have been *base begotten child*.

baser A member of a gospel-singing chorus; or the lines that are sung by the gospel-singing chorus.

basket meeting A picnic or other social gathering to which food is brought in baskets. Its purpose isn't entirely social but may be religious, political or educational.

bastard oak; bastard white oak Other names for the common Durand oak, pin oak or Bigalow oak.

bathcloth A washcloth used for washing the face or body.

batter bread A light cornbread made with eggs and milk; pronounced *baddy bread* or *batby bread*. Other Southern names for it include SPOON BREAD and *egg bread*.

battercake A pancake; also called a *batter* or *flittercake*.

battle To wash clothes by pounding them with a paddle after they are boiled in water, "whuppin' the dirt out of 'em." *Battle* in this sense is an old English word first recorded in 1570.

Battle in the Clouds The Civil War battle of Lookout Mountain, near Chattanooga, Tennessee.

baubee A little thing not worth much, a trifle, from the Scotish *bawbee* for a half-penny. "I don't care a baubee for that." Also spelled *bawbee* and *bobee.*

bay In South Carolina a *bay* refers to a low swampy area with many bay trees, also called bay laurels *(Laurus nobilis);* in Florida a *bay* is a watergrass meadow or flooded forests of cypresses and other trees.

bay chicken A term used in Louisiana for an umbrella-shaped edible mushroom that grows on wood, not on the ground, and is said to taste like chicken.

bayou A marshy, sluggish outlet of a lake or river; any slow-moving body of water. Used chiefly in the lower Mississippi Valley and Gulf States, it probably derives from the Choctaw *bayuk* for a river forming part of a delta.

Bayou State An old nickname for the state of Mississippi, whose inhabitants were sometimes called *tadpoles;* now a nickname for Louisiana.

bazooka The weapon takes its name from the trombone-like musical instrument invented in the 1930s by Arkansas comedian Bob Burns from two gas pipes and a whiskey funnel.

be Am. " 'Oh, I be mean, be I?' " [Marjorie Kinnan Rawlings, *The Yearling,* 1938]

bead tree Another name for the chinaberry tree, so called because its berries were once used to make beads.

bear-hug To shinny up a tree; the technique is also called *bear-climbing* and *bear-walking* in the South.

bear sign The droppings or tracks of a bear. " 'When kin we go, Pa?' 'Soon as we git the hoein' done. And see the bear sign.' " [Marjorie Kinnan Rawlings, *The Yearling,* 1938]

beast back An old term for riding horseback. "I rode beast back all the way to town."

beat around To putter or to loaf around. "He's not doing much, he's just beating around."

beat bobtail To beat or exceed all expectations. "Don't it beat bobtail what she did!"

beat-down Feeling low or beaten down by life. See example of usage at GOT A LOW EYE FOR A HIGH FENCE.

beaten biscuit A light Southern biscuit made by beating the dough before rolling it out.

beatin'est Most unusual, remarkable, surprising. "I declare, he's the beatin'est child I ever saw." [John Faulkner, *Men Working,* 1941]

beating the devil around the stump An expression equivalent to hemming and hawing, or beating around the bush.

beat out Worn out. "She's plumb beat out."

beats pickin' cotton Said when one is having an easier time of it than he might have had. "This sure beats pickin' cotton."

beat the devil and carry a rail To beat someone decisively, the expression deriving from the rural custom of having the favorite runner in a race carry a rail as a handicap. "For a sample of honesty this beats the devil and carries a rail." [(Little Rock) *Arkansas Gazette*, August 25, 1872]

beat the hound out of To give someone a bad beating. "He beat the hound out of him."

beau Boyfriend, lover. See example of usage at CONFEDRIT.

beaucoup Many, a lot, an abundance. A Southern term (from the French *beaucoup*, a great deal) pronounced *boocoo, boocoos* or *bogoobs*, which has gained wider use in recent years, and is sometimes lengthened to *boogoodles*. "He's got boocoo of money."

beau dollar A silver dollar. Many fanciful explanations have been given for the origins of this term, but the *beau (bo) dollar* probably derives from the French *beau*, dandy.

beauticious Very beautiful, especially of face. ". . . I knew I wasn't beauticious but that I was bodily and bountiful . . . He said I was more glorious . . . than two bare-assed Queens of Sheba getting in from both sides of the bed with him at the same time." [Erskine Caldwell, *The Earnshaw Neighborhood*, 1971]

beautifuller Sometimes heard instead of more beautiful. "She's more beautifuller than her sister."

because Why. "Give me a good reason because."

become to be To come to be, to come about. "This event become to be held annually."

be dawg Euphemism for "be damned." " 'Yes, sir. Be dawg if I ain't lived to be a great-grandpaw after all.' " [William Faulkner, "Wash," 1934]

bed baby An infant who can't crawl yet, who remains mostly in his or her crib or bed.

bedrid Confined to bed for a long time, bedridden. "He's been bedrid over a year now."

bedroom shoes House slippers; also called *bed shoes*.

bee gum A hollow tree or log used as a beehive; any beehive.

been to the bushes Been to the bathroom. " 'Durn it [Mink said], let me out on that bridge. I ain't been to the bushes this morning.' " [William Faulkner, *The Mansion*, 1959]

been try Tried to; heard mainly in Cajun speech. "You been try make me mad."

beerhead Someone who habitually drinks beer. "You better stop running around with those beerheads."

beeswax One's business or own concern. "Mind your own beeswax." Common in other regions of the United States as well.

before-day The time just before daybreak; pronounced *afore-day* or *fore-day*.

beforetimes Early. "That plant's blooming beforetimes for such."

beggar-trash Low-class, worthless people. "He comes from beggar-trash and acts like it."

begone An old scolding expression, meaning "be off, get out of here," that is still heard in the South.

beholden Frequently used instead of indebted, as in "I'm beholden to you."

beignet A French-style doughnut popular in New Orleans and other parts of Louisiana. It is also spelled *bignet* and is sometimes pronounced *ben-yā.*

being Because, since. "Being it's you, I'll take a dollar for it."

belike Probably; perhaps. " 'You gave it to your foster mother to keep for you, belike?' " [William Faulkner, *Light in August,* 1932]

belittle To disparage; an Americanism widely used today that was invented by Thomas Jefferson in 1787.

bell A dog's baying during the chase in hunting; from the Old English *bellan,* to bark, bellow.

bell cow The lead cow of a herd, the one that wears a bell. By transference the term has come to mean any leader or big shot. *Bell ox* is also used. "He's the bell ox of that town."

belling Synonymous for a big party in West Virginia. "You coming to the belling?"

bell ox See BELL COW.

bellyache root Southern plant *(Angelica lucida canadensis fortasse)* used as a tonic for stomachaches.

belly rub To dance closely, belly to belly, with someone to slow music.

belly timber An old English term for food or provisions; sometimes used in the South, though not nearly as often as in the past. It was widely used in England three centuries ago.

belly washer Soda pop; lemonade. "I'd rather have water than that belly washer you're drinking."

belong Sometimes means should, ought. "Please paint that boat as it belongs to be." It can also mean must. "Do I belong to clean the room?"

benasty A verb meaning to befoul or make dirty.

bench-legged Bowlegged; applied to dogs and sometimes to people.

benefit Advantage. " 'Ain't no benefit in farming. I figure on getting out of it soon as I can.' " [William Faulkner, *The Hamlet*, 1940]

benne A name used mainly in South Carolina for sesame seeds. *Sesamum indicum* is said to be the oldest herbaceous plant cultivated for its seeds. Benne, as the seeds are called in Africa and the South, or *sim sim*, another African name for them, were brought to the South on the first slave ships. They have been used for everything from ink to cattle feed to flour to oil, and are a popular ingredient in cookies, crackers and candies. *Benne* is a Wolof word for the sesame seed. *Sesamum* is the Greek version of the Arabic word for sesame.

be on someone like a South Texas wind To be so mad one is immediately ready to fight violently. "I'm gonna be on you like a South Texas wind."

bereft Crazy. "I'll be clean bereft before I finish this." *Bereft* here is short for "bereft of sense or reason."

bescrow and bescrew An old term meaning "to curse." "She bescrowed and bescrewed him."

be-shame bush The mimosa (*mimosa pudica*) or any sensitive plant that closes its leaves when touched. This mimosa should not be confused with the mimosa tree.

best Often used in place of better. "You'd best not do that."

bestest A double superlative primarily used by Southern blacks. "He's the bestest there is."

best good The best result of an action, morally or otherwise. " 'Dear God [Bessie prayed], we poor sinners kneel down . . . to pray for a blessing on this new automobile trade . . . And these two men here who sold the new car to us need your bless, too, so they can sell automobiles for the best good.' " [Erskine Caldwell, *Tobacco Road*, 1932]

best-goodest A redundancy sometimes used for "a favorite," as in "Are you wearing your best-goodest dress?"

bestmost Double superlative for best, one's very best. "I'll do my bestmost to win."

best woman Sometimes used for the maid or matron of honor at a wedding. Variations are *best maid, best lady* and *best girl*, which is also used in the sense of a girlfriend or a favorite girl.

betimes An old English dialect word meaning "occasionally." "I've worked betimes in the city."

bet straightening A term used mainly by blacks for giving unsolicited, often unwanted, advice while others play cards. "They weren't in the game, but they was standing around bet straightening."

better had Had better. " 'Maybe he'll change his mind.' 'He better had.' "

bettywood Probably another name for the buttonwood tree or sycamore. The expression is rarely, if ever, used today, though it was once common, especially in Kentucky.

between hawk and buzzard Twilight time, when it is too dark to tell a hawk from a buzzard.

betwixt Between. "He let him have it betwixt the eyes."

betwixt a balk and a breakdown In fair or middling health.

Beulah land A Biblical term (*Isaiah* 62:4) used in the South and other regions for heaven or the promised land; also called *Beulah shore*.

bias road A road that cuts off at a sharp angle from the main road.

Bible Belt H. L. Mencken coined this term to describe parts of the United States where the literal accuracy of the Bible is widely believed, which of course is not limited to the South, despite the first use of the term: "The Baptist Record, in Jackson, Mississippi, [is] in the heart of the Bible and Lynching Belt." [H. L. Mencken, *American Mercury*, 1926] More recently the term has been used to refer to the South as an area of religious or moral fervor.

biblefish See PADDLEFISH.

biddable Obedient, docile, tractable. "He's not a biddable servant."

biddy A just-hatched or young chicken; probably derives through Gullah from the African Kongo *bi-dibidi* for a bird.

bidness A pronunciation of business. "I ain't going to stand fer this bidness any longer, I ain't."

bien Good; a French word often used in the Southern Louisiana-French dialects.

biff A very hard or quick blow with the fist. "He give him a biff in the eye."

big (1) As an adverb *big* can mean "very, exceedingly," as in "He got big rich." (2) Pregnant. "If you hadn't said you were big, he wouldn't have married you." (3) As a verb, to make or become pregnant; to have sex with. " 'Lov's going to big her,' Dude said. 'He's getting ready to do it right now, too. Look at him crawl around—he acts like an old stud horse.' " [Erskine Caldwell, *Tobacco Road*, 1932]

big as the broad daylight Vast, immense. " 'You're lying as big as the broad daylight, Jeff Newsome!' Aunt Annie said . . ." [Erskine Caldwell, "Uncle Jeff," *The Complete Stories of Erskine Caldwell*, 1953]

big-butt A conceited, self-important person; an aristocrat or big wig.

big church An ironic expression meaning "no church at all": "I'm not religious, I belong to the big church."

Big D A popular nickname for Dallas, Texas.

Big Daddy An affectionate term for one's grandfather or the paternalistic head of a family, the term made famous by Tennessee Williams as the nickname of the wealthy cotton planter in his play *Cat on a Hot Tin Roof* (1955). Variants include *Big Papa, Big Grandpa* and *Big Gonpy*.

big dog A conceited, pompous person; also called BIG DUDE. This is apparently a shortening of the old, rarely used *big dog with the brass collar*. "There goes the big dog with the brass collar."

Big Drink Obsolete name for the Mississippi River.

big dude A conceited, pompous person; also called BIG DOG.

Big Easy Possibly a jazz term that refers to the pleasant easy-going life in New Orleans. No dictionary records the fact, but New Orleans' nickname among its residents is the *Big Easy,* as is noted in the 1987 film of that name.

big end The most important part of something. "The big end of it [running a marathon] is to pace yourself so you can finish."

big-eye Covetousness or greed. Someone who has the *big-eye* for food, for example, is the same as someone who has *eyes bigger than his belly*. The term is said to be a Gullah expression that is a translation of an African Ibo word meaning the same. *Big-eyed* means greedy. "She's big-eyed, wants everything she sees."

big feeler Someone who believes (feels) he is very important, who is proud and haughty.

big frost A black, killing frost.

bigged To have made pregnant. "He bigged her, that's the truth."

biggety; biggity; briggety Conceited; a show-off. "Stop being so biggety."

biggety bantam A feisty little person who acts tough. "Lum said, 'Die and good riddance. Biggety bantam.'" [Marjorie Kinnan Rawlings, *The Yearling,* 1938]

big hat A policeman, sheriff or state trooper.

big hominy An old term for a hominy dish with meat or fowl in it.

Big Hound A Greyhound bus. "If he'd taken my pickup that'd be real uncool and I'd have to catch the Big Hound going north emptyhanded." [Larry Brown, "Gold Nuggets," 1990.]

big house A manor; the main house on a plantation. *Big house* is also used for the living room, sometimes called BIG ROOM, of a house.

Big Hungry An old nickname for the poor country area around Tuskegee, Alabama. The famous Tuskegee Institute is located in this area.

Big Ike A disparaging term meaning "a self-important person, a big wheel, a loud offensive person." "He's a real Big Ike."

big laurel A Southern name for the rhododendron or a large variety of magnolia (*Magnolia grandiflora*).

big lazies A state of inertia. "He had the big lazies most of the time."

Big Mama A grandmother; a woman regarded as the head of a family; a man's wife, sweetheart or girlfriend. See also BIG DADDY.

Big Mama's Everlasting Rolls A delicate, slightly sweet and sour special occasion bread (made in the form of rolls) known throughout the South.

bigmouth A species of fish, *Chaenobryttus coronarius;* also called the *warmouth* and the *bigmouth perch* in Louisiana.

big road Any main road or highway.

big rock A jail or state prison. "He's up at the big rock two years now."

big room The living room of a house; also called BIG HOUSE.

big stick A policeman or other person of authority.

big time An enjoyable party or celebration; any good time. "They had a big time at the Joneses."

big water (1) A very bad flood. "Remember that big water of 1946?" (2) The Mississippi River. "The boat was slipping along, swift and steady, through the big water in the smoky moonlight." [Mark Twain, *Tom Sawyer, Detective,* 1896]

big word book A dictionary.

billdown See PADDLEFISH.

binnyache A bellyache.

bip into To attack with either words or blows. "They had some argument. She really bipped into him."

bird dog The buttocks. "He knocked him on his bird dog."

bird minder A South Carolina term for someone who frightens birds away from crops by shooting a gun, cracking a whip, etc.

Bird o' Satan A colorful name used in Virginia for the bluejay, especially among black speakers. In folklore the bird is associated with hell and Satan.

birth Used as a verb, to give birth to. "She was a midwife that helped a lot of women birthin' their babies."

biter Another term for the claw of a crab, used in Maryland and Virginia.

biting frost A severe frost that damages plants.

black ankle See BRASS ANKLE.

black-assed pea A humorous term for black-eyed peas, used mostly by black Southern speakers.

Black Belt Any Southern region, especially in Alabama and Mississippi, with rich black soil and a large population of black people.

blackberry baby An illegitimate child, perhaps because the child was thought to be conceived in the brush. Also called a *blackberry patch baby*.

blackberry winter A period of cool weather in spring, usually May or June, when the blackberries are in blossom. Robert Penn Warren wrote a highly regarded story entitled "Blackberry Winter." It is also the title Margaret Mead used for a memoir she published in 1972. See also DOGWOOD WINTER.

black bottle Any poisonous drink; an opiate; knock-out drops. Giving one the *black bottle* was said to be a way of getting rid of patients in hospital charity wards. "Black," of course, has always been associated with death.

black bottom A low-lying section of a town inhabited solely by blacks. The dance called the *black bottom*, which originated among blacks in the South, is not named for this geographical description. The *New Yorker* (October 7, 1926) said the hip-moving dance "was constructed to sim-ulate the movements of a cow mired in black bottom river mud."

black Christmas A snowless late December.

black codes Southern state laws passed in 1865 and 1866 to retain white control over blacks. Also called bloody codes. As early as 1840 the term *black code* was used to mean a legal code applying to blacks in Southern states.

black drink A former ceremonial drink and medicine made from the leaves of the Yaupon holly by Indians of the Southern states.

black-eye gravy Ham gravy that is poured over dishes like rice and grits.

black-eyed pea See COWPEA.

black flesh A term used for black slaves in the South before emancipation.

black hand A witchcraft spell or charm; a term originating with Gullah speakers.

blackjack (1) A Southern term for a heavy, sticky black soil not much valued because it clods when wet and is very hard when dry. (2) The *blackjack oak (Quercus marilandica)* common to the South, or wood from the tree. Some sources call this scrub oak good firewood, but Erskine Caldwell writes in *Tobacco Road* (1932): "People argued with Jeeter about his mule-like determination to sell blackjack for fuel, and they tried to convince him that as firewood it was practically worthless . . ."

black moss The famous Spanish moss of the South; it takes this name from the black fiber beneath the stem's outer covering.

Black Republican Long an insulting nickname for a Republican in the South, the term was first used to describe a Republican favoring emancipation of the slaves but came to be applied to any Republican and is still occasionally heard.

blacksnake A term for a black man's penis; used in Erskine Caldwell's famous story "Blue Boy" (*The Complete Stories of Erskine Caldwell,* 1943) and by a black character in the film *Platoon* (1986), among other works.

black stock A term used for black slaves in the South before emancipation.

blast my old shoes! An emphatic expression not much used anymore. "I'll see you a fair fight, blast my old shoes if I don't." [Augustus Longstreet, *Georgia Scenes,* 1835]

bleed Another term for "to sweat." "It's so hot I'm bleedin' to death."

bless Katy! An old term meaning "Bless me!"

blind mosquito See CHIZZWINK.

blind pig A somewhat old-fashioned, chiefly Southern expression for a speakeasy. The origin of the term,

first recorded in 1857, is uncertain but according to one tale the name *blind pig* comes from the nickname of a band of soldiers called the Public Guard serving in Richmond, Virginia about 1858. Their militia hats had the initial P.G. on them, the sobriquet originating because "P.G. is a pig without an *i,* and a pig without an eye is a blind pig." Also called a *blind tiger.*

blind tiger See BLIND PIG.

blip An old-fashioned term for a sudden blow. "He took him a blip in the back and knocked him off." [Mark Twain, *Tom Sawyer Abroad,* 1885]

blood kin Related by blood, not marriage. " 'It's got to be done by the fellow's own blood kin, or it won't work.' " [William Faulkner, *The Hamlet,* 1940]

bloodnoun A bullfrog, chiefly in South Carolina. Also heard as *bloodynoun.*

blood pig A New Orleans dish made with hog's blood.

blood pudding A dark sausage with a high blood content; also called *blood sausage* and *black pudding.*

blood's thick Blood is thicker than water. " 'I don't know nothing about that one Varner hired. But blood's thick.' " [William Faulkner, *The Hamlet,* 1940]

Bloody bill In 1833 Congress passed a law providing for the enforcement of the federal tariff laws in South Carolina. South Carolinians called this the *Bloody bill,* predicting that it would lead to bloodshed.

Bloody bones A boogeyman children are threatened with when they don't behave. "Old Bloody bones'll get you."

bloody bucket See BUCKET OF BLOOD.

bloody codes See BLACK CODES.

bloody flux See quote. "As for dysentery—the 'bloody flux' as the ladies delicately called it—it seemed to have spared no one from private to general . . . 'Dey ain' a soun' set of bowels in de whole Confedrut ahmy,' observed Mammy darkly . . ." [Margaret Mitchell, *Gone With the Wind,* 1936]

bloodynoun See BLOODNOUN.

blow fire To heal a burn simply by reciting some magic words and blowing on it, blowing the fire out of it; in the past, and still to some extent today, certain people were believed to have this magical power.

blow gum Sometimes used as a synonym for bubblegum. "I'd sure like a piece of that blow gum."

blown up like a toad Very angry, silently seething with anger. "There he was in the corner, blown up like a toad while I danced with Jim Bob."

blue A very darkskinned black person, the term common among black speakers.

bluebacks Paper money used by the Confederates during the Civil War; also called *graybacks.* "During the Civil War . . . the original Blue Backs of the Confederacy (so-called in opposition to Green Backs of the Union) soon became known as Shucks, a name sufficiently significant of their evil repute . . ." [Maximillian Schele De Vere, *Americanisms,* 1871] Over a billion dollars worth of bluebacks and graybacks were issued by the South during the Civil War, the bills worth about 1.7 cents in gold to the dollar by the end of the hostilities.

bluebelly A Northerner, a Yankee or a New Englander. The word, which first meant an American, was applied to Northerners shortly before the Civil War in reference to the blue uniforms worn by Union soldiers. It is sometimes used in a derogatory or humorous sense today.

bluebird weather Unusually warm weather in autumn; used mainly in Maryland and Virginia.

blue devils The blues, low spirits. "He lost the game and got the blue devils."

blue hen's chicken One who is a good fighter, because blue hens are said to breed the best fighting cocks; the term also means someone highspirited, aggressive, quick-tempered or high-class and was applied to soldiers from Delaware during the Revolutionary War, resulting in the nickname *Blue Hen's Chicken* for a native of Delaware.

bluegrass (1) The bluegrass used so widely for American lawns isn't very blue, having only a slightly blue tinge at most. The green grass takes its name from another grass, a pest grass that settlers on the Atlantic coast so named because its leaves were distinctly bluish in color. When these settlers moved into what is now Kentucky, they found another grass of about the same size and shape as the Atlantic coast bluegrass and gave it the same name. (2) U.S. country music played on unamplified stringed instruments, with emphasis on the banjo.

Bluegrass and Bourbon State A nickname for the state of Kentucky.

bluegrass country The region in Kentucky and central Virginia noted for its bluegrass.

blue-gum A derogatory term for a black person with a blue tint to his gums; applied, but less frequently, to a Creole or a Cajun. "They making a bluegum out of you . . ." [William Faulkner, *The Sound and the Fury,* 1929]

blue John Skim milk, because it sometimes has a bluish appearance.

Blue Lodge See SONS OF THE SOUTH.

blue tick A hound with blue flecks on its white coat. "That big Bluetick hound running like a greyhound . . ." [William Faulkner, *The Mansion,* 1959]

bluff Used in the South as early as 1687 in place of the British "river bank," *bluff,* according to the late Stuart Berg Flexner in *I Hear America Talking* (1976), "has the distinction of being the first word attacked as being a 'barbarous' American term."

Bluff City A nickname for both Memphis, Tennessee and Hannibal, Missouri because they are located on bluffs overhanging water.

board To beat someone with a board on the rump. Apparently in days past a punishment for thieves involved the whole town turning out to punish offenders in this way. One account says the board used measured "four feet long and six inches wide."

bobbasheely To walk in no great rush but to move on, to saunter. " 'Ha ha ha,' Butch said, without mirth, without anything. 'How's that for a idea? Huh, Sugar Boy? You and Sweet Thing bobbasheely on back to the hotel now, and me and Uncle Remus and Lord Fauntleroy will mosey along any time up to midnight, providing of course we are through here.' " [William Faulkner, *The Reivers,* 1962] A *bobbasheely* can also mean "a very close friend"; in fact, it is said to derive from a Choctaw Indian word meaning "my brother." See also MOSEY.

bobble A mistake or error. The word, which originated in the South or West, is commonly used as a verb for a mishandled chance in baseball.

bobo A word, heard in Louisiana, especially New Orleans, and generally reserved for children, describing a bump, a cut or a sore. Derives from the French *faire bobo,* to hurt oneself. *Booboo* is an equivalent heard in other areas of the country, including the South.

bobolition Whether this was a humorous black pronunciation of "abolition," in the South and elsewhere, is open to question; it may have been a word scornful whites attributed to blacks. In *Customs of Old New England* (1893) Alice Earle writes: "The 14th of July was observed for many years to commemorate the introduction of measures to abolish the slave trade. It was derisively called Bobolition Day, and the orderly convention of black men was greeted with a fusillade of rotten fruit and eggs and much jesting abuse."

bobtailed flush A worthless flush in poker, only three or four cards of same suit. *Bobtailed* means "short, deficient."

bobtailed straight A worthless four card straight in poker. See also BOBTAILED FLUSH.

bobwire A common pronunciation of *barbed wire.* See usage example at UNHEALTH.

bodacious Bold, audacious; unceremonious. Can also mean thorough, as in "He's a bodacious idiot," and

completely, as in "That jug was bodaciously smashed."

bog A Southern dish made with wine and chicken or game, such as chicken bog or squirrel bog.

bog bugle A Southern name for the pitcher plant *(Sarracenia purpurea),* which grows in bogs and has bugle-shaped leaves.

bogue (1) A stream or creek, from the Choctaw *bog,* stream. "They'd see only their heads swimming across the bogues . . ." [William Faulkner, *Mosquitoes,* 1927] (2) Fake, phony; either from *bogus* or from the African Hausa *boko,* fake. (3) To grope or wander aimlessly. "He was bogueing around in the dark."

bohunkus Backside. "Well, honey, they can just rest back on their little bohonkus . . ." [Eudora Welty, *Petrified Man,* 1941]

boil Water that bursts through a break in a levee is called a boil.

boil cabbage Boiled cabbage.

boiled bacon Bacon that is boiled instead of fried or broiled. "She had finished eating a late breakfast of Texas pink grapefruit, boiled bacon, grits-and-gravy, and biscuits and gravy . . ." [Erskine Caldwell, *The Earnshaw Neighborhood,* 1971]

boiled custard A Southern custard dessert made with eggs, milk, sugar, vanilla and other ingredients.

boiled pie   A pie or dumpling cooked in boiling water.

boiled shirt   A formal dress shirt starched in the front; this term has general as well as Southern usage. " '. . . Whitfield was standing jest like pap said, in his boiled shirt and his black hat and pants and necktie . . .' " [William Faulkner, "Shingles for the Lord," 1943]

boiler   (1) A saucepan for cooking. (2) A whiskey still. (3) The stomach. "He ate so much he like to bust his boiler." (4) A pipe for smoking tobacco.

boiling   A crowd, a whole group. " '. . . the whole damned boiling of you . . .' " [William Faulkner, *The Town*, 1957]

boiling corn; boiling ear   Sweet, eating corn, not field corn for livestock.

boiling up   Said of storm clouds growing in size.

boiling with   Filled up to the brim with, packed with. " '[He] was born where what few other people he knew lived, in log cabins boiling with children like the one he was born in . . .' " [William Faulkner, *Absalom, Absalom!*, 1936]

boil potatoes   Boiled potatoes.

boil shrimp   Boiled shrimp.

boil the pot   To make a boiled dinner, such as pot roast.

bold stream   A swiftly running stream. "He took the raft down that bold stream."

bolichi roast   A roast beef stuffed with hardboiled eggs; the Cuban Spanish *boliche* means "round of beef."

bolliwog   Nonsense, belly wash, hog wash; also pronounced *bolly wash*.

bollixed up   Thrown into confusion; an expression common in the South, though it is often regarded as a Northern expression. The word derives from the old English *bealluc*, testicle. Faulkner uses it several times in his work. " 'Nothing,' Butch said. 'Nothing a-tall. Me and Sugar was kind of bollixed up at one another for a while.' " [William Faulkner, *The Reivers*, 1962]

boll weevil   Pronounced *boweevil*. *Weevil* comes from the Old English *wifel*, beetle, and *boll*, first spelled *bowl*, refers to the pod of the cotton plant, which the beetle attacks. In Enterprise, Alabama there is a monument to a boll weevil—erected at the turn of the century after the beetle so devastated the cotton crop in the area that farmers were forced to plant peanuts and as a result became more prosperous than they had ever been as cotton growers. *Boll weevil* has some use in the South as a term for a tenderfoot and for a contempt-ible person.

boll weevil weather The cold wet weather in which the boll weevil thrives.

bomb A term children in South Carolina and elsewhere use for the big marble, or aggie, in marbles.

bombazine Because the silk and wool fabric called bombazine was often used to make umbrellas, a *bombazine* was humorously used as a synonym for an umbrella in the South and other areas. The term is rarely heard today.

bombo According to John Bartlett in his *Dictionary of Americanisms* (1877), a *bombo* is "an animal of North Carolina, said to resemble the hedgehog and by some called a badger." The term is obsolete today.

bomb-proof A historical expression used in the South during the Civil War to describe a man who occupied a safe place at home while the war raged on. "Able-bodied bomb-proofs" were the object of much derision.

bone felon A *felon* is an acute and painful inflammation of the deeper tissues or of a finger or toe. Because it seems to ache right down to the bone, it is often called a *bone felon* in the South. The expression is found as far back as the tales of Uncle Re-mus. Rather than a redundancy, it seems like an improvement on the original.

boneset A plant *(Eupetorium pur-pureum)*, also known as *Joe-Pye weed,* regarded in folk medicine as a rem-edy for broken bones. *Boneset* is heard in other regions of the country also.

bonnet squash The common vege-table sponge *(Luffa cylindrica)* was once so named in the South because women made bonnets out of its fi-brous matter. "The girls made their hats of rye and wheat straw, and some very pretty bonnets were made of the fibrous substance that grows in the vegetable known as the bonnet squash." [Joel Chandler Harris, *On the Plantation,* 1892]

bonnet walker A colorful name for the purple gallinude, because the bird walks on lily pads, or bonnets, in ponds and lakes.

Bonnie Blue Flag The secession flag of South Carolina, which had a blue field and a single star; also the name of a popular secessionist song. It was at a state convention at Jackson, Mis-sissippi, when that state voted to secede from the Union, that the fa-mous patriotic song of the South was inspired by an immense blue silk banner with a single star that some-one carried through the crowd. Ac-cording to one old story, Arkansas comedian Harry Macarthy witnessed the scene and began writing the song's lyrics, which he finished when the rest of the Southern states seceded:

> First gallant South Carolina nobly
>   made the stand;
> Then came Mississippi, who took her
>   by the hand;

Next, quickly Florida Alabama and
  Georgia,
All raised on high the Bonnie Blue
  Flag that bears a Single Star . . .
Hurrah, hurrah! for Southern Rights
  Hurrah!

boocoodles See BEAUCOUP.

boody (Often pronounced *booty*)
Originally meaning a woman's sexual
organs and sexual intercourse, this
term has come to mean "buttocks"
and is widely used in this sense today, even in the names of tanning
parlors, such as "Tan Your Booty."

booger A ghost or hobgoblin; also
called the *boogerman, boogerbear* and
bookity Sam, among other terms. Derives ultimately from the Middle English *bugge,* ghost. " 'I still think you
have found a booger where there
isn't one,' the sheriff said." [William
Faulkner, *The Mansion,* 1959]

boojy A disparaging term, deriving
from *bourgeous,* that is used by
Southern blacks to describe rich blacks
who put on white elitest airs.

book (1) The third stomach of a
cow; possibly so called by farmers
who slaughter their cattle because
this stomach has so many "leaves" in
it but perhaps deriving from the
Middle English *bouk,* belly. (2) Often
used to describe a pile or stack of
tobacco leaves. (3) Common term
for a magazine or pamphlet throughout the South.

booked on out Left hastily. "We
booked on out of there, and I think

it was like 3:47 when I got on in
home . . ." [Larry Brown, "Wild
Thing," 1990]

bookie sug A sweetheart or lover;
sug is short for "sugar."

bookity-book Quickly; used mainly
by black speakers to imitate the sound
of running feet, as in "Here he comes,
bookity-book, bookity-book."

bookooing Loud talking, from the
French BEAUCOUP, a great deal.

books School or schooltime, as in
"Books began at eight o'clock." In
days past "Books, books!" was a call
to school.

book-writer An author of books; to
book-write means "to write a book."

boomalally A soldier, especially one
parading to music, the term apparently deriving from the sound of
drums; first applied to cadets at the
South Carolina Military Academy.

boot (1) A lagniappe or premium,
a little extra inducement in a sale;
can also be the children a woman
brings to a second marriage. The
chiefly Southern term is first recorded in the early 19th century but
possibly derives from an Old English
word meaning "good, advantage,
profit." (2) *Boot* for the trunk of a
car, chiefly a British term, was sometimes used in Georgia and other
Southern states earlier in the century
but apparently has little or no use
there today.

bootkisser A sycophant; also called *bootlicker*.

bootlicker See BOOTKISSER.

booze A Mr. E. G. or E. S. Booze of Kentucky, circa 1840, was a distiller who sold his *booze*, liquor, under his own name, the bottles often made in the shape of log cabins. But *booze* probably has its roots in the Middle English verb *bousen*, drink deeply. However, the English use *booze* only for beer and ale, and there is no doubt that the labels on Mr. Booze's bottles strengthened the general American use of the word for hard liquor. Today *booze*, in the South and the rest of the country, most often signifies cheap, even rot-gut whiskey, though it also often refers to any alcoholic drink.

bopper A hard blow. "He socked him a real bopper."

bore for the hollow horn A probably obsolete phrase once common in the South, among other regions. "A hole is bored in the horn of a cow (having a hollow horn) with a gimlet. This custom gave rise to the epithet applied to people who behaved foolishly (suggesting a hollow head): "He ought to be bored for the holler horn." [*Dialect Notes*, volume 5, 1919]

boresome Boring. "He's a kind of boresome man."

borga; booga A paper sack or POKE, the word's origin unknown.

born To give birth to, as in " 'She got help to born that child.' " [William Faulkner, "Tomorrow," 1940]

born on crazy creek Stupid. "He wasn't born on crazy creek, you know."

born tired and raised lazy Said of someone completely worthless.

boss dog Person in authority, top dog, big dog, an important person. "He's boss dog around here."

boss-man; boss-lady; boss-woman The man or woman in charge; an employer or supervisor. "Watch it—here comes the boss-man."

bosom bread These were large, flat loaves of bread that black stevadores working the Mississippi steamboats carried in their shirt fronts (against their chests or bosoms) for snacks throughout the day. They needed such fuel, as these longshoremen expended more energy than almost any other workers at the time.

bothered up Disturbed, agitated, apprehensive. "They're all bothered up about it."

botherment A bother, trouble. "It's really a botherment putting all those parts together."

both two Both one and the other. "I don't want one, I want both two of them."

bottle A widespread pronunciation of *battle*, which, according to one joke, may have led to the outbreak of the Civil War. (See Introduction.)

bottle-arsed tupelo A humorous Southern name for the tupelo gum tree *(Nyssa aquatica)* because of its bulging trunk base.

bottle drink A somewhat old-fashioned Southern term for any soft drink.

bottom Low land near a river; also called *bottomland.*

bought Attached to bread (bought bread), clothing, champagne, and so forth, *bought* indicates something not made at home, something commercially made. See also BOUGHT CHAMPAGNE.

bought champagne Champagne purchased from a store as opposed to homemade wine. See also SCUPPERNONG CLARET and SCUPPERNONG WINE.

boughten Something commercially made, as opposed to homemade. See BOUGHT.

bought flowers Cut flowers purchased from a florist. "They held the funeral on the second day with the town coming to look at Miss Emily beneath a mass of bought flowers . . ." [William Faulkner, "A Rose for Emily," 1930]

bound To bet, as in "I bound he'll be there" or "I bound you he'll win"; heard throughout the South but especially among black speakers.

bound and determined Irrevocably committed to do something. "He's bound and determined to leave home."

bounden Obligatory. "It's his bounden duty."

bourbon A whiskey that takes its name from a whiskey originally made only in Bourbon County, Kentucky. The county, in turn, was named for France's Bourbon Kings.

bourbon ball A candy flavored with bourbon whiskey made in Kentucky and other Southern states.

Bourbon Street A famous street in the French Quarter of New Orleans. In *Love and Money* (1954), Erskine Caldwell called it "that Southern gentleman's skid row."

Bowie knife See ARKANSAS TOOTHPICK.

bow the blinds To bring the shutters together so that they are almost closed.

bow up to The opposite of bow down to; to stand up to someone. "You have got to bow up to him."

box (1) A coffin. "Addie Burden could not want a better one, a better box to lie in." [William Faulkner, *As I Lay Dying,* 1930] (2) A stringed musical instrument such as a guitar or banjo.

box-ankled Someone who has ankles that strike together when he or she walks. "He was a clumsy, knock-kneed, box-ankled S.O.B."

boxing A term widely used in Mississippi and other Southern states for wooden siding on a house. See also SHIPLAP.

boy An insulting term for an adult black male that dates back to days of slavery and has become much less common in recent times.

boys in gray Confederate soldiers; a term coined in 1861 after the color of Confederate uniforms. See also BUTTERNUT.

Bradley According to Gary Jennings in *Personalities of Language* (1965): "All of the few Chickahominy Indians still existing in Virginia are surnamed Bradley. This commemorates either the popularity or the fecundity of an early English colonist, a runaway indentured servant, who joined and married into the tribe."

brag Excellent, fit to be boasted about. A prize dog for example is a *brag dog;* superlative cotton is *brag cotton.*

braggable Something that can be boasted about. "We're doin' all right, but nothing' braggable."

braggadocious Boastful, bragging.

branch A tributary stream or any stream that is not a large river or bayou.

branch water Pure, natural water, water from a pure creek or stream, as in *bourbon and branch water.*

brang Bring (see quotation for PECKERWOOD); sometimes used as the past tense of bring.

brass ankle An often derogatory name for a person of mixed race that was first recorded in 1930 but is probably considerably older. One possible explanation has the term deriving from Portuguese settlers in South Carolina who intermarried with local blacks. These racially mixed people then tended to marry within their own group. Noted for the brass anklets they liked to wear and their dark skin, they came to be known as *brass ankles* or *black ankles.*

bray To prepare or pound up a medicine. "I brayed him a powder of elderberries and strawberry leaves." The word dates back to at least 1386 but still has limited use in the South, or at least did up until recent times.

bread Often means corn bread in the South and can mean biscuits as well.

break (1) A blunder, a mistake. "She made a terrible break at that meeting." (2) To age or show one's age. "Her prettiness was breaking."

break a breath To speak. "He didn't break a breath with no one."

break a leg; break a toe To become pregnant when unmarried. "She broke her leg."

break bad To behave in a violent manner for no good reason. "He just broke bad last night and the po-leece got him."

breakbone A chicken's wishbone; also called the breaking bone or pulleybone.

breakdown A noisy, rollicking country dance; also called a *Virginia breakdown*, an *Old Virginia breakdown*, an *Ethiopian breakdown* and a *Negro breakdown*.

breakfast bacon Sliced, smoked bacon, not salt-cured bacon.

breaking corn Picking corn (breaking it off the stalk).

breaking one's arm Bragging about yourself. "That's really breaking your arm and patting yourself on the back."

break it off in someone To hurt someone with a cutting, sarcastic remark. "She broke it off in him with that last wisecrack."

break land To plow. " 'When their mule died three or four years ago, him and her broke their land working time about in the traces with the other mule.' " [William Faulkner, *The Hamlet*, 1940]

break one's manners To become intentionally rude. " 'It was all that bumping and jolting you done,' Ned said. 'You talk like I brake my manners just on purpose to get caught.' " [William Faulkner, *The Reivers*, 1962]

break one's neck To get married. "He broke his neck, and he hardly knew her."

break out a path To clear snow from a road or walk.

break western To "talk rough," talk harshly, usually in temper and sometimes with profanity.

breast complaint; breast disease Tuberculosis.

breath-and-britches Someone of no worth. "Don't come around here with your breath-and-britches friends."

breath harp A harmonica.

breathing image of Very close in appearance to (someone). "She's the breathing image of her mother." See SPITTIN' IMAGE.

breath of spring Honeysuckle, because of its sweet smell early in spring.

breeding vein A varicose vein, because varicose veins are common after pregnancies.

breeding woman A term used by slaveowners for a slave woman who was kept to bear children. Frederick L. Olmsted's *A Journey in the Seaboard Slave States* (1856) reported, "A breeding woman is worth from one-sixth to one-fourth more than one that does not breed." The term *breeder* was used to refer to men as well as women who were kept to produce children.

brer A black pronunciation of *brother,* made famous in the Uncle Remus tales of Joel Chandler Harris.

brickle; brickly Brittle. Sometimes heard in *peanut brickle* (peanut brittle).

brierhopper A poor farmworker or farmer.

brierpatch child; brierpatch kid An illegitimate child, from the idea of a child conceived in a brier patch.

bring To yield a crop. "That field brings beautiful tomatoes."

britches Pants, trousers.

britches riding high Very proud. "His britches are riding high."

British lady A nickname for the redwing blackbird.

broad See ABROAD.

broadhorn dialect An old term once applied to an exaggerated language believed to be typical of Kentuckians and keelboatmen.

broad open daylight Broad daylight.

broadus Something given as a bonus, lagniappe, apparently deriving from the American-Spanish *barata* (bargain).

brogan A heavy, sturdy workshoe, from the Irish *brogan* meaning the same. The term has widespread use but is especially common in the South.

broken arms; broken victuals Leftover food.

Bronze John A now mostly historical term for yellow fever, from *bronze* and the French *jaune* (yellow).

brother Commonly used as a form of address by parents to male children (brothers) in many Southern families, as it is indeed in other regions. " 'Wonderful,' she [Mother] said, sitting forward. 'What's she like, Brother? What is your impression of her?' " [Calder Willingham, *Rambling Rose,* 1972]

brother, I'm bobbed A parlor game, once widely played in the South, in which a blindfolded player is touched by the other players. When a player touches him, he responds, "Brother, I'm bobbed" and the reply is, "Who bobbed you?" If he can identify who "bobbed" or touched him, that person takes his place as the blindfolded player.

broughten Brought; imported.

brown-eyed peas Black-eyed peas with a brown rather than black spot where they were attached to the pod; sometimes called *brown-eyed crowder peas.* See also CROWDER. " 'But where can we get fresh-shelled brown-eyed peas to can?' he said, shaking his head. 'Everybody in New Orleans eats brown-eyed peas, but nobody here grows them.' " [Erskine Caldwell, "Miss Paddleford," *Gulf Coast Stories,* 1956]

brownie A penny. "All I got is one brownie."

Brown Mule A brand of chewing tobacco once very popular in rural parts of the South.

bruder; brooder A woman who has given birth to many children.

Brunswick stew A stew usually made of squirrel meat, lima beans and green corn seasoned with salt and pepper and said to have been invented by a cook in Brunswick County, Virginia, according to Ruth Berolzheimer's *The United States Regional Cookbook* (1947). William Faulkner, Marjorie Kinnan Rawlings and many other Southern writers mention it.

brush-ape A derisive term for a hillbilly.

brush colt An illegitimate child.

brush mouth A drink of whiskey; used mainly among Gullah speakers.

brush mover A heavy rainfall.

bubba Bubba, chiefly among blacks in the South, is a term of address meaning "brother" and is used by friends as well as relatives. But reference works generally fail to note that the word is also commonly used to mean a white Southerner. An essay in the *New York Times* by Molly Ivins put it this way: "In theory, the battle for Southern voters revolves around the stereotypical white Southerner, usually known as 'Bubba,' who is partial to country music and conservative politics. But as Presidential politics move into the states of the Confederacy, the biggest question about Bubba may not be how he will vote but how to find him."

bubbe A woman's breast.

bubblegum machine The revolving light atop a police car, or the car itself; sometimes called a *gumball machine.*

bubby The strawberry shrub *(Calycanthus glaucus),* so named because of the globular blossoms' resemblance to a woman's breast, or BUBBE. According to Thomas Anburey in his *Travels Through the Interior Parts of America* (1791), the word derives "from a custom that the women have of putting this flower down their bosums . . . till it has lost all its grateful perfume." Also called *bubby blossom, bubby brush, bubby flower* and *bubby shrub.*

buck (1) A bull or a steer. (2) A derogatory term, dating back to slavery times, for a strong young black man. (3) From early times, short for a sawbuck, or sawhorse. (4) See BUCK; BUCK A DANDY.

buck a bull off the bridge To perform a very difficult job, meet a difficult challenge.

buck; buck a dandy Both can mean either a young virile man or a woman-chasing fop, depending on how they are used.

bucket Often used instead of *pail* in the South.

bucket candy An old term for candy sold loose from buckets or other open display containers.

bucket letter A historical term for any anonymous letter, deriving from a series of letters signed under the pseudonym Edward Bucket and sent to President John Quincy Adams by David Bucket of Georgia.

bucket of blood; bloody bucket An old-fashioned term for a cheap, tough dive or speakeasy. A number were named the Bucket-of-Blood or Bloody Bucket.

buckeyed Bugeyed, the word influenced by *bucktoothed* and most used by black speakers.

buckhead A derisive term for a person of mixed race, perhaps deriving from *bughead*.

bucking at the halter Resisting, trying to break away or break free. " 'Yes, sir,' Miss Jenny said. 'Horace has been bucking at the halter for some time now. But you better not run against it too hard, Horace; it might not be fastened at the other end.' " [William Faulkner, *Sanctuary*, 1931]

bucklety-whet An old-fashioned term for *lickety-split*, very quickly.

"Afore you could snap your finger, he was there bucklety-whet."

buck like a colt To vehemently object to something. " 'And when my family wanted me to marry a second cousin, I bucked like a colt.' " [Margaret Mitchell, *Gone With the Wind*, 1936]

buck load An old term for a large portion of liquor.

buck-nekked Completely naked. " 'They got drunk and crashed the door in on him and found him buck-nekked, dancing the highland fling. A man fifty years old, seven foot tall, with a head like a peanut.' " [William Faulkner, *Sanctuary*, 1931] Other similar terms are *buck ass-naked*, *buck born-naked* and *stark buck-naked*.

buckra A Gullah term from the African Elik language *mbakara* (white leader or man), which can be a derogatory term for any white person or mean "white boss" or "poor white person."

buckra yam A name given to a white yam in the South.

buckskin A term used in the past to describe a backwoodsman, especially a Virginian.

buckshot soil (land) Poor clay soil that when dry forms little pebbles that resemble buckshot.

buddy; buddy up To pair up. "We buddied up and went for a trip."

buddy gee A black term for any friend or a fellow black.

budge An old-fashioned term for a fit of fidgety nerves. In *The Deliverance* (1904), Ellen Glasgow wrote: "Having unfortunately crossed her knees in the parlour after supper, she suffered untold tortures from 'budges' for three mortal hours rather than be seen to do anything so indelicate as to uncross them."

buffalo A name used to describe a North Carolinian favoring the North during the Civil War; the name was also given to the poor whites of North Carolina.

bug To cheat. "You sure got bugged when you bought that car."

bug-eater An obsolete term once used to describe a worthless or insignificant person.

bughouse A humorous term for a jail.

Bugtown; Bughill; Bugtressle; Bugscuffle Southern nicknames for small, insignificant, sometimes bug-infested towns or villages.

bug under the chip An old expression, common in the South, meaning an ulterior motive. "I can't understand why he'd being so generous, but there must be a bug under the chip."

build the fence To get married when a child is on the way. "They planted their corn before they built their fence."

built from the ground up Sturdy, stocky. "We could use him on the line; he's built from the ground up."

bull ant The large black, stinging carpenter ant.

bull bay The southern or great-flowered magnolia (*Magnolia grandiflora*).

bulldocia Boasting, threatening language, probably deriving from *bull* and *braggadocio*.

bulldozer The earth-moving *bulldozer* takes its name from a band of political terrorists. After the Civil War a group of Louisiana vigilantes, who brutally prevented freed slaves from voting freely, were termed *bulldozers*, the word first printed in an 1876 newspaper account of their activities. It is not certain whether they were whites forcing blacks to vote Democratic, Republican Negroes forcing their brothers not to vote Democratic or groups of both. Neither is the exact origin of their name clear—it probably came from *bulldose*, to mete out a "dose of the bull" with the long heavy bullwhip often made from the animal's penis. *Bulldozer* was soon used for "a revolver" and to describe anyone resembling the original terrorist bullies. Later the huge earth-moving machine, which brutally pushes everything in its path aside, became a national candidate for the designation. Few people realize that when someone is called a *bulldozer* today he is being named not for the machine but for the vigilantes so much like him.

bulleye To hunt game at night by shining a light in an animal's eyes and momentarily stunning it. "They bulleyed some deer last night."

bullfeathers! "Nonsense, horsefeathers!"

bull-footed Clumsy.

bull gang A crew of laborers.

bull-goaded Pestered or irritated, as a bull is by a goad. "He stood against the desk, huge, bull-goaded, impatient and outraged." [William Faulkner, *The Hamlet,* 1940]

bull of the woods Someone who is an important person, or thinks he is.

bumblebee cotton; bumblebee crop A name given to cotton or any crop stunted by drought. "The cotton's so low that the bees lie on their backs and suck the juice from the blooms— a real bumblebee crop."

bumfidgets A case of nerves or the figets.

bum fodder Toilet paper.

bumfuzzle To confuse, used in Mississippi and other parts of the South.

bum jacket A short, durable everyday jacket, often made of denim.

bummer During the Civil War, Union soldiers who deserted the ranks and looted and burned property, among other offenses, were called *bummers* by Southerners. The word had meant a loafer or sponger before this. See also SHERMAN'S BUMMERS.

bump A pimple or boil.

bumps A rash.

bunch oysters A Southern term for oysters that grow in clusters rather than singly.

buncle A carbuncle.

bundle A woman; one's wife.

bungo A type of canoe or small boat, the word probably deriving from the West African *bongo,* canoe or large raft.

bunk The Missouri Compromise was being hotly debated that morning of February 25, 1820, when longwinded Congressman Felix Walker of Buncombe County, North Carolina rose on the floor of the House of Representatives and insisted that he be heard before a vote was taken. "Old Oil Jug," as his fellow congressmen called him after his well-lubricated vocal cords, did not address himself to the monumental question of the extension of slavery; his interminable oration actually had little to do with anything important and members began interrupting him with cries of "Question, Question!" On being asked what purpose his speech served, Walker calmly replied, "You're not hurting my feelings, gentlemen. I am not speaking for your ears. I am only talking for Buncombe." Walker apparently had written his speech some time before and believed he would ingratiate himself with the voters back home if he delivered it in the midst of a great debate, but the strategy didn't work, judging by the fact that he lost the next election. Yet his reply, "I am talking for Buncombe," was widely published in newspapers covering the debate and became a synonym for talking nonsense. Eventually, *Buncombe* became *bunkum* and then took the shortened form of *bunk* (in the 1850s) meaning not only "bombastic political talk" but "any empty, inflated speech obviously meant to fool people."

burgoo The rich Southern stew of meat and vegetables called burgoo probably takes its name from a similar stew that American seamen used to make, which, in turn, may derive its name from the Arabic *burghul* (bruised grain). The word, however, was first recorded in the West as *burgou* in 1837 and may be a corruption of "barbecue." Someone has noted about burgoo: "No two people tell the same story about its origin and no two people will give you the same recipe." Kentucky is especially noted for its burgoo, and the word there can also mean a picnic at which the stew is served.

burk To vomit or to break wind.

burn To cook; especially common among blacks. "I have to go and burn supper."

burn down To kill with a gun.

burning a river Being dressed up for an occasion, dressed to kill. "You're burnin' a river, girl. You look better than the bride!"

burning green wood for kindling Performing a futile task.

burnt-out on Tired or sick of. " 'I can't imagine no tragedy worse than being burnt out on strawberry ice-cream.' " [William Faulkner, *The Town*, 1957] " 'U'm burnt out on sowbelly,' [Mink said]." [William Faulkner, *The Mansion*, 1959]

burn the britches off To spank severely. ". . . that boy that his paw ought to burned his britches off for not being home in bed two hours ago . . ." [William Faulkner, *The Mansion*, 1959]

burr artichoke A globe or French artichoke, as opposed to a Jerusalem artichoke.

burrhead A derogatory term for a black person.

bush baby An illegitimate child.

bush hog A mower for cutting brush or clearing ground.

bush line A fishing line thrown into the water and attached to brush or a tree on land.

bushwhackers See COPPERHEADS.

busk An old-fashioned term meaning "to buss or kiss." "I felt like busking him on his bald spot."

buss-eyed Old-fashioned term for calf-eyed. "The winner can call the loser a slew-footed, buss-eyed, cattywampus." See also CATAWAMPUS.

busthead Bad or illicit whiskey that can produce violent headaches; also called *bustskull*.

bust out the middles To plow between the rows in a field.

bustskull See BUSTHEAD.

busy as a cat with fur on fire Very busy, agitated. "Singing Sal had been stirring around as busy as a cat with fur on fire, and she was out of breath." [Erskine Caldwell, "Big Buck," *The Complete Stories of Erskine Caldwell*, 1953]

busy as a three-pricked goat Extremely busy, using the reference to the goat because of its renown for its procreative abilities.

butter bean A small lima bean.

butter bean teeth Buck teeth.

butternut A term used during the Civil War for Confederate soldiers, because their uniforms were often homespun colored brown with dye made from butternut tree bark. See also COPPERHEADS.

butt-headed Stubborn. "He's a butt-headed S.O.B. if there ever was one."

but what A common expression, usually following an expression of doubt, to introduce what the speaker thinks is probably true; often used as in the following examples: "I don't know but what I'll eat some of them" (I think I'll eat some of them). "I'm not sure but what he's right" (He's probably right).

by God and by Jesus! A mild oath or exclamation. " 'By God and by Jesus, Dude,' Jeeter said, 'ain't you ever going to stop bouncing that there ball against that there old house?' " [Erskine Caldwell, *Tobacco Road*, 1932]

by godfrey! Euphemism for "By God!" " 'Well by godfrey [Father said], that puts you one up on Manfred de Spain, don't it?' " [William Faulkner, *The Town*, 1957]

by sun Before sunset. "I'll be there by sun to get the job finished."

by the hardest With great difficulty. "He got on the horse by the hardest."

C

cabbage patch Something, especially a place, of very little importance. "He lives in that cabbage patch town down by the river."

cabin song A song sung and often created by blacks who lived in cabins on Southern plantations in slavery days.

cachinnant To laugh loudly or immoderately; has some use among educated Southerners, as in the following: "Then he began to laugh, though almost at once it stopped being laughing and Ratliff knew that it had never been laughing, cachinnant, sobbing, already beyond the creature's power to stop it . . ." [William Faulkner, *The Hamlet,* 1940]

cackle To laugh; used widely outside the South today.

Caddo An Indian tribe formerly living in Louisiana, Arkansas and part of Texas.

Cajan See CAJUN.

Cajun A group of people of French Catholic ancestry who were expelled from Acadia in the late 18th century and settled in Louisiana and Maine. The word, deriving from *Acadian,* is also applied to any of their characteristics, such as the French dialect they speak. Also *Cajan.*

cakewalk See TAKE THE CAKE.

cala A rice fritter made principally by Creoles in New Orleans, the word deriving from the African Bambara *kala,* meaning the same, or the Nube *kare* (a fried cake).

calaboose A small town jail; also used frequently in the West and other parts of the country.

Calhounery A historical term once used to describe political crimes such as stuffing ballot boxes, permitting illegal votes to be cast and so forth because supporters of Southern statesman John C. Calhoun (1782–1850) were known to engage in these practices.

call hogs To snore, an old Scottish and English expression, from the Scots' *call* (to drive). "He really called some hogs."

Cal-lina A common pronunciation of Carolina. " 'Yeer'd think he would learn in three years that he ain't going to catch ere Cal-lina fox with them Yankee city dogs,' the youth said." [William Faulkner, "Fox Hunt," 1931]

47

call one's name To call oneself by a name. "How do you call your name?" "I calls me Sally."

call out of name To call someone abusive names. "He called me out of my name."

call pigs See CALL HOGS.

callyhooting Moving at a breakneck pace, very rapidly and noisily; moving recklessly; moving licketety-split. "Here he comes a callyhootin'!" It possibly derives, according to one source, from "the confusion and noise that accompanies a calliope."

camelback house A house, usually in New Orleans, that is higher in the back than in the front.

camel cricket A Southern nickname for the insect more widely known as the mantis, which has a long thorax that suggests the neck of a camel.

camel walk A dance step once popular among blacks in the South.

camp A name for slave quarters on a plantation before the Civil War; also called the *quarters*.

camp meeting A religious revival meeting held outdoors in a camp for several days or longer; in days past, an important social event as well.

candy Sometimes used to mean "candid" in the South. " 'Give me your candy opinion.' " [Carson McCullers, *The Member of the Wedding*, 1946]

candy ankle A sissy; a weak effeminate man. "You know I heard you was a candy-ankle because you got a little book sense." [Jesse Stuart, "Uncle Joe's Boys," 1938]

candy breaking A once-popular social gathering at which individuals are paired by having the male and female guests match broken ends of candy sticks (candy canes).

candy knocking An old party game at which a candy stick is tied to a string hanging from the ceiling. A person is blindfolded and given a wooden stick to hit the candy stick with. If he hits it, he is given a stick of candy.

candy pulling A social gathering at which molasses candy is made and pulled.

candy roaster A squash variety, usually roasted or baked with butter, brown sugar and cinnamon.

cane beer Beer made with the skimmings taken from boiling sugar cane juice that is being made into molasses; the beer has a sweet-sour taste.

canebrake An area overgrown with canes, a thicket of canes, especially southern cane, small cane or switch cane. *Mississippi canebrake* is another common designation for such a region.

canecutter A large swamp rabbit found in many Southern states.

cannonball A slow Southern train; this expression is used nationally, however, as a name for a fast or express train.

canoe To have sexual intercourse; to neck passionately.

can-see to can't-see Dawn to dusk. See usage example at TROMP.

can't hardlies Same as the *all-overs* (q.v.).

can't-help-its A joking name for any imaginary disease. "He must have the can't-help-its today."

can't-see to can't-see Before dawn to after dusk. "I got boys in the woods from can't see to can't see gettin' me squirrels." [Marjorie Kinnan Rawlings, *Cross Creek*, 1942]

caouane The name, taken from the French, given to the Southern alligator snapping turtle *(Macrochelys lacertina)*, which ranges from western Texas to Florida and as far north as Missouri.

cap To beat, outdo, surpass. "Well, he capped all."

cape bonnet "There is a kind of bonnet very commonly worn [in Virginia], which, in particular, disfigures them amazingly; it is made with a caul, fitting close on the back part of the head, and a front stiffened with small pieces of cane, which projects nearly two feet from the head in a horizontal direction." [Isaac Weld, *Travels Through the States of North America*, 1799] Another writer said the bonnet "makes a face look as it were at the far end of a cavern . . ."

cape jasmine The gardenia. "She could look down upon the cape jasmine and syringa." [William Faulkner, *Sartoris*, 1929]

cape merchant An archaic term for the owner or man in charge of a general store.

Capital of Miserable Huts See GREAT AMERICAN MUDHOLE.

capper A corn popper.

captain (1) Any man who excels at something. "He's a captain to tell a tale." (2) A form of address to white men by blacks, often obsequious. " 'What is it, captain?' the Negro said. 'I ain't done nothing.' " [William Faulkner, "Dry September," 1931] (3) A courtesy title, usually capitalized. ". . . in the South and West, nearly all tall men are called generals, stout men judges, and men of middling proportions, captains or colonels!" [James Robertson, *A Few Months in America*, 1855]

Captain Bill vine A designation, origin unknown, for a common Southern vine that often overruns fences.

Captain Lynch Another name for the "lynch law": the administration of summary punishment, especially death, upon a suspect by a mob without legal authority. "Being cut off from all opportunity of bringing the offender to justice through the regular legal tribunals . . . they reved to have recourse to that well-known arbiter vulgarly yclept [called] Captain Lynch." [Henry S. Foote, *Texas and the Texans,* 1841] See LYNCH.

captain's beat A historical Southern term, now obsolete, meaning the limits within which members of a military company reside and within which the votes are received on election day.

carbox A boxcar on a train.

carcass Joking term for a person's body or buttocks. "Park your carcass over there."

careen To lean or bend the body to one side. "I noticed a ketch in my back ever since I careened to get that pencil."

car house A garage; also *car shed*.

Carolina bean The lima bean.

Carolina glass A glass, often colored, used in the border of windows or for windows themselves. "Beside the window (the sash was raised now, with its narrow border of Carolina glass which in the winter framed her head and bust like a hung portrait) an old woman sat in a wheelchair." [William Faulkner, "There Was a Queen," 1933]

Carolina gouger See VIRGINIA GOUGER.

Carolina jasmine The yellow jasmine.

Carolina potato An old, seldom-used term for a sweet potato.

Carolina racehorse A humorous term for a razorback hog.

Carolina rice Some sources say that the first rice successfully grown in Carolina was introduced into Charleston in 1694 by a Dutch brig out of Madagascar, while others hold that Yankee shipmaster Captain John Thurber presented a packet of Madagascar rice to one of the early settlers on pulling into Charleston harbor late in the 1680s. According to the latter story, the settler planted the rice rather than dining on it, and after it sprouted, he gave seed to his friends, who in turn raised rice on their fertile land. Charleston and the Carolina low country soon became the "Rice Coast," rice fortunes building Charleston and marking the beginning of a plantocracy considered by many to be the New World aristocracy. In any case, the Madagascar rice raised there was being called *Carolina rice* or *golden rice* by 1787.

Carolina robin A smoked herring, probably because herring takes on the color of a robin's breast when smoked according to the North Carolina recipe.

Carolina rose The Cherokee rose.

Carolinian A native of South or North Carolina, the term first recorded in 1707.

carpetbag corruption See CARPETBAGGER.

his expression, long / the American South, / ts origins in England, / ictorian times, luggage / plush red carpet became / tion and was so popular / mbezzling bankers as a place / their loot that the embezzlers / elves were dubbed *carpetbag-* / After the U.S. Civil War, car- / bags were used by many of the / scrupulous northern political ad- / enturers, often poor whites, who packed their few worldly possessions in them to satisfy state property evidence requirements and moved to the South to take advantage of the newly enfranchised blacks and to win power and future wealth by controlling elections. Such greedy, unprincipled men, carrying their red carpetbags, and the previous association of the bags with men who milked banks just as these men were milking the South, gave birth to their name *carpetbaggers*, as well as the *Carpetbag Era* of American history.

carpetbag Yankee Another term for a CARPETBAGGER.

carpet sack An old term for a carpetbag, a piece of luggage made from carpet.

carried Brought. " 'Young lady, I carried you some Bigbee pecans. I thought you might not harvest the like around here.' " [Eudora Welty, *The Optimist's Daughter*, 1972]

carried on to Carried on at a place or function; acted improperly or even immorally. "My how we carried on

to the pa... / times used ... / incessantly."

carrion crow The t... / the black vulture, both

carrot A historical term in tr... / for a compressed roll of leaf to... / 12 to 15 inches long.

carry (1) To take or bring, as in "Carry me back to ole Virginie." (2) To drive someone somewhere in an automobile. (3) To escort, take, lead, accompany; sometimes heard as *carry out*. "Are you going to carry Miss Alice to the theater?" (4) To haul by truck. "He's carrying that wood to market."

carry guts to a bear Said of someone very stupid. "He ain't got sense enough to carry guts to a bear."

car shed A garage; also *car house*.

cart To transport by car or truck. "I've been cartin' him all over town."

Carter's oats An old term used in expressions of exaggerated comparison, as in "We had more whiskey than Carter had oats." It is said that a Georgian named Carter, in bragging of his oatfield's yield, claimed that "the oats were so thick that he had to move the fence to find room to stack the bundles."

cascade An old euphemistic term, originating in England, meaning to vomit a lot at one time, "from the resemblance to a waterfall," as Bartlett says.

... supply ... "Cash down, ... off at the next

... Cash, coins or bills ... checks or credit. "We'll ... a heap o' cash money selling at the game."

cast up To vomit.

cat (1) Short for *catfish* since the early 18th century. (2) A term used by blacks that has passed into general use meaning "a good performer or lover of jazz"; "a good guy"; and "a prostitute or woman of loose morals." (See also CATTING.) (3) To fish for catfish. "When we goes a catting, we goes a catting, and throws trout back into the water to pay 'em for their imperdence of biting." [John Wilkes, *Spirit of the Times*, August 19, 1865]

catabias Askew, out of line. "You've got it turned catabias."

Catahoula hound dog (cur) A large blue-spotted hound dog associated with Louisiana's Catahoula parish and used in hunting wild hogs. Also called *leopard dogs,* they are said to have first been used by Indian tribes in Louisiana.

cat-and-clay Clay mixed with sticks or straw and used as a mortar for chimneys.

cat-and-rat rifle A small-caliber rifle used for small game. "We had an air-rifle, but wanted a cat-and-rat rifle,

which used real cartridges . . ." [H... L. Mencken, *Happy Days,* 1940]

catasterfy An old humorous pronunciation of *catastrophe.*

catastrastroke Catastrophe. Used in Calder Willingham's *Rambling Rose* (1972) but nowhere else that can be firmly established: " 'This is a total catastrastroke,' said Daddy. 'That's what it is, a catastrastroke out of the blue.' " (The story takes place in Great Despression era, small-town Mississippi.)

catawampus (1) Cater-cornered. "He walked catawampus across the street." Also heard as CATTYWAMPUS. (2) A hobgoblin or fierce imaginary monster; also called *wampus.* See usage example at BUSS-EYED.

Catawba grapes A light reddish variety of grape, the *Catawba* was developed by John Adlum in his vineyard near Georgetown, Washington, D.C. in 1829. It was named three years later for the Catawba Indians of the Carolinas or for the Catawba River, which takes its name from the Indian tribe. The *Catawba,* long a traditional favorite, contains some vinifera blood and is one of the best grapes for white domestic wines. By 1860 nine-tenths of all grapes grown east of the Rockies were *Catawbas,* but they were thereafter replaced by the Concord, perfected in 1850, as the leading American variety. They are now making a comeback.

catbird seat To be in the catbird seat means "to be sitting pretty, to be in

carpetbagger This expression, long associated with the American South, actually has its origins in England, where, in Victorian times, luggage made from plush red carpet became an institution and was so popular among embezzling bankers as a place to stash their loot that the embezzlers themselves were dubbed *carpetbaggers*. After the U.S. Civil War, carpetbags were used by many of the unscrupulous northern political adventurers, often poor whites, who packed their few worldly possessions in them to satisfy state property evidence requirements and moved to the South to take advantage of the newly enfranchised blacks and to win power and future wealth by controlling elections. Such greedy, unprincipled men, carrying their red carpetbags, and the previous association of the bags with men who milked banks just as these men were milking the South, gave birth to their name *carpetbaggers*, as well as the *Carpetbag Era* of American history.

carpetbag Yankee Another term for a CARPETBAGGER.

carpet sack An old term for a carpetbag, a piece of luggage made from carpet.

carried Brought. " 'Young lady, I carried you some Bigbee pecans. I thought you might not harvest the like around here.' " [Eudora Welty, *The Optimist's Daughter,* 1972]

carried on to Carried on at a place or function; acted improperly or even immorally. "My how we carried on to the party." *Carried on* is sometimes used in the sense of "talked incessantly."

carrion crow The turkey vulture or the black vulture, both scavengers.

carrot A historical term in the South for a compressed roll of leaf tobacco 12 to 15 inches long.

carry (1) To take or bring, as in "Carry me back to ole Virginie." (2) To drive someone somewhere in an automobile. (3) To escort, take, lead, accompany; sometimes heard as *carry out*. "Are you going to carry Miss Alice to the theater?" (4) To haul by truck. "He's carrying that wood to market."

carry guts to a bear Said of someone very stupid. "He ain't got sense enough to carry guts to a bear."

car shed A garage; also *car house*.

cart To transport by car or truck. "I've been cartin' him all over town."

Carter's oats An old term used in expressions of exaggerated comparison, as in "We had more whiskey than Carter had oats." It is said that a Georgian named Carter, in bragging of his oatfield's yield, claimed that "the oats were so thick that he had to move the fence to find room to stack the bundles."

cascade An old euphemistic term, originating in England, meaning to vomit a lot at one time, "from the resemblance to a waterfall," as Bartlett says.

cash down; cash over To supply cash; to pay at once. "Cash down, quick, or I'll put you off at the next station."

cash money Cash, coins or bills rather than checks or credit. "We'll take in a heap o' cash money selling these at the game."

cast up To vomit.

cat (1) Short for *catfish* since the early 18th century. (2) A term used by blacks that has passed into general use meaning "a good performer or lover of jazz"; "a good guy"; and "a prostitute or woman of loose morals." (See also CATTING.) (3) To fish for catfish. "When we goes a catting, we goes a catting, and throws trout back into the water to pay 'em for their imperdence of biting." [John Wilkes, *Spirit of the Times,* August 19, 1865]

catabias Askew, out of line. "You've got it turned catabias."

Catahoula hound dog (cur) A large blue-spotted hound dog associated with Louisiana's Catahoula parish and used in hunting wild hogs. Also called *leopard dogs,* they are said to have first been used by Indian tribes in Louisiana.

cat-and-clay Clay mixed with sticks or straw and used as a mortar for chimneys.

cat-and-rat rifle A small-caliber rifle used for small game. "We had an air-rifle, but wanted a cat-and-rat rifle, which used real cartridges . . ." [H. L. Mencken, *Happy Days,* 1940]

catasterfy An old humorous pronunciation of *catastrophe.*

catastrastroke Catastrophe. Used in Calder Willingham's *Rambling Rose* (1972) but nowhere else that can be firmly established: " 'This is a total catastrastroke,' said Daddy. 'That's what it is, a catastrastroke out of the blue.' " (The story takes place in Great Depression era, small-town Mississippi.)

catawampus (1) Cater-cornered. "He walked catawampus across the street." Also heard as CATTYWAMPUS. (2) A hobgoblin or fierce imaginary monster; also called *wampus.* See usage example at BUSS-EYED.

Catawba grapes A light reddish variety of grape, the *Catawba* was developed by John Adlum in his vineyard near Georgetown, Washington, D.C. in 1829. It was named three years later for the Catawba Indians of the Carolinas or for the Catawba River, which takes its name from the Indian tribe. The *Catawba,* long a traditional favorite, contains some vinifera blood and is one of the best grapes for white domestic wines. By 1860 nine-tenths of all grapes grown east of the Rockies were *Catawbas,* but they were thereafter replaced by the Concord, perfected in 1850, as the leading American variety. They are now making a comeback.

catbird seat To be in the catbird seat means "to be sitting pretty, to be in a favorable position." It is a Southern Americanism dating back to the 19th century but popularized nationally by Brooklyn Dodgers baseball announcer Red Barber, of Southern origin, and James Thurber's short story "The Catbird Seat." The catbird, or North American thrush, usually sings its song from a high place in a tree. It has the name catbird because "its ordinary cry of alarm . . . somewhat resembles the mew of a cat."

catbrier A sharp, tangling bramble growth (*Smilex rotundfolia*) that is a nuisance to farmers and gardeners and is called *catbrier* because its leaves are as sharp as the claws of a cat; also known as *blaspheme vine,* among other names.

catch a fly Said of someone who is staring or gawking open-mouthed. "Watch out now you don't catch a fly."

catch air To run with great, sudden speed. "He saw the police coming and did he catch air!"

catcher A synonym for the game of tag children play.

catch 'im! A command to a dog meaning "Get im!" or "Sic 'im!"

catch one redhand To catch someone redhanded. " 'Ah, hah!' she said. 'I set a trap for you and caught you red hand!' " [Calder Willingham, *Rambling Rose,* 1972]

catch-pain A sudden sharp pain in the side or in the back.

catchpenny Used in the South for any low-priced fraudulent item, this term has its origins in England, having been first recorded there in the mid-18th century.

catface A scar or knot in a tree or on a piece of fruit, such as a tomato; also a disease in tomatoes and the cracks that naturally occur on a tomato near the stem. The term is used in other regions as well.

cat fever Short for the catarrhal fever respiratory infection.

catfish hole A hole in a stream where people fish for catfish. "Let's go down to the old catfish hole."

catfish row The poor black section of a town.

catfish stew A Southern dish made with catfish that is similar to a chowder.

cat-hauling A cruel punishment used mostly on slaves in which a man was fastened down and a huge fierce tomcat was taken by the tail and hauled down along the man's bare back, the cat's claws ripping flesh all the way.

cathead A large biscuit.

catmint A Southern name for catnip.

catmocker Another name for the *catbird.* See also CATBIRD SEAT.

cat on a hot tin roof Best known today as the title of Tennessee Williams' famous play, the expression has been in wide use since the turn of the century. Apparently it came to the South and then the rest of the country via a similar British phrase, *like a cat on hot bricks,* which has been traced back to about 1880 and means "someone ill at ease, uncomfortable, not at home in a place or situation."

cat's fur to make kitten britches A humorous answer to the question "What for [pronounced *fur*]?"

catstepping Walking quietly. "Out he went, catstepping down the walk."

catting A term originating with blacks that usually means "fooling around" or "going out chasing women," but it can also mean "to fish for cats (catfish)."

cattle Low, contemptible people.

cattle droppings A Southern term for cattle dung or cow flops, as they are called in other parts of the country. "[My dog] had a few little idiosyncratic oddities about him that didn't exactly endear him to some people, like rolling in fresh cattle droppings and then climbing up on somebody's truck seats . . ." [Larry Brown, "Big Bad Love," 1990]

cat-tongues Small but long and slender oysters.

cat track A disease of the eyes, trachoma.

cattywampus (1) Catawampus, askew, awry, positioned diagonally, cater-cornered, oblique. (2) Very big, a monster of its kind. " 'I'll bet we kin ketch us a cattywampus in one o' them ponds.' [Jody said]." [Majorie Kinnan Rawlings, *The Yearling,* 1938] See also CATAWAMPUS.

caught Become pregnant. " 'So there was an old woman [Varner said] told my mammy once that if a woman showed her belly to the moon after she had done caught, it would be a gal. So Mrs. Varner taken and laid every night with the moon on her nekid belly, until it fulled and after. I could lay my ear to her belly and hear Eula kicking and scrouging like all get out, feeling the moon.' " [William Faulkner, *The Hamlet,* 1940]

caught short To become pregnant while not married.

the Cause A Southern name for the Civil War. " 'And I know Charlie would like you to help the Cause he died for.' " [Margaret Mitchell, *Gone With the Wind,* 1936.]

cawked An old, perhaps obsolete term for exhausted. "I'm all cawked." Possibly a pronunciation of *corked* or *caulked.*

cease (1) Used among blacks to mean a decrease in the wind. "It's beginning to cease." (2) As a verb, *cease* can mean "to die," as in, "Now that he ceased, we got no one can fix things here."

cedar pencil An old Southern term for a cheap, unpainted pencil.

cedar pine A name for the spruce pine *(Pinus glabra)*.

cedar robe A small piece of cedar furniture to hang clothes in, a cedar wardrobe.

ceiling Can be a synonym for an attic or a loft.

ceitful Deceitful; usually heard among Gullah speakers.

celery A frequent pronunciation of *salary*.

cent The singular *cent* is often used as a plural, as in "He had 10 cent."

center shot An old historical term for a great marksman with a rifle, one who would always hit the center of the target.

certain-sure Absolutely certain. "He had all those certain-sure cures."

c'est vrai It is true; a French expression often used in the Louisiana-French dialects.

chain-gang pea The black-eyed pea, because it was commonly grown on farms where chain gangs worked.

chairbacker A part-time lay preacher who has no formal training in the ministry and has no church of his own, perhaps because such a preacher once carried a chair, which he turned around back to him, for his street-corner pulpit.

chaland A term used in Louisiana for a small rectangular flat-bottomed boat. *Chaland* is French for "flat-boat."

chamber lye An old term or euphemism for urine or urine mixed with another substance used as a medicine. "She used chamber lye to treat her chapped skin."

cham-chack The red-billed woodpecker *(Centurus carolinus)*, in reference to its cries.

chance An old term for an amount, number or quantity. "He lost a right smart chance of blood."

chance off To raffle off something.

change An euphemism meaning to castrate or alter an animal.

change over See CHANGE.

change-up A change. "We'll have to have a change-up pretty soon."

change words To converse, exchange words. "I'd like to change a few words with you."

chanky chank A term Cajuns use for their music.

channel catfish A Southern term for a number of different catfish but generally *Ictalurus punctatus*, which goes by the names *blue catfish, silver catfish* and *black warrior*, among others.

chap (1) A baby or young child. "There's a new baby downstairs. Little chaps like that can't be comfortable on a long journey, you know." [Mark Twain, *Life on the Mississippi*, 1883]. (2) To have children, reproduce. " 'You and me ain't nigh done chapping yet, with just two.' " [William Faulkner, *As I Lay Dying*, 1930]

chappie Same as CHAP.

charcoal An old derogatory term for a dark-skinned black person.

charcoal out To barbecue a meal outside. "We gonna charcoal out tonight."

charge it to the dust and let the rain settle it A sassy term meaning "charge it on the books, it probably won't be paid anyway; in any event, it's not my responsibility and I'm not going to worry about it"; also "charge it to the sand."

charge it to the sand See CHARGE IT TO THE DUST AND LET THE RAIN SETTLE IT.

charging school A private school where tuition is paid, as opposed to a public school. The term was popular during the Great Depression when public schools could only stay open five to seven months a year, due to budget cuts, and parents were allowed to use the facilities, paying teachers themselves to teach their children.

Charles See MR. CHARLIE.

Charleston This peppy dance, symbolic of the Roaring Twenties, takes its name from Charleston, South Carolina where it was probably first introduced as a variation of an earlier dance originated by American blacks. The word is first recorded in 1925.

Charleston brim The sheepshead fish; *brim* here is a variation of *bream*.

Charleston butterfly A palmetto bug or water bug; a roach.

Charleston buzzard See CHARLESTON EAGLE.

Charleston eagle The black vulture (*Coragyps atratus*); also known as the *Charleston buzzard*.

Charlestonian A native of Charleston, South Carolina. In 1828 Mrs. Basil Hall wrote in her *Aristocratic Journey,* "I must do the Charlestonians the justice to say that I have not seen any chewing amongst them nor spitting."

Charlie See MR. CHARLIE.

charm string Buttons displayed on a string like a necklace. According to the *Miami Herald,* at the turn of the century: "Young girls . . . sometimes collected buttons or received them as gifts. They would be strung and counted. Supposedly when the girl reached 999 buttons, her final prize would be Prince Charming, who would come and take her away and they would live happily ever after."

chartered whiskey Whiskey that is strained through charcoal, a relatively good whiskey as opposed to ordinary moonshine. William Faulkner wrote of "good red chartered whiskey."

chase the gator A game of tag in a pool with the chaser called the "gator."

chaw (1) A common pronunciation of *chew* in the South, though it is used in New England and other areas as well. (2) To embarrass or belittle somebody. "He chawed her so much her face turned red."

chawbacon An old, perhaps obsolete, term for a country hick that dates back to the early 19th century.

chawed See CHEWED.

chaw tobacco An old term for *chewing tobacco*.

Chay! A cry for cattle; used in the vicinity of Williamsburg, South Carolina, whereas *Cowench!* is used in other parts of South Carolina. One writer points out that *Chay!* is duplicated in County Antrim, Ireland, "linking the present residents in a tiny area of the South with their ancestors in the old country."

cheapwad A very cheap person, a combination of *cheapskate* and *tightwad*.

checks The playing pieces in a checkers set. The game itself is some-times called *checker* (singular) in the South.

cheep To reveal something, to betray a secret. "I didn't cheep it to anybody."

cheese The singular *cheese* is often used as a plural, as in, "Pass me them cheese."

cheesebox upon a plank See YANKEE CHEESEBOX ON A RAFT.

cheese-eater A person who cheats, informs or doublecrosses, deriving from the slang expression *rat*, which means the same.

chere (sher) A term of endearment for a woman or girl in New Orleans and other parts of Louisiana; from the French *chère* (dear, beloved).

cherie Darling. A French word often used in the Louisiana-French dialects.

chermany A variety of the game of baseball once played in the Southern United States. According to the *Dictionary of Americanisms,* the origin of the word is unknown.

Cherokee rose The evergreen white rose *Rosa laevigata* or *Rosa bracteata* (also known as the *prairie rose* and *Chickasaw rose*), both of which often grow wild in the South and are cultivated as hedges.

cherry phosphate A favorite soft drink in the South of old, still available in some areas. "All the trails converged upon the crossroads store . . . with . . . its flyspecked window, and the bottles of Coke and cherry phosphate on a counter inside." [Cecile Matschat, *Suwanee River,* 1938] Cherry phosphate was often mixed with Coca-Cola to make cherry Coke.

chess pie   A pie filled with a creamy mixture of eggs, butter and sugar. *Chess* here was probably *chest* originally, possibly because the pie was baked in a pan resembling a small chest.

chew-bubble   A synonym for bubble gum; also called *Blow gum.*

chewed   Can mean either angry or defeated. "He feels chewed."

cheweeka   A name for the killdeer, in imitation of the sound of the bird's song.

chew one's bit   Deriving from the expression *to champ at the bit,* like a horse does, this old expression means the same—to be impatient or to be angry.

chew one's tobacco more than once   To repeat oneself. "I ain't gonna chaw my tobacker twice." It can also mean "to be cheap; to think something over."

Chewsday   A common pronunciation of *Tuesday.*

chew your own tobacco   Rely on yourself, no one else.

Chicago of the South   A name used to describe Houston, Texas.

Chickasaw   A horse of mixed colors once used by the Chickasaw Indians.

Chickasaw plum   The common wild plum *(Prunus angustifolia),* found in abundance where the Chickasaw Indians lived.

chicken asshole   See CHICKEN BUTT.

chicken-bone   The wishbone of a chicken or turkey.

chicken butt   A humorous name for the navel; a coarser variation is *chicken asshole.*

chicken coop   A humorous term for an outdoor privy.

chicken corn   A variety of sorghum *(S. vulgare drummondii);* also called *Chinese sugarcane* in the past.

chicken-eater   A name given to any animal (a hog, dog, etc.) that eats chickens.

chicken-eating   (1) Something mean, little or generally despised. "You chicken-eatin' fool!" (2) A word used when referring to a CHICKEN-EATER. "That chicken-eatin' sow made short work of him."

chicken feed   Something trifling, of no importance. "A hundred dollars. That's chicken feed today." The term apparently originated in the South in the early 19th century, but it is now a national expression.

chicken flutter An old dance popular among slaves on antebellum plantations in which the dancers imitate the fluttering of a chicken.

chicken grape The purple medium-sized grape *Vitis riparia*, which grows wild and is valued for its fragrant blossoms.

chicken guts (1) A humorous term for the gold trim on the cuffs of Confederate uniforms during the Civil War. (2) A name used by children for the symbol *&*, the ampersand.

chicken meat A turtle's white meat.

chicken money An old term similar to *egg money*: a small amount of spending money, originally earned by farm women who sold eggs or chickens.

chicken 'n' egg Another name for the zinnia.

chicken preacher A part-time lay preacher, usually black, so named because women often served such preachers roast chicken when they preached.

chicken ranch A brothel; after the name of a real brothel made famous in the play *The Best Little Whorehouse in Texas*.

chickenweed Ragwort, because its seed used to be mixed with chicken feed as a remedy for various maladies of chickens.

chick nor child No one. " 'So you ain't got father, mother, brother, sister, husband, chick nor child. Not a soul to call on, that's you.' " [Eudora Welty, *The Optimist's Daughter*, 1972]

chifforobe A blending of *chiffonier* and *wardrobe*, this word, for a piece of furniture with drawers on one side and a space for hanging clothes on the other, is common in the South but used in other areas of the country as well, even in New York City.

chigger This word, meaning the larva form of certain mites, especially the red bug, *Trombicula irritans*, is found in several African languages and may have been brought to the South by slaves.

chill bumps Gooseflesh; also *cold bumps, cold pimples*.

chillin; chillun; chillum Common black Southern pronunciation of *children*, also heard among whites.

chimbley; chimbly Chimney. ". . . even when it was staring him in the face out yonder at Miz Hait's chimbley Saturday night . . ." [William Faulkner, *The Town*, 1957]

chinchy Stingy, miserly. "He got chinchy as he grew older."

chin music Loquacious, inconsequential talking made by those who like to hear themselves talk.

chinning Talking a lot. "He never stopped chinnin'."

chipperdale; chippendale A whore, prostitute, chippy. " 'If she's nothin' but one o' them lettle ol' chipperdales, why do he mess up with her?' " [Marjorie Kinnan Rawlings, *The Yearling*, 1938] See also CHIPPY.

chippy A prostitute. Dating back to about 1800 and perhaps deriving from prostitutes chipping (*chip:* to chirp, to hiss) at men passing by in the street, the expression is common throughout the country now.

chippyhouse A brothel.

chitlins (1) See CHITTERLINGS. (2) Insides, guts of a man or woman. "His chitlin's is made of iron." [Marjorie Kinnan Rawlings, *The Yearling*, 1938]

chitlin strut A party at which chitlins (CHITTERLINGS) and beer are sold.

chittamwood The small American snake tree, *Cotinus obovatus*, of the central-southern United States, with yellow flowers and clusters of fleshy fruits with silky plumes. *Chittam* is apparently of unknown Indian origin.

chitterlings Hog intestines made into a popular Southern dish; usually pronounced *chitlins*.

chizzwink A Floridian name for the crane fly, also called the *blind mosquito* in Florida.

chizzywink A white midge of the family Chironomedae that is prolific in the Everglades.

choaty Fat, chubby; possibly deriving from *shoat* and often a nickname.

choicy Very fussy or choosy. "I'm tired of her choicy ways."

cholmondely (pronounced *chumley*) The Charleston, South Carolina pronunciation of *chimney,* according to Lord Ashley Cooper's (Frank B. Gilbreth's) *Dictionary of Charlestonese,* which gives examples of Southern pronunciation that border on becoming new words.

choog See CHUG.

choose To wish or want. "How about some pecan pie?" "Thank you, no, I don't choose any."

chop To weed or thin crops. "He got his hoe and begun choppin' out young cotton plants."

chop-mouth hound, chop-tongue hound A dog with a strong steady bark or chop.

chouette The French name in Louisiana for what is also called there the screech owl or "gimme bird" (*Otus asia floridonus*).

Christian Besides its religious usage, a Christian can mean "a person who abstains from all liquor, a nondrinker."

Christmas (1) Can mean whiskey. "Put some Christmas in that punch." (2) Sometimes means the gifts given at Christmas. "Look at this Christmas I got."

Christmas at you! A greeting on Christmas day.

Christmas gift! A greeting used on Christmas morning, with the first person saying it traditionally receiving a gift. The custom, which has been traced back to as early as 1844, is no longer observed, but *Christmas gift!*, which used to be a far more popular Christmas greeting than *Merry Christmas!* is still heard among older people. "[The black children] with branches of mistletoe and holly for excuses, already lurking about the rear of the big house to shout 'Christmas gift' at the white people . . ." [William Faulkner, *Absalom, Absalom!*, 1936]

Chuck See MR. CHARLIE.

chuckheaded catfish The blue catfish *(Ictaclurus furcatus)*.

chuffle-jawed Large or full jaws, the word *chuffle* here probably deriving from an early word for jowl.

chuffy (1) Plump and healthy-looking; from a Scottish dialect word meaning the same. (2) Short and fat. See also CHOATY.

chug; choog To hit, jab, poke. "He chugged me in the ribs."

chune A pronunciation of *tune*.

chunk (1) To throw a stone, ball, etc. "He chunked a rock at her." (2) As an adjective, moderately good. "He owned a chunk of a house back then."

chunk-floater A heavy rain that comes on suddenly (and can float or move chunks of wood, etc.).

chunking Throwing, chucking. "'Quit chunking that durn ball at them there weatherboards,' he said. 'You don't never stop doing what I tell you.'" [Erskine Caldwell, *Tobacco Road*, 1932]

chunk up To throw up, vomit. "He chunked up all over the rug."

church stick A staff with a rabbit foot on one end and a fox tail on the other, once used in the South and other areas to awaken people who had fallen asleep in church.

chute See TAKE THE CHUTE.

City of Monuments A nickname for Baltimore, Maryland.

City of Rocks A nickname for Nashville, Tennessee.

City of the Hills A nickname for Richmond, Virginia.

City of White Sand A nickname for Pensacola, Florida, long noted for its white beaches.

city sparrow The English sparrow *(Passer domesticus)*.

city whiskey Commercially manufactured whiskey as opposed to moonshine. " 'Now, fellers, let's all have a drink of this-here nice city whiskey . . .' " [William Faulkner, *The Town,* 1957]

civil A fairly widespread term today describing either a kind, polite, civilized person or mannerly actions.

Civil War The Northern name for what some Southerners called the War, the Revolution, the War of Independence, the Second War of Independence, the War of Secession, the Glorious Cause, the War Between the States, the Unpleasantness, the Second American Revolution, the War for Constitutional Liberty, the War for Nationality, the War for Separation, the War for Southern Freedom, the War for Southern Independence, the War for Southern Nationality, the War for Southern Rights, the War for States' Rights, the War of the North and South, the War of the Sixties, the War to Suppress Yankee Arrogance and the Yankee Invasion, the Late Unpleasantness, the Little Unpleasantness, and Mr. Lincoln's War. All of these terms, including the *Civil War,* were first recorded in 1861.

clabber Sour, curdled milk.

clabber cheese Cottage cheese.

clabberhead Someone foolish or, less often, foul-mouthed.

clam A common pronunciation of *climb.* "He clammed up the tree."

clap one's fists To strike one's palm with one's fist in order to emphasize a speech. "He not only preached against them [the Ku Klux Klan] in his four-hour sermons but he went out on the road and clapped his fists and preached against them." [Jesse Stuart, *Beyond Dark Hills,* 1938]

clapper-clawing A violent fight in which someone is badly mauled or beaten; by extension a fiery denunciation, a tirade. "There were three of them involved in that clapper-clawing, and none of them came out looking good, I can tell you."

clawthumper A Marylander, erroneous pronunciation of *crawthumper.* "Those [soldiers] from Maryland were called claw-thumpers." [Walt Whitman, *November Boughs,* 1888]

Clay In the 19th century numerous terms bore the name of Kentucky statesman Henry Clay (1777–1852), including a breed of trotting horse called the *Clay.*

claybank A horse of a cream or yellowish color; called either a *claybank* or a *claybank horse.*

clay-eater One who eats clay for its nutritional content, especially a Southern poor white or black. "He was a little, dried up, withered atomy—a jaundiced sand-lapper or clay-eater from the Wassamasaw county" [William Gilmore Simms, *The Scout,* 1854] The term has often been used disparagingly, along with terms like POOR WHITE, *hillbilly* and REDNECK. *Clay-eating,* also called *dirt-*

eating, is still practiced in parts of the South, especially in the South Carolina and Georgia low country. " 'Coming down here every year and staying two months, without nothing to see . . . except these clay-eaters and Nigras.' " [William Faulkner, "Fox Hunt," 1931]

clean An expression used mostly among blacks meaning "well-dressed."

cleanly An old term for clean. "Get us some cleanly clothes."

clean one's plow To beat someone up in a fight. "As we say in Texas, he cleaned his plow."

clean up your own backyard Don't talk about others when you can stand improvement yourself.

clearseed See CLEARSTONE.

clearstone A freestone peach, as opposed to a *clingstone;* also called a *clearseed.*

clever (1) Nice, pleasant, agreeable, good-natured; sometimes heard as *clever-hearted.* "He was a right clever person, never a mean word from him." (2) Kindly, hospitable. "The new miller treated him real clever, and let him sleep in Old Master's mill room." [Willa Cather, *Sapphire and the Slave Girl,* 1940]

cleverness An old term for amiability in Virginia and other Southern states.

climb (crawl) one's frame To attack someone abusively, either physically or verbally. " 'Don't let 'em climb your frame, son.' " [Thomas Wolfe, *Look Homeward, Angel,* 1929]

clinch peach The clingstone variety of peach, in which the flesh clings to the pit, as opposed to the freestone variety; Also called *cling-fast.*

cling-fast See CLINCH PEACH.

clip and clean Completely, entirely. "He missed the target clip and clean."

clod buster A heavy sudden rain.

clome Climbed; used by uneducated speakers in parts of Virginia. "He clome the tree."

clomper To walk with a heavy foot. "His clompering could wake up the dead."

closed for flu Sign in a store window in a small Alabama town meaning that the store is closed because the owner and/or a number of his employees have come down with the flu (recorded in the movie *My Cousin Vinnie,* 1992).

clothespress An old term for a large wardrobe used to hold hanging clothes and which also has drawers in which to store clothes flat or folded.

clothes to die in Good clothing set aside for one's funeral. "Ada, too, talked about getting clothes to die in. She wanted a silk dress, and it mattered little to her whether the

colored A common term, now considered derogatory by many African-Americans, for a black person or black people in the South, though it is frequently heard in other regions as well; short for *colored person*.

colored people's time; C.P.T. This phrase, meaning a different time system, or a time later than the prescribed time, possibly originated among blacks, perhaps in the South; in any case, it is considered derogatory by many African-Americans.

color-struck A derogatory term apparently originating among Southern blacks and referring to a black person who acts conceited because his or her skin is lighter than that of most blacks.

come a Used of weather that is going to develop, as in "It's going to come a storm."

come across To occur to. "It come across me that I might be wrong."

come back A farewell expression, sometimes expanded to *come back again,* meaning "come again." "Y'all come back, y'hear?"

come by An invitation to pay a short visit. "Come by and stay for dinner."

come-by-chance A euphemism for an illegitimate child. "All her kids are come-by-chance."

come ci Come here; a combination of the English *come* and the French *ci* (here); used in Louisiana to call children.

come easy, go easy Southern variation of *easy come, easy go;* an easygoing person; also *come easy, come go.*

come here A southwest Virginia term for a person not born in the community. *Come heres* are a group of such people.

come off An often unfortunate outcome or circumstance. "Well, that's a fine come off. I thought I was going to win, and I lost by ten points."

come on at one's own gait Do things at one's own pace or in one's own good time. " 'Won't you please go to hell and let me come on at my own gait?' " [William Faulkner, "Uncle Willy," 1936]

come on to rain To begin raining. "Along in the afternoon it came on to rain."

come over one's head To hit someone over the head. "He come over my head with his cane."

comer-and-goer An old term for a tourist. "We get a lot of comer-and-goers in summer."

come-see A lovely word in Gullah for a delicate child, one who has come to see this world and decide whether or not it wishes to stay, which might make its life very brief.

come sick To menstruate; also *coming sick.*

come stout To go beyond a certain limit. "That's coming pretty stout, interpreting it so liberally."

come the giraffe over An unusual, though obsolete, Southern slang expression relating to cheating or getting the better of someone. " 'No, you don't,' said the watchman, 'you don't come the giraffe over me that-a-way.' " [*New Orleans Picayune,* October 14, 1844] *Giraffe* itself meant to humbug or cheat.

come through To make a religious conversion, especially at a revival meeting. "He come through yesterday at the big meeting."

come to fetch fire To come quickly and leave.

come to the end of one's row To run out of patience or be at the end of one's rope.

come-too-soon Euphemism for an illegitimate child or a child born less than nine months after a couple marries.

come up (1) Used of developing weather, as in "Looks like its coming up a storm" or "It come up a storm." (2) To grow up. "When I was coming up in Alabama."

comeuppance An advantage. "That way we'll all share alike and no man have air comeuppance over no other man." [John Faulkner, *Men Working,* 1941]

comfort A comforter, coverlet; also *comfort-quilt.*

comical An old term for strange or peculiar. "She's a comical-looking one."

comings One's just deserts. "He'll get his comings yet."

coming up a cloud A storm is approaching; it is going to rain. "Don't wander far. It's comin' up a cloud."

commence to Often used for "to begin or start." "They commence to fight as soon as they see each other."

comme ça Like that; French phrase often used in the Southern Louisiana-French dialects.

comment? How?; French word often used in the Southern Louisiana-French dialects.

common (1) When Henry Wallace campaigned with the slogan that this was "the century of the common man," many Southerners had trouble understanding at first, for *common* is often a term of contempt in the South, far more than in the rest of the United States. (2) A complimentary term for an unassuming, friendly person. It is most frequently heard in the Appalachians and Ozarks. "He's a real common man."

common as pig tracks Very common; used mostly in rural Texas.

commonest A pronunciation of Communist. ". . . in fact they were both fighting on the commonist side in that war." [William Faulkner, *The Mansion*, 1959]

companion Often a synonym for *wife*. "She's been his companion 20 years now."

compersation Conversation, from a black pronunciation of the word.

complainy (1) Disposed to complain. "Hit makes us all feel ailish and complainy sort of." [John Faulkner, *Men Working*, 1941] (2) Ill. "She was quite complainy yesterday."

complete Sometimes used as an adverb meaning "completely," as in "It's almost complete gone."

complicate up To complicate, confuse. " '. . . because for a feller in the nekkid photograph business . . . to complicate it up with peddling whiskey, would be jist pleading for trouble.' " [William Faulkner, *The Mansion*, 1959]

conch (1) Pronounced "conk," this is the often derogatory term for a white resident of the Florida Keys, though conchs in the past also lived along the south coast of Florida and in North Carolina. The term dates back to the early 19th century when white native Bahamians were called conchs because they were skilled in diving for the large shellfish called the conch *(Strombus alatus)*, an important item in their diet. The descendants of a band of Cockney Englishmen called the Eleutherian Adventurers who migrated from London to Bermuda in about 1649 in search of religious and political freedom, they came to the Florida Keys from Eleuthera in the 19th century. One persistent old story has the conchs able to dive fathoms in search of their quarry. "Nearly half of all residents [of Key West] are natives of the Bahama Islands. They are called Conch-men or Conchs [pronounced conks], by reason of their skill in diving (for conchs, which they are said to locate underwater and crack open with their teeth!)." [*New York Weekly Tribune*, May 1, 1852] (2) The dialect spoken by the Conchs in the Florida Keys.

Confed Short for both a CONFEDERATE during the Civil War and for Confederate currency issued by the Confederacy. "For one dollar greenbacks, we can get five to ten dollars Confed." [Louis Boudrye, *Fifth New York Cavalry*, 1865]

Confederacy The Confederate States of America, the term used in this sense some 30 years before the Civil War.

Confederate (1) A citizen of the CONFEDERACY; the term appears to have first been used in May 1861, after the Civil War began. (2) For a time after the Civil War the word signified the highest praise in parts of the South. "When a Texan wishes to express the strongest possible approval . . . he will exclaim, 'You're mighty Confederate!' " [*Overland Monthly*, March 1867]

Confederate beef A humorous description Southerners gave to mule meat when beef was scarce during the Civil War.

Confederate brigadier In post-Civil War days, a U.S. congressman or senator who had served as an officer in the Confederate States of America. The term was also applied to very loyal, patriotic and vocal Southerners after the Civil War. *Southern brigadier* was a synonym.

Confederate coffee A substitute coffee made of chicory, beans, etc., during the Civil War when coffee was in short supply.

Confederate candle "Another light in great vogue [during the Civil War] was the 'Confederate' or 'endless' candle. It was constructed by dipping a wick in melted wax and resin and wrapping it around a stick, one end of the wick being passed through a wire loop fastened to the end of the stick." [*Century Magazine,* volume 36, 1888]

Confederate cotton Cotton that had to be used in the South because the Union blockade of Southern ports prevented it from reaching its markets.

Confederate duck This Civil War dish wasn't duck at all but "a tender and juicy beefsteak rolled and pinioned around stuffing of stale bread crumbs." No one appears to know why it was so named.

Confederate grayback The official currency of the Confederacy during the Civil War, so-called because of its gray back.

Confederate jasmine The star jasmine, because it has been commonly cultivated in the South for well over a century.

Confederate money A term that means "money not worth the paper it is printed on," referring to the worthless banknotes of the Confederacy after the Civil War. After the war, according to Margaret Mitchell in *Gone With the Wind* (1936), an anonymous poem entitled "Lines on the Back of a Confederate Note" circulated in the South, sometimes written in hand on a piece of paper pasted to the backs of the "useless" Confederate notes:

Representing nothing on God's earth now
And naught in the waters below it—
As the pledge of a nation that's passed away
Keep it, dear friend, and show it.

Show it to those who will lend an ear
To the tale this trifle will tell
Of Liberty, born of patriots' dream,
Of a storm-cradled nation that fell.

Confederate paper Homemade writing paper. "Dear old quire of yellow, coarse, Confederate homemade paper, here you are again." [Mary Chestnut, *Diary,* 1865]

Confederate rose The hibiscus; also called the *cotton rose.*

Confederate shinplaster A humorous derogatory term for *Confederate* *money* during the Civil War. "In the North a carpenter got three dollars . . . In the South he got fifty—payable in Confederate shinplasters worth a dollar a bushel." [Mark Twain, *A Connecticut Yankee in King Arthur's Court*, 1889]

Confederate War Once a common term among Southerners for the Civil War.

Confedrit Common pronunciation of Confederate. " '. . . like in the photographs [Ratliff said] where the Confedrit sweetheart in a hoop skirt and a magnolia is saying goodbye to her Confedrit beau just before he rides off to finish tending to General Grant . . .' " [William Faulkner, *The Town*, 1957]

confidence To have trust in. "I don't reckon I could even confidence her nohow."

congealed salad A gelatin salad made with vegetables and/or fruit.

Congo A name in pre-Civil War days for a black person from the Congo area in Africa or the language of that person; also a popular dance invented by blacks in the South. *Congo* is also used for things black in color, such as a *congo eel*.

conjure bag A collection of magic charms tied together in a ball and kept in a small bag that is used to ward off evil spirits or gain control over someone; also called a *conjure ball* and *kungu*. "The conjurer's bag of the Africans . . . is called 'waiter'

or 'kunger' by Southern blacks, and is supposed to have the power to charm away evil spirits, and do all manner of miraculously good things for its wearer." [Edmund Kirks, *My Southern Friends*, 1863]

conjure; conjuree To practice voodoo.

conjure ball See CONJURE BAG.

Conjuer John The Solomon's seal, a member of the lily family; so-called because the plant was considered a powerful charm in conjuring; also called *Big John the Conjueror* and *Big John the Conqueror*.

conk A hairstyle worn by African-Americans that straightens and waves curly hair; probably takes its name from the slang *conk* for head and/or from the commercial preparation Congolene used to so fashion hair; also called a *process*. The term is used widely throughout the United States, and its point of origin is unknown but might be Southern.

consarn Damn, darn. "Consarn it!"

considerable A great deal. "It was a kind of mixed hound, with a little bird dog and some collie and maybe a considerable of almost anything else." [William Faulkner, "Shingles for the Lord," 1943]

considerable more A lot more. " 'That cow wasn't worth eight dollars last fall,' Houston said. 'But she's worth a considerable more now.' "

[William Faulkner, *The Mansion*, 1959]

consumpted Consumptive, having tuberculosis.

contintment A common pronunciation of *contentment*.

contrary Stubborn. "He's one contrary old boy."

cooling board A board once commonly used for laying out a corpse before putting it in the coffin. See also LAY ON THE COOLING BOARD.

coon (1) An often derogatory term for a country person; hayseed. (2) An offensive term for a black person that apparently originated in the South. (3) As a verb, to crawl on all fours like a raccoon; to climb a tree or pole. "He cooned up that tree."

coon ass Crazy. "He's real coon ass, man," or "He's a real coon ass, man."

coonass A vulgar offensive term for a Cajun, used chiefly in Louisiana. The word is probably a corruption of the French *conasse* (vulva) and a contemptuous term for a woman. A variation is *coonie*.

coon bottom A part of town where poorer people live; used especially in Florida and Georgia.

coon dick An old term for homemade liquor.

coon dog; coon hound A dog trained to hunt raccoons on coon hunts.

coonfine A derogatory term used in days past to describe the rhythmic gait and movement of black roustabouts when loading or unloading freight on ships. The workers, who also sang as they worked, were often called *coonfiners*. The word may refer to the waddling walk of the raccoon.

coon juice Homemade liquor.

coon oyster Small oysters (*Lapha frons*, usually) that grow in clusters along salt marshes and are a favorite of raccoons.

cooter Applied to sea tortoises, the obsolete verb *coot* meant "to copulate," a usage recorded as early as 1667. It may also be responsible for the common name (cooter) for two amorous American turtles (especially *Chrysemys concinna*). The first recorded use of the word is "The tortoises . . . coot for fourteen days together." However, some authorities say that *cooter* is not from *coot* but from the African Bambara word *kuta*, meaning "turtle that was brought by slaves to America."

copperheads Not Southerners during the Civil War but Northerners who sympathized with the Confederate cause. They were also called, in various places, *butternuts, guerillas, bushwhackers, jayhawkers* and *Vallandinghamers* (after Ohioan copperhead leader Clement Vallandigham, who was convicted of treason).

Cork ball; corks ball A variety of baseball played in the St. Louis area with four or more players, a small ball and a thin bat.

cork high and bottle deep Very drunk.

corn Corn whiskey, made by distilling corn.

corn beer Corn made into a beer, or such beer fermented into whiskey.

corn bread See CORN PONE.

corncakes See FLITTERCAKES.

corn coffee (1) A coffee made from parched corn and other ingredients. "The supper consisted of . . . and coffee made of burnt acorns and maize . . . He laughed at our fastidiousness and advised us to drink some of the corn coffee." [George Featherstonhaugh, *Excursion Through the Slave States,* 1844] (2) Can also mean corn whiskey.

corncracker (1) Once a common nickname for residents of Kentucky and other Southern states. (2) A derogatory term for a poor white farmer.

Corncracker State A nickname given to Kentucky.

corn dodger A corn bread cake or cornmeal dumpling.

cornfield pea Black-eyed pea.

cornfield school A now historical term for a small schoolhouse set in a man-made clearing in the cornfield.

corn juice Whiskey made from corn.

corn light bread Bread made completely of cornmeal or of cornmeal and very little wheat flour.

corn pone (1) A famous Southern cornmeal cake or bread, defined by Bartlett in 1859 as "a superior type of corn bread, made with milk and eggs and cooked in a pan." It is often called *corn bread.* (2) A derogatory term for someone or something rural and unsophisticated: "That's a corn-pone accent."

cornrow A hairstyle worn by African-Americans consisting of rows of small flat braids.

corn shucking A traditional social gathering at which corn is shucked.

corn song A song field workers sang when harvesting corn; the custom originated with slaves in the South.

corporosity An old-fashioned term for one's body or its state of health; probably derives from *corpulence.* "How's the state of your corporosity today?"

correspond the idea An old term of limited, mostly black usage meaning "to give up on a plan": "I done corresponded the idea of going."

corruption A term for pus of any kind.

cotton bale A bale of ginned cotton, closely packed and weighing up to 500 pounds.

cotton brag An expression used in pre-Civil War times of overseers who boasted of harvesting the largest cotton crop with a certain number of slaves. "The Southern newspapers, at the crop season, chronicle carefully the 'cotton brag' and the 'crack cotton picking' and 'unparalleled driving' . . . We recollect . . . the editor of a religious paper at Natchez, Miss., in which he took care to assign a prominent place and capitals to the 'cotton brag.' " [Theodore Weld, *American Slavery As It Is,* 1839]

cotton broker One who brokers cotton, or in Erskine Caldwell's words (*God's Little Acre,* 1933): " 'Do you know why they're called brokers?' 'Why?' 'Because they keep the farmers broke all the time. They lend a little money, and then they take the whole damn crop. Or else they suck the blood out of a man by running the price up and down forcing him to sell. That's why they call them cotton brokers.' "

cotton chopper A laborer who chops out or thins young cotton plants. "The cotton-chopper straddles the row, and chops wide gaps, leaving the plants in hills." [Edward Knight, *Practical Dictionary of Mechanics,* 1874]

cotton chopping time The time during the growing season when cotton is chopped or thinned. "It was cotton-chopping time when the long rows of thickly planted stalks had to be thinned with hoes." [*Century Magazine,* May 1885]

cottonclad A play on *ironclad,* this term was applied to Civil War vessels "armored" with bales of cotton. "He was in command of the tin-clad *Indianola* at Vicksburg; and after running the batteries there was engaged single-handed with two Confederate rams and two 'cotton-clad' steamers." [Jacob Dunn, *Indiana and Indianans,* 1919]

Cotton Confederacy A humorous term for the Southern Confederacy.

cotton-eyed Eyes prominently white, as in the folk song "Cotton-eyed Joe."

cottonhead A person, especially a child, with white or very light blond hair.

cottonmouth-bit Bitten by a cottonmouth snake.

cotton pickers A humorous term for the hands.

cotton pickin' Despicable, wretched, damned; now sometimes used in a humorous sense. The expression has its roots in the inferior status of poor farmers and field hands in the Southern United States. "Keep your cotton pickin' hands off me."

cotton picking In pre-cotton-gin times, social gatherings of friends and neighbors to remove the seed from cotton were called cotton pickings. Such gatherings were also held to harvest cotton.

cotton rebel A nickname for a Southerner during the Civil War. "If there's anything civil between us and the Cotton Rebels, we don't exactly see it." [*Vanity Fair,* May 4, 1861]

cotton rose The large-flowered hibiscus; also called the *Confederate rose.*

cotton senator A senator representing a Southern state. ". . . there are 'silver Senators' and 'wheat Senators' and 'labor Senators' and 'cotton Senators' and 'big business Senators' and too few United States Senators." [*Readers Digest,* March 1947]

couillon A stupid foolish person, a hick; used chiefly in Louisiana, deriving from a French word meaning the same.

could talk a cat down out of a tree Very persuasive, loquacious. "At any rate, she could talk a cat down out of a tree and I was one of the very few people who could really listen to her." [Calder Willingham, *Rambling Rose,* 1972]

couldn't hit a bull in the ass with a bass fiddle A terrible shot or marksman; any inept person.

couldn't hit the ground if he (she) fell A clumsy, inept person.

coulee A term used mainly in Louisiana for a number of types of waterways, including a streambed that runs dry in summer and a small bayou; from the French word meaning "a flow."

counterpin This folk etymology of *counterpane* is an old word for a coverlet or bedspread.

country block See COUNTRY MILE.

country coin A countrified person.

country cousin A euphemism for menstruation. "Her country cousin is visiting, if you know what I mean."

country cracker A rustic or hick.

country fever An old term for malaria.

country fries Sliced fried potatoes, home fries.

country ham Salt-cured, unsmoked hams.

country hotel The county jailhouse.

country joke A yokel, a rustic.

country man One who lives in a rural area, usually a farmer. " 'Except that like you said, nobody named Vladimir Kyrilytch could make a living as a Mississippi country man.' " [William Faulkner, *The Town,* 1957]

country mile Any long distance; a widely used expression that apparently originated in the South. "He hit the ball a country mile." Also called *country block.*

country pin A COUNTERPIN, bedspread.

country steak A Southern favorite, steak cooked in a frying pan. "I'll cook you a nice meal, Milo. You can have fried chicken and yams, or ham and red-eye dish gravy, or country steak." [Erskine Caldwell, *Jenny By Nature*, 1961]

courage Sexual desire or potency. "He told the doctor that he had sexual problems, couldn't get his courage up."

courage bump A pimple on the face.

courting fool One who courts in high style, not necessarily one who makes a fool of himself for love. " 'Just look at that courting fool,' Jimson whispered. 'Ain't he the biggest sport you ever did see? He's all dressed up in yellow shoes and red necktie ready to flash them colors on the first gal he sees. That courting fool can do courting where courting's never been done afore. Man alive, don't I wish I was him!' " [Erskine Caldwell, "Big Buck," *The Complete Stories of Erskine Caldwell*, 1953]

covered him (her) like the dew covers Dixie To fall all over someone, usually with amorous intention. "She covered him like the dew covers Dixie."

covering the waterfront A euphemism for attending to menstruation or diapering a baby; it can also be used to indicate someone's bisexuality.

cow alligator The female alligator as opposed to the male, called the bull gator, in Louisiana and other states. "In dimmer recesses [was] the cow alligator, with her nest hard by." [George Washington Cable, *The Grandissimes*, 1880]

coward-hearted Chiefly a Gullah term describing a cowardly person.

cowbelly A term, used mainly in Louisiana, for the soft mud on the banks of rivers.

cowcumber A name for the cucumber in North Carolina, Louisiana and other Southern states, especially among older speakers.

cow cutter An old-fashioned euphemism for a bull; can also mean a cow or steer.

cow doctor A poorly regarded physician.

cow-dung cooter The striped mud turtle or the box turtle, both of which sometimes eat manure.

cowhide (1) A whip made from straps of rawhide. (2) As a verb, to beat someone with such a whip.

cowpea Another name for the BLACK-EYED PEA extensively cultivated in the South for forage and soil improvement as well as for food.

cow-pen tea Medicinal tea made from cow manure; widely used in the 19th century.

cow's gentleman friend An old-fashioned euphemism for a bull.

C.P.T. See COLORED PEOPLE'S TIME.

crab-apple switch A large pocket-knife with folding blades.

crabburger A hamburger-shaped pattie made of crabmeat and served on a hamburger roll; used mainly in Louisiana.

crab cake See CRABBURGER.

crab soup See SHE-CRAB SOUP.

crack To open slightly; has some national use but is primarily a Southernism. "Crack open the door a little to let in some air."

cracker A poor white person, especially one from Georgia (the Cracker State), so called, perhaps, from their use of cracked corn. Originally the expression was *corncracker,* one who cracks corn to make grits or cornmeal. At one time (1766), *cracker* meant "a liar," but when, after the Civil War, many people in the South became too poor to buy cornmeal and had to make their own, *cracker* came to mean a backwoodsman and then a poor white, generally a person living in the Southern states of Georgia and Florida. Others say that cracker was originally applied to Florida cowboys and derived from their cracking their whips as they herded cattle. In any case, the term is generally an offensive one and is now regarded as a racial epithet that is a violation under the Florida Hate Crimes Act. Many people, however, are proud to call themselves *Georgia Crackers, Florida Crackers,* etc., just so long as they're doing the calling.

cracker sack See CROCUS SACK.

Cracker State A nickname given to Georgia since the 19th century.

crackling The crisp skin from a hog or other animal that remains after fat has been rendered. Used as food, it is famous in crackling bread, a cornmeal dish. Cracklings are also used to make soup.

crackling bread See CRACKLING.

crack of day Dawn or daybreak.

crack one's sides To laugh so hard you hurt yourself. "I like to crack my sides."

crack one's teeth To talk. " 'E [he] nebber crack 'e teet." A Gullah expression of which a variation is *crack one's breath*.

Cradle of the Confederacy A nickname given to Montgomery, Alabama, where the seceded Southern states met on February 4, 1861, to form the Confederate States of America.

cramp-colic Stomach spasms.

crank-sided Lopsided, twisted or carried to the side.

crank up the car Common, especially in South Carolina, for "start up the car" or "start the car."

cranky A term used mainly in Virginia for the great blue heron.

crany-crow An old-fashioned term for a CARRION CROW. A popular rhyme in the game "Old Witch" goes: "Chicky-ma, chicky-ma, crany-crow, I went to the well to wash my toe."

craps The game of dice as all America knows it today dates to the early 19th century and may owe its name, craps, to a Louisiana Frenchman. Johnny Crapaud was the nickname of gambler Bernard Mariginy, who introduced dice to New Orleans in about 1800 (*Crapaud* being slang for any Frenchman, owing to the belief that three crapauds, or toads, were the ancient arms of France.) High-roller Mariginy became associated with the game, which was named *Johnny Crapaud's game* after his nickname, this eventually shortened to *craps*. It is said that Mariginy even named the present Burgundy Street "Craps Street" in honor of his favorite pastime. Another theory holds that *craps* derives from the English *crabs,* the lowest throw in the game of hazard, which passed into French as *craps* and came into American usage in the present sense in early 19th century New Orleans.

Craps Street See CRAPS.

crawdad; crawdab (1) A crawfish (crayfish). (2) To crawl like a crawfish. "I craw-dabbed from under the house."

crawfish The crayfish.

crawfish boil A party in Louisiana at which crawfish are boiled and eaten.

crawfishing A term once applied to wet lowlands in Alabama and other Southern states because such areas were inhabited by crawfish.

crawl Chasten, punish. " 'I reckon I'd ought to have crawled him about it,' he thought. In his day he would have been thoroughly thrashed for slipping away and idling." [Marjorie Kinnan Rawlings, *The Yearling,* 1938]

crawl on broken glass through hell for The ultimate in devotion. "She'd crawl on broken glass through hell for him."

crawl one's frame See CLIMB ONE'S FRAME.

crawthumper An old name for a native of Maryland, in reference to Roman Catholics (considered crawthumpers [chest beaters] by some) having played a prominent part in settling Maryland.

crazy Broken; out of line.

crazy as a betsy bug Very crazy; after the large black beetle called the *betsy bug,* because to some it seems to say "bessy" when touched. This bug, of the family Passalidae, is also called the *horn beetle* and *pinch bug.*

crazy as a peach-orchard boar Said of a wild crazy person.

creaker An elderly person; a term used mostly by African-Americans.

cream cheese A term used mainly in Louisiana for what is cottage cheese elsewhere.

creamed potatoes   Mashed potatoes.

cream gravy   Gravy made with fat, flour and cream or milk.

cream of the pot   The ultimate, best of its kind, state of the art; said of a person or a thing.

creamy ass   The bird generally known as the old snow is called the *creamy ass* along the coast in North Carolina.

crease   To barely wound with a shot. "I just creased him in the leg, is all."

creation!   An old-fashioned euphemism for the expletive "Christ!" "Creation, man, what's wrong with you!"

creature   (1) Colloquial term for a horse in the South, especially in the form of *critter* or *crittur*. (2) Wild animal. " 'You no-account creature! Homin' in on our rations and leavin' sich as this to happen.' " [Marjorie Kinnan Rawlings, *The Yearling*, 1938]

creek   A small brook.

Creek claims   A historical term for lands in Alabama and Georgia claimed by the Creek Indians, who formerly occupied the area as the Creek Confederacy.

Creek Confederacy   See   CREEK CLAIMS.

creepified   Scared, creepy.

creepmouse   "Here comes a little mouse/creeping up to baby's house" is the rhyme often used in this familiar game played with infants. Most common in the South under the name "creepmouse," the game is played everywhere, the idea being to make babies laugh by tickling them slightly with one's fingers as if a mouse was running over their bodies. The usage of *creepmouse* is first recorded in 1899.

creep the goose   A Cajun method of hunting geese where the hunters creep through the sawgrass, evading eye contact with the sentinel goose in a flock, and suddenly spring up and fire their weapons.

Creole   (1) A white person descended from French or Spanish settlers in Louisiana. (2) A person of mixed black and French or Spanish heritage. (3) The language used by Creoles in Louisiana. (4) A nickname for a native of Louisiana. (5) A spicy type of food or method of cooking that is common in southern Louisiana.

Creole coffee   Strong dark black coffee laced with chicory. Popular in New Orleans.

Creole State   Louisiana.

Crescent   The state flag of South Carolina. "They tore down the U.S. flag and raised the Crescent in its place."

Crescent City   Nickname for New Orleans, because, according to Joseph Ingraham in *The South-West*

(1835), "it is built around the segment of a circle formed by a graceful curve of the Mississippi River."

cribber A horse that gnaws or sucks at trees or stumps; a stump-sucker.

crimpy Cold, nasty weather. "It's been right crimpy the last few days."

crip Something simple to do, easy. "That puzzle was a crip."

Critter See CREATURE.

Croatan Someone of mixed Indian, white and black ancestry living mainly in North Carolina. The name is objectionable to many of these people, who, however, at first asked to be called Croatan Indians after Sir Walter Raleigh's lost colony of Croatan off North Carolina. They consider the name "Cro" given to them by blacks and whites in the area even more offensive.

crocodile A Southern name for the American alligator, *Alligator mississipiensis.*

crocus sack A gunny sack, a sack made of coarse material like burlap; so named because crocus, or saffron, was first shipped in sacks made of this material; also called a *croker sack, tow sack* and *grass sack* in the South. " 'What you got in that there crocus sack, Lov?' Jeeter said." [Erskine Caldwell, *Tobacco Road,* 1932]

croker sack See CROCUS SACK.

crooked as a barrel of fishhooks Very crooked, dishonest. "He was the mayor of Memphis but crooked as a barrel of fishhooks."

crooked rail fence The name for a rail fence in Virginia.

crope Crept; used chiefly by blacks. "I crope up behind him."

cropper; crapper A sharecropper, a small or tenant farmer.

cross-breed A derogatory term sometimes applied to people of mixed white and Indian origins.

crossed up To oppose someone. "We're all crossed up on that one, we can't find any common ground at all."

crossways In a bad, ill-tempered mood; also *crosswise.* "I'm all crossways today."

crosswise See CROSSWAYS.

crow A derogatory term for a black person.

crowder A variety of black-eyed pea that grows crowded together in the pod; in his diary, George Washington records growing them.

crumb crusher An expression used mainly by blacks for a baby or young child, one who is still crawling.

crystallized pickle A kind of cucumber pickle.

Cuban sandwich A name, generally confined to Florida, for a submarine or hero sandwich.

cubbitch A term from Gullah, deriving from *covetous,* meaning stingy, cheap, miserly.

Cuby Cuban. " 'And leave me tell you, do you fill a demi-john with 'em [berries of the saw palmetto] and pour Cuby rum over 'em and leave 'em stand five months, you've got a drink would make even your Ma shout Hallelujah . . .' " [Marjorie Kinnan Rawlings, *The Yearling,* 1938]

cuda A common name for the barracuda in some Southern states.

cue (1) Short for *barbecue* or for barbecued food. "We gonna have a cue tonight." (2) A small, round variety of muskmelon; probably based on *cueball.*

cuffy A term commonly used for a black man before the Civil War; it derives from *Kofi,* a name used on the African Gold Coast for a boy born on Friday.

cunnin' Very cute. "She's a cunnin' thing, ain't she?"

cup towel A towel used to dry dishes.

curb market An outdoor market; originally one where farmers sold produce.

cur dog A mongrel or any worthless dog.

curious (person) An eccentric, old or strange person. "He's a curious one all right."

curiouser More curious. " 'But what's curiouser than that is what you want with it.' " [William Faulkner, *The Hamlet,* 1940]

curioussome Curious; used chiefly by blacks. "He looked at me kinder curioussome."

curly dirt Fuzzy balls of lint that collect, especially under beds.

curly flower A folk pronunciation of *cauliflower.*

currying A very sharp scolding. "I sure got some currying for coming home so late."

cush Sweetened and fried cornmeal; the word is an African one brought into this country by slaves. *Cush* is now also slang for money reserved for a special purpose.

cut (1) *n* A portion of land or a field. "[I] took to laying off the 20-acre cut designed to carrots." [George Washington, *Diaries,* 1787] (2) *v* To stab, wound with a knife. "They cut each other real bad."

cut a hog To make an embarrassing mistake or fail in some way; Derives from *to cut a gut,* referring to a mistake made when dressing an animal.

cut a rusty To play a prank on someone or show off.

cute as a kitten on down South Very cute, adorable. "She's as cute as a kitten on down South."

cute as a speckled pup Very cute, adorable. "That child's cute as a speckled pup."

cut off To switch off; also *cut out.* "She cut off the radio."

cut off the light Widely used in the South for *turn off the light;* also *outen the light.*

cut on To switch on, to turn on. "He cut on the lights."

cut one's eyes To glance furtively out of the corner of one's eyes.

cut one's foot To step in cow dung. The Southern euphemism, first re-corded in 1899, still has some currency in rural areas today.

cut the cake To be married. "When are you going to cut the cake?"

cut the fool (1) To behave in a stupid way. "You really cut the fool last night." (2) To play tricks on people, joke around.

cut the tail off the dog Make a long story short. "Wal, to cut the tail off the dog, he finally married her."

cutting (1) A stabbing, a knife fight. (2) When applied to rodents, cutting often means chewing, as in "That squirrel's sure cuttin' away on those nuts."

Cyclops An officer in the KU KLUX KLAN; often called *Exalted Cyclops* or *Grand Cyclops.*

cymling head A stupid person, after the small round variety of melon or squash called the cymling.

D

dab A small quantity, a spot, a splotch. "All we saw was cornfields and dabs of woods."

Daddy An old-fashioned term, mostly used by blacks, for an old black man. See also AUNTIE.

daddy longlegs A stallion or the male of any species kept for breeding.

dad-gum Euphemism for *damn*. "I'm dad-gum tired trying!" [Huey Long, 1935 speech]

Damnation to the Yankees! A favorite drinking toast in the South from the time of Fort Sumter to Appomattox and beyond.

damn-blasted A common expletive meaning "damned." " 'All my turnips has got them damn-blasted green-gutted worms in them, Lov,' [Jeeter said]." [Erskine Caldwell, *Tobacco Road,* 1932]

Damn to blue blazes! A common expletive, " 'Them Indians!' " Luke says. 'They was fixing to ———' 'What?' Major hollers. 'Damn to blue blazes, what?' " [William Faulkner, "A Bear Hunt," 1934]

damn Yankee A Northerner. In early America, Yankee peddlers generally had a bad name, being "proverbial for their dishonesty," according to one early observer, and Northerners probably got the name *damn Yankee,* coined long before the Civil War, from Yankee peddlers who worked the rural South. The opprobrious term *damn Yankee* appears to have first been used in the South in about 1812. By Civil War times we find a Northern soldier writing home about a Virginia woman who "wasn't going to let the damned Yankees drink out of her well." The term is often written as one word: *damyankee.*

dan Common black and Gullah pronunciation of *than*.

dang An old euphemism for *damn,* dating back to before 1790.

daren't The old English contraction of *dare not* is still heard, though rarely, among older speakers in the South.

daresome Afraid. "I'm daresome to go through those woods."

Dark and Bloody Ground An old name for Kentucky, possibly a translation of an Indian name. "*Dark and Bloody Ground* alluded not to battles between Indians and the first white settlers, but to contests between Northern and Southern tribes of Indians." [H. L. Mencken, *The American Language, Supplement II*, 1948]

darkey A derogatory old-fashioned term for a black person; also *darky*, *darkie*. " 'Poor Handsome Brown. He was the best darkey we ever had.' " [Erskine Caldwell, *Georgia Boy*, 1943]

darling A common affectionate term used by Southern men to address all women. "It's nice to meet you, dahlin'."

dassant Dare not. ". . . he just could not believe that; he dassant to believe that . . ." [William Faulkner, *The Town*, 1957]

dat A common black and Gullah pronunciation of *that*.

daube A kind of stew well-known in New Orleans.

Davisdom An old nickname for the Confederate States of America, whose president was Jefferson Davis.

day and time Era, period of time. "In his day and time, they didn't do it that way."

daybust Sunrise. "We started out at daybust."

dayclean A Gullah term for *daybreak* that may be the translation of an African expression.

dazed as a goose with a nail in its head Stunned. "We found him wandering around after the fight dazed as a goose with a nail in its head."

dead as a beef Completely dead, with no life. " 'Are you Rosie Caldfield? Then you better come out yon. Henry has done shot that deem French feller. Kilt him dead as a beef.' " [William Faulkner, *Absalom, Absalom!*, 1936]

dead as a hammer Without any life at all, stone-cold dead. "My dog died. I went out there in the yard and looked at him and there he was, dead as a hammer." [Larry Brown, "Big Bad Love," 1990]

dead cat on the line Field workers for the *Dictionary of American Regional English* found 21 people who used this expression, meaning "there's something suspicious, something wrong"—but not one of the 21 could explain it. When William Safire asked readers of his nationally syndicated word column for help, an old man in Louisiana scrawled a letter explaining that the expression has its roots in fishing for catfish, when trotlines with many hooks on them are set in the water. The lines are checked every day, so if a fisherman checks a neighbor's line and finds a dead catfish (cat) on the line, he knows there is something wrong, suspicious or fishy going on (his neighbor may be ill, be in trouble, etc.).

deaden A method of killing trees by cutting through the bark all around, girdling them. "A house was half erected, and some fifty acres of trees deadened." [A. Van Buren, *Jottings of A Year's Sojourn in the South*, 1859]

dead hearing Deafness; very poor sense of hearing. "She remembered her grandmother, thinking of the old woman with her dead hearing and her inescapable cold eyes . . ." [William Faulkner, "Elly," 1934]

dead to know Very anxious to know. "Just cast your mind back and try to remember who your lady was yestiddy who happ'n to mention that my customer was pregnant, that's all. She's dead to know," [Eudora Welty, "Petrified Man," 1941]

dear goodness! A common exclamation. "Oh dear goodness!" [Marjorie Kinnan Rawlings, *The Yearling*, 1938]

deef Deaf. " 'That's Pap.' the man said. 'Blind and deef both.' " [William Faulkner, *Sanctuary*, 1931]

dee-po Depot. " 'So they're down at the dee-po now.' " [William Faulkner, *The Town*, 1957]

delta dog A Mississippi name for a HUSH PUPPY.

dem A common black and Gullah pronunciation of *them*.

demoiselle Miss; French, often used in Southern Louisiana-French dialects.

dese Common black and Gullah pronunciation of *these*.

devil To fool or tease. "I knew he'd devil you."

devil's grandmother A shrewish or otherwise undesirable woman. An old Southern rhyme goes: "I married another,/ The devil's grandmother./ I wish I was single again."

dewberry An old name, common in the South, for the low brush blackberry.

dey Common black and Gullah pronunciation of *they*.

dicty Stylish or wealthy; a snob, aristocrat; mainly a black term.

diddled Cheated. "Though even in his extremity Montgomery Ward had more simple sense and judgment . . . than to actively believe that ten thousand Lawyer Stevensons . . . could a diddled Flem Snopes." [William Faulkner, *The Mansion*, 1959]

didapper The Carolina grebe, *Podilymbus podiceps*. "Besides these birds we have . . . the Didapper or Dapchick." [Thomas Jefferson, *Notes on the State of Virginia*, 1788]

diddly Nothing, very little, as in "It's not worth diddly."

diddly-squat Nothing or very little. "He don't know diddly-squat."

didn't nobody go A common double negative for *nobody went*. "Didn't nobody go because of the rain."

dientical A pronunciation of *identical* sometimes used by uneducated speakers in Mississippi and other Southern states.

die up To die. "He'll die up shore if he gets no care."

differ not To matter not. "It differs not to me whether we go or stay home."

digging one's grave with one's teeth Said of someone who eats too much. "She's diggin' her grave with her teeth."

dilbert-head A dope, a fool. "Boy. I bet David Lynch is just losing his lunch right now because you and your boyfriend thought his movie was sick. You dilbert-head." [Larry Brown, "92 Days," 1990]

dinges A derogatory name for blacks that is also used in the North and other sections of the country. " 'I haven't seen you since Abraham Lincoln put on long pants and grew a beard and freed the dinges.' " [Erskine Caldwell, *The Earnshaw Neighborhood*, 1971]

dinner The midday meal in North Carolina and other Southern areas.

dinner on the grounds A meal, often served at church gatherings, that was once an outdoor picnic meal but now can indicate a meal eaten either inside or outside.

dinners Southern slang for a woman's breasts.

dip (1) To take snuff. "The old man sat in his rocker and dipped." (2) Gravy. "His youth, passed largely in New Orleans and in Georgia, had left him two notable survivals, the use of the phrases 'I reckon'—instead of the Yankee 'I guess'—and 'dip' instead of 'gravy'." [Arthur Pease, *Sequestered Vales of Life,* 1946]

directly As soon as. "Come out of there directly as you finish." It can also mean "before long." "I'll cook dinner directly."

dirt-dog poor Very poor, living in poverty.

dirt-dauber A mud dauber, a kind of wasp; also *dirt-dobber*. " 'Why, boy, I knowed you when you was no bigger'n a dirt-dauber.' " [Marjorie Kinnan Rawlings, *The Yearling,* 1938]

dirt-eater See CLAY-EATER.

dirty rice A Creole rice recipe, so named for its appearance.

dirty-up To soil, dirty. " 'Bessie,' she said, 'You'll have to make Dude wash his feet every once in a while, because if you don't he'll dirty-up your quilts." [Erskine Caldwell, *Tobacco Road,* 1932]

dis Common black and Gullah pronunciation of *this.*

discomfit To inconvenience. "I hope I won't discomfit you."

disconvenient Inconvenient. "It was really disconvenient for me."

disgust An old-fashioned term meaning "to be disgusted with something or somebody." "He disgusts eggs."

dish face A slightly concave face with the lower jaw jutting out and the mouth drawn in.

dismal Any lonely, forbidden swamp. "Rice is yet the grand staple production of South Carolina, and for which the planters neglect the healthy, pleasant back country in order to live in the Dismals on the coast, for so the Americans justly call the swamps." [*American Husbandry,* 1775]

Dismalite A resident of the DISMAL SWAMP.

Dismal Swamp A name given to the large marshy area extending from southeastern Virginia into northwestern North Carolina; also called the Dismal. "We ordered several men to patrol on the edge of the Dismal." [William Boyd, *Histories of the Dividing Line,* 1728]

dis night Gullah for tonight. "Don't want nothin' 'to happen here dis night."

disputed bounds "North Carolina formerly was the South part of Virginia . . . There is a very long List of Land fifteen Miles broad between both colonies (called the disputed bounds) . . . which is an asylum for Runagates of both Countries." [Hugh Jones, *The Present State of Virginia,* 1724]

disremember To forget. " 'Miss What-you-may-call-her, I disremem-

ber her name.' " [Mark Twain, *The Adventures of Huckleberry Finn,* 1884]

distressing one's ears Making one feel bad. " 'Don't reproach yourself like that. You're distressing my ears,' he says." [Eudora Welty, *The Optimist's Daughter,* 1972]

ditch-edge child An illegitimate child.

ditch hunter A Southern soldier during the Civil War, the designation arising because the Confederates were determined to "fight to the last ditch." Similarly, the South was nicknamed *ditch land.*

ditch land See DITCH HUNTER.

Dixie; Dixieland It sounds incredible, but the first Dixieland or Dixie may have been in New York City, not the South. Some etymologists lean to the following derivation of the word given by the *Charleston Courier* of June 11, 1885: "When slavery existed in New York, one Dixie owned a large tract of land on Manhattan Island, and a large number of slaves. The increase of the slaves and of the abolition sentiment caused an emigration of the slaves to more thorough and secure slave sections, and the Negroes who were thus sent off (many being born there) naturally looked back to their old houses, where they had lived in clover, with feelings of regret, as they could not imagine any place like Dixie's. Hence it became synonymous with an ideal location combining ease, comfort, and material happiness of every description." Although no slave "lived in clover," the explanation seems somewhat less doubtful than other theories about Dixie—that it derives from the 18th century *Mason-Dixon line* or that the word comes from the French Creole word *dix* which was prominently printed on the back of $10 notes issued by a New Orleans bank before the Civil War.

"Dixie" The title of a song, in full "Away Down South In Dixie," which songwriter and minstrel Daniel D. Emmett composed on his violin in 1859 while living in New York City and wishing he were back home in Dixie. It became very popular in the South and was the favorite marching song of the Confederacy, but it was first sung as a war song in 1861 by Yankee troops heading South aboard the *Star of the West* in the attempt to reinforce Fort Sumter. A war correspondent reported that the song was sung over and over again on that ill-fated voyage.

Dixie cup The American Water Supply Company's vending machine sold a drink of water in a disposable cup for one cent beginning in 1906, the cup possibly called a Dixie cup because it was so reliable—like the old ten-dollar bills issued in Louisiana prior to the Civil War (see DIXIE; DIXIELAND). In years to come, *Dixie cup* was frequently applied to ice cream sold in a small cup as opposed to ice-cream cones and ice cream on sticks.

Dixie mafia Organized criminals operating in the Southern United States.

the dizzies A dizzy spell. "I'd never make a good pilot; I get the dizzies just looking down from a tall building."

do (1) Used in its plural form, *do* is a euphemism for dung, especially of animals. "The yard was littered with chicken doos." (2) An old-fashioned word for duty, the best a person can do. "He's DONE done his do." (3) Does, as in, "That do beat all."

do about To get busy, hurry up, move oneself. "Do about, boys, do about!"

dobbin' An old term for the mud chinking used to fill in between the logs of a log cabin.

do don't Please don't. "Do don't let me fall now."

doctor woman A woman who practices voodoo; the term is also used for a midwife.

does Do. "You got to keep in mind he is a Northerner. They does things different from us." [William Faulkner, *The Hamlet*, 1940]

doesn't know B from bull's foot Is very ignorant, illiterate. "He doesn't know B from bull's foot."

dofunnies Knick-knacks. "She has a cabinet full of dofunnies."

dofunny; doofunny A thingamajig. "What do you call that doofunny on the top [of the machine]?"

dog bite it!   Common exclamation. " 'Dog bite it!' Ray would say with a sad expression on his long thin face when he took one more last look at his box and left the post office." [Erskine Caldwell, "Letters in the Mail," *Gulf Coast Stories,* 1956]

dogbread   A bread made with cornmeal and similar to CORN PONE.

dog drunk   Thoroughly drunk. "We got dog drunk and forgot all about the party."

dog-faced liar   A lowdown, contemptible person.

dog finger   Believed by some people to be the index finger and by others to be the middle finger, the *dog finger* is said to be the "bad luck finger," bringing bad luck to those at whom it is pointed.

dogged   Damned. "Dogged if they don't grow tall ones up there, Ben." [Thomas Wolfe, *Look Homeward, Angel,* 1929]

dog my cats!   An exclamation of surprise. "Well dog my cats if he ain't come home!"

dog trot   A covered area connecting two parts of a cabin.

dog take it!   An emphatic expletive common at least since the turn of the century.

dogwood winter   Similar to BLACK-BERRY WINTER. In 1907 an issue of *American Folk-lore* reported this explanation by a contributor: " 'Don't you know what dogwood winter is?' demanded the man from Hickory, North Carolina. 'There is always a spell of it in May, when the dogwood tree is in bloom. For several days there is cold disagreeable, cloudy weather, and often a touch of frost.' "

do like that   Do that; do something similar. " 'You're the only man I ever knowed of who wanted to sleep in his overalls [Ada said]. Don't nobody else do like that.' " [Erskine Caldwell, *Tobacco Road,* 1932]

doll baby   A doll or child's toy; also a silly young girl or woman.

done   (1) Often used among uneducated speakers, as in "He done did it," "She done said it" and "He's done gone and done it." (2) Have. "They done killed him." (3) Already. "He's done eaten his lunch."

done and gone   Gone. "He has done and gone."

done to a finish   Done to perfection. "Take the ham out of the oven; it's done to a finish."

done told   Told. "I already done told you to stop."

don't   (1) Frequently used in Cajun for am not, is not, are not: "I don't going to go." ("I'm not going to go.") (2) Often used for doesn't. " 'Father and Ratliff say "she don't" all the time, and so do you when you are talking to them. And Ratliff says "taken" for "took" and "drug" for "dragged" and so do you when you are talking to country people like Ratliff.' " [William Faulkner, *The Town,* 1957]

don't amount to a bucket of spit Said of a worthless no-account person. "He don't amount to a bucket of spit."

don't cut no ice Makes no difference. This phrase has widespread use now in the United States but possibly originated in the South. " 'He yelled some, and kicked a great deal, but that didn't cut no ice with the boys and me.' " [Erskine Caldwell, *God's Little Acre,* 1933]

don't get crosslegged Don't lose your temper.

don't give a hoot in hell's hollow Don't care at all, don't give a damn. " 'I don't give a hoot in hell's hollow what it means to her, I have blown a gasket on this thing.' said Daddy." [Calder Willingham, *Rambling Rose,* 1972]

don't go back on your raisin' Don't act like a boor; don't pretend to be something you're not.

don't got Haven't or hasn't. "He don't got no more better boat." ("He hasn't a better boat.")

don't got but Only have; heard mainly in Cajun speech. "I don't got but a dollar, me."

don't guess Don't think so or suppose. "I don't guess I know that one."

don't look back; something might be gaining on you Don't dwell too much on the past, go forward. Sage advice from baseball great Leroy "Satchel" Paige, who would have been one of the greatest pitchers in the major leagues if the color barrier had been broken earlier. The words may have their origins in an old Southern adage.

don't never A common double negative, as in, "He don't never go."

don't piss on my back and tell me it's raining Don't take me for a fool.

don't that beat a hen a-flying? Isn't that surprising or astonishing?

don't that take the whole biscuit! Doesn't that take the cake; isn't that the most outrageous thing you've ever heard.

don't you fret Don't worry. " 'But don't you fret, Miss Scarlett, it'll be over in a month [the Civil War] and we'll have them howling.' " [Margaret Mitchell, *Gone With the Wind,* 1936]

doodle A name for a Northern soldier during the Civil War, in allusion to the song "Yankee Doodle."

dooley Another word for a sweet potato in the South, possibly named for someone who developed a superior variety.

do one bad To do harm to someone. " 'Then why was he so bad?' screamed Fay. 'Why did he do me so bad?' " [Eudora Welty, *The Optimist's Daughter*, 1972]

dope "Gimme a dope" still means "Give me a Coca-Cola" in the South, especially among teenagers, and dates back to the 19th century when the fabled soft drink was touted as a tonic and contained a minute amount of cocaine. Coca-Cola's inventor, druggist John S. Pemberton, brewed the drink in his backyard and knew it was done when he smelled the cooked cocaine—no reactions in the man or among his neighbors are reported.

dose Common black and Gullah pronunciation of *those*.

double-dog dare To issue a defiant, often insulting, challenge to someone to do something. "I double-dog dare you to swim across that river!"

downright Very, really. "That's downright kind of you."

down to a gnat's eyebrow Exactly, precisely. "She had it planned down to a gnat's eyebrow."

dozens The art of hurling invectives at one's enemies is an ancient one, and American slaves probably brought the verbal exchange called the *dozens* or *dirty dozens* with them from Africa, basing it on the Tuareg and Galla game of two opponents cursing one another until one man lost his temper and began fighting with his hands instead of his mouth; he was considered the loser. Alive and thriving today among blacks, the game takes its name not from dozen (twelve) but probably from the Americanism *bulldoze,* which meant "to bullwhip someone," especially a slave, the insults likened to whip lashes.

dozenth Twelfth. "For the dozenth time, she ran out onto the porch . . ." [Margaret Mitchell, *Gone With the Wind,* 1936]

draftee First recorded in an 1866 Civil War memoir, *draftee* was surely used before this during the war, probably as soon as the Confederate Conscription Act of 1862 and the Union Draft Law of 1863 were passed. In the North single men ages 20 to 45 and married men ages 20 to 35 were drafted, while the South conscripted all men ages 18 to 35. Most men volunteered, however; for example, only about 2% of the Union Army consisted of draftees.

drag one's foot To bow deeply, dragging the right foot far back while bowing at the waist. " 'Welcome to Warwick' [she said]. He and Uncle Buck dragged their foot." [William Faulkner, *Go Down, Moses,* 1942]

drank Sometimes used for "drunk", as in "I have drank." In days past, even fastidious, educated Southern people used the expression, to avoid the association with *drunk* (intoxicated).

drap Drop; used chiefly by blacks. "He drapped his hoe."

drappin' Raining; used mostly by blacks.

drat! Damn, darn, as in "Drat their hides!"

draw up To shrink. "It was all drawn up into a ball."

dressed egg A deviled egg topped with parsley.

dressed up like gals going to meeting Dressed up in one's best. "They're all dressed up like gals going to meeting."

dressed within an inch of her life Dressed to the nines, but sometimes glaringly, to the point of vulgarity, overdressed. "And here he was now, stepping out of an elegant carriage and handing [helping] down a woman dressed within an inch of her life." [Margaret Mitchell, *Gone With the Wind*, 1936]

dress the bed Make the bed.

drew Drove. " 'Just say it was following along behind the wagon when Snopes drew up to the house.' " [William Faulkner, *The Hamlet*, 1940]

drinking mash and talking trash Said of someone drunk for whom liquor is doing the talking, who isn't reasoning properly. "You're drinkin' mash and talkin' trash, man."

drinkin' liquor A good quality, smooth whiskey.

drip-drop A little bit, a small amount. "My recipe calls for just a drip-drop of nutmeg."

drive a nail To make a perfect shot with a rifle or handgun; also *drive the center* and *drive the cross*. "To drive a nail is a common feat, not more thought of by the Kentuckians than to cut off a wild turkey's head, at a distance of one hundred yards." [John James Audubon, *Ornithological Biography*, 1831]

drive a nail into a plank To have sexual intercourse. " 'To tell the truth,' she said, 'you've got me worried [about becoming pregnant].' 'You ought to be [Will said]. When I drive a nail into a plank, it stays driven.' " [Erskine Caldwell, *God's Little Acre*, 1933]

drive one's ducks to a poor market To enter into a poor marriage or fall in with a bad crowd. "She had everything going for her, but she drove her ducks to a poor market."

drive the center See DRIVE A NAIL.

drive the cross See DRIVE A NAIL.

drop his (her) candy To blunder badly and lose out as a result. The phrase may have originated at an outdoor CANDY PULLING when someone dropped a piece of candy he or she had made in the dirt and thus lost it. "He dropped his candy, and the Democrat won the election."

drivin' like a blue ass fly Driving very fast.

Drop in the grease A saying common in Texas meaning to involve someone in the thick of things, in big trouble, especially when a scandal is involved. "He'd better have a better excuse than that or I'll leak his name to the press. I'll drop him in the grease with all the others."

dropped like an ox Dropped suddenly and heavily like a slaughtered ox. " '. . . while he was shaking her loose, number one ups and hits him over the head with his rail, and he dropped like an ox!' " [William Faulkner, "The Liar," sketch, *New Orleans Times-Picayune,* July 26, 1925]

drug Dragged. See Introduction for a good usage example by William Faulkner of *drug.*

drunk as a bowdow Extremely drunk. The phrase is apparently a corruption of "drunk as a boiled owl".

drunk as a coot Very drunk, the Coot being an American duck noted for its laugh-like cry and, to some people, its crazy or drunk-like behavior. " 'You wasn't here, Buck, when ol' man Twistle died o' snakebite. Penny must o' been right about whiskey not doin' no good [to cure one of it]. Twistle were drunk as a coot when he stepped on the rattler.' " [Marjorie Kinnan Rawlings, *The Yearling,* 1938]

drunk as Cooter Brown; drunker than Cooter Brown Very drunk indeed. Who the proverbial Cooter Brown is no one seems to know, but this may have originally been a black expression from the Carolinas. "In Texas we'd call him drunker than Cooter Brown."

drunk as a fiddler's bitch Extremely drunk. " '. . . I heard her scream and I ran into the kitchen and there he was, drunk as a fiddler's bitch . . .' " [Margaret Mitchell, *Gone With the Wind,* 1936]

drunker than who shot John Uncontrollably drunk. "There he was in the Beeville bar drunker than who shot John."

druthers Choice, preference, as in "If I had my druthers, I wouldn't be leaving"; sometimes *ruthers.* See also YOUR DRUTHERS IS MY RUTHERS.

druv Drove. "He druv off quickly."

dry grins An embarrassed sheepish smile; a forced smile without any pleasure; possibly a folk etymology deriving from *chagrin.* "They found him out, and he got a bad case of the dry grins."

dry so Plain, straight, unadulterated. "I always take my whiskey dry so."

dry-weather stock Said of horses and, by extension, people who can't cope with all the problems of life, especially when the going gets rough. " 'They'll do fine on a dry track, a fast track, but mark my words, I don't believe the Wilkes can run on a mud track . . . when the emergency arises I don't believe they can run against odds. Dry-weather stock. Give me a big horse that can run in any weather!' " [Margaret Mitchell, *Gone With the Wind*, 1936]

dry wilts State of advanced physical deterioration, as from age, also used in the Midwest.

duck fit A state of great excitement or anger. "He throwed a duck fit when I broke the window."

due me a compliment Owe me an apology. "You due me a compliment for the way you acted."

du'in' Mark Twain gave this as the Southern pronunciation of during. (See usage example at THE WAR.)

durn Damn. "Because she is a durn woman." [William Faulkner, "Mule in the Yard," 1930]

durned Euphemism for *damned*. "Is that what they call him? Well, I'd be durned. Hawkshaw." [William Faulkner, "Hair," 1931]

dust-dawn to dust-dark The whole day. " 'So how is Jefferson going to be steady-blessed [Het said] without me steady willing from dust-dawn to dust-dark, rain or snow or sun, to say MUCH OBLIGE?' " [William Faulkner, *The Town*, 1957]

Dutch A term for a Southerner who sympathized with the North during the Civil War. "Every steamer at the levee was laden with families, who . . . had hastily packed a few articles of clothing, to flee from the general and bloody conflict supposed to be impending between the Americans and the Dutch, as the Secessionists artfully termed the two parties." [Albert Richardson, *The Secret Service . . .*, 1865]

E

e The Gullah pronunciation of *she*. "E sho is nice."

Earbobs; earscrews Earrings. " 'Now you jist give me them ear-bobs, you pirate,' [Grandma said]." [Marjorie Kinnan Rawlings, *The Yearling*, 1938]

earthslide A landslide.

easy rider Popularized by the film *Easy Rider*, this term for a sexually satisfying male lover originated among Southern blacks. Faulkner in *Soldier's Pay* (1926) quotes a line from an old blues song: "Oh, oh, I wonder where my easy rider's gone."

easy walker Easy Walkers, a trademarked sneaker, have been popular in the South for over 30 years, so much so that *easy walkers*, in the lower case, has become a synonym for sneakers.

eat cooter liver To tell a secret. "He must have been eatin' cooter liver. Now everybody knows."

eat good Tastes good. " 'They do eat good,' she said." [Marjorie Kinnan Rawlings, *The Yearling*, 1938]

eatin' a green 'simmon The *'simmon* in this 19th century Southern Americanism is a persimmon, which takes its name from the Cree *pasiminan* (dried fruit). Although the fruit is delicious when thoroughly ripe, a green unripe persimmon is so sour it could make you whistle, which led to the expression *he* (or *she*) *looks like he's been eatin' a green 'simmon*. On the other hand, ripe persimmons suggested *walking off with the persimmons* (walking off with the prize), which also dates back to the 1850s.

eating apron A kind of bib used to cover children while they were eating. "My poor mother led me out bareheaded with a big eating-apron on." [Daisy Campbell, *The Proving of Virginia*, 1915]

eat oneself full To stuff oneself with food. "Don't eat yourself full, Pop, there's pie back (in the kitchen) yet."

ebony See SON OF EBONY.

egg on To urge someone to do something. "They egged her on." Originally a Southern expression, it now is used throughout the United States.

eight-day man A disparaging term for one who joined the Confederate forces during the Civil War for just a short time.

Elberta peach The Elberta peach, the most widely sold of American peaches, was probably imported from Shanghai in 1850, but more than one source records a story that shows more imagination. According to this tale, Samuel Rumph of Marshallville, Georgia received peach tree buddings from a friend in Delaware, planted them and eventually harvested a good crop. His wife, Elberta, accidentally dropped a few pits from these peaches in her sewing basket and when their grandson wanted to start an orchard 10 years later, she dug them out and asked her husband to plant them. By 1870 trees from the pits were flourishing, and by an accidental cross-pollination, a new golden variety resulted, which Rumph named for his spouse.

elsehow A Gullah term for "or else."

Empire State of the South A nickname that has been applied to Georgia, South Carolina and rarely, to Texas, which is of course best known as the Lone Star State.

enduring During, "I'll be back sometime endurin' the week."

English peas A term used for green peas to distinguish them from the blackeyed or browneyed varieties.

enough to choke a shoat Big, a large amount. ". . . they all watched Mr. Flem . . . draw out a roll of bills . . . 'Fore God,' old Het said. 'You could choke a shoat with it.' " [William Faulkner, *The Town,* 1957]

enough to make a Texas preacher lay his Bible down Enough to make anyone mad enough to fight.

entitlement Name; old-fashioned term. "What is your entitlement?"

enty A Gullah term for *isn't it* (and for aren't they, wasn't it, haven't they, didn't it, etc.), as in "But it's gwine to rain, enty?"

-est Often used as a suffix of superlative adjectives, as in, *beautifulest, believingest, dancin'est, drinkingest, God-fearingest, hurringest, kissinest, knowinest, lovingest, talkinest, vote-gettinest* and so forth. This is also common in Cajun speech, as in "He the bestest child."

et Ate; eaten. "Ain't you et yet?"

Ethiopian breakdown Scc BREAK-DOWN.

Evacuation Day Sunday, April 14, 1861, the day Northern troops evacuated Fort Sumter off Charleston, South Carolina after being defeated in the first battle of the Civil War.

even his in-growed toenails is on the outside of his shoes An open, unsecretive person, one whose life seems an open book. ". . . he was, Ratliff said, 'a feller that even his in-growed toenails was on the outside of his shoes.' " [William Faulkner, *The Town,* 1957]

evening Sometimes used, especially among older speakers, as the time between noon and dark (instead of beginning at sunset). "We'll be going this evening about three o'clock." An anonymous Virginia woman observed in 1909: "We Southerners sometimes say 'Afternoon' on formal occasions, but in our hearts we feel this is affectation; our natural diversions of time are 'morning,' 'evening,' and 'night.' "

evening was already finding itself Darkness was falling. "And then it became late, what with the yet short winter days; when she came in sight of the two gaunt chimneys against the sunset, evening was already finding itself." [William Faulkner, "Mule in the Yard," 1940]

ever (1) Always. "She was ever a pretty one." (2) Whenever. "Ever he was grown, never would he marry!"

ever' Every. " 'He was laying there going without water and he reached himself over and bit that tube in two and drunk that glucose. And drunk ever' drop that was in it." [Eudora Welty, *The Optimist's Daughter*, 1972]

ever body Everybody. "I got to get to the Warden in time, before they try it maybe tonight even and wreck ever body." [William Faulkner, *The Mansion*, 1959]

Everglades Since the early 19th century this term, apparently an Americanism, has been applied to the low, marshy region overgrown with tall grass in Florida. It has been suggested that the "ever" in the word

is used loosely in the sense of "interminable."

ever I saw I ever saw; a common reversal of usual English word order, as in "He's the ugliest man ever I saw," or the song lyric "The first time ever I saw your face."

everthin' Everything.

everwhat Whatever; a term used mostly by older Southerners. "Everwhat is happening down there."

everwhich See EVERWHICHWAY.

everwhichway In all directions; can also be *everwhichways* or *everwhich*. "Everwhichway I turn, I see him."

everwho Whoever; another term used mostly by older Southerners. "Everwho do you think you are?"

every which way In every way, in all directions. The first recorded use of this expression, in 1824, says it was originally an "odd phrase" taught by slaves to the children of Virginia gentry.

Exalted Cyclops See CYCLOPS.

excusin' Except. " 'I ain't done much today, excusin' fret and worry, and mess with sausage.' " [Marjorie Kinnan Rawlings, *The Yearling*, 1938]

exoduster A term most likely based on *exodus* and describing a black person who left the South in the mass migration to the Northwest of 1878–1880.

extry Rural pronunciation of *extra*. "Let's get some extry brief ones."

eye-eating Staring at a member of the opposite sex with sexual desire. "You was eye-eatin' that girl all night, Henry!"

eyes Burners on a stove. "'Son you've heard me tell. Stuffed up the windows, stuffed up the door, turned on all four eyes of the stove and the oven,' said Mrs. Chisom indulgently. 'Fire department drug him out, rushed him to the Baptist Hospital in the firewagin, tried all their tricks, but they couldn't get ahead of Roscoe. He was in Heaven already.'" [Eudora Welty, *The Optimist's Daughter*, 1972]

F

fabling Lying; telling exaggerated stories. "His fabling was well-known." [William Faulkner, "The Liar," sketch in the *New Orleans Times-Picayune*, July 26, 1925]

face hurt Blushed. "His face hurt him." ("He blushed.")

failing disease Tuberculosis.

faintified Fainthearted; in a state in which one is ready to faint. "Suddenly, Jody could not endure the sight . . . 'Don't go gittin' faintified on me,' [his father] said." [Marjorie Kinnan Rawlings, *The Yearling*, 1938]

fair Moderately. "It was fair late in the fall."

fairly An adjective roughly equivalent to "nearly, almost." "I fairly screamed when I heard what he did."

fair off To clear up, when applied to the weather. "It's gonna fair off by tomorrow."

fallacy A mistake or error. "That was our fallacy, and it won't happen again."

fall out To faint; principally a Southern expression but today heard as far north as northern Wisconsin, northern Indiana and southeastern Pennsylvania. "He was standing at attention, and suddenly he fell out."

false An old-fashioned term with limited use for the wooden box in which a coffin is placed before being lowered into the grave.

family woman A pregnant woman, a woman in the family way.

fandaddies A colorful Southernism of unknown origin for fried clams.

fanfoot A promiscuous woman, but not a woman who is *paid* for sexual favors.

far-gone By all standards, far and away. "He was known to be far-gone the best shot in the county."

farrer; farrest Farther; farthest. "He lives farrer on down the road."

Far South The Deep South. "Save, in fact, for a few oddities in vocabulary, it was perfectly possible to understand any man encountered along the road, even in the Far South . . ." [H. L. Mencken, *The American Language, Supplement II,* 1948]

fast as (or as the) Forty An old expression meaning very fast. Inspired by an express train nicknamed

"The Forty" that ran from Atlanta to New York City.

fat as a nigger's hog An old, derogatory, probably obsolete phrase. "The negroe's hogs are always fatter than those of their master. 'Fat as a nigger's hog' has become a proverb with us in Virginia." [*Harper's*, May 1858]

fatback The fat and fat meat from the upper part of a side of pork, often salt-cured and a Southern favorite.

fatnen' hog Very heavy. "She needs to go on a diet, looks like a fatnen' hog."

Father Mississippi A nickname for the Mississippi River. See also FATHER OF WATERS.

Father of Floods A nickname for the Mississippi River. See FATHER OF WATERS.

Father of Rivers A nickname for the Mississippi River. See FATHER OF WATERS.

Father of Waters A nickname for the Mississippi River that may derive from an Indian name, *Meact-Chassipi* (the ancient Father of the Rivers), a word the French corrupted into *Mississippi*. For another possible derivation of *Mississippi*, see the entry MISSISSIPPI.

fatty-bread CRACKLING bread.

fault To blame; used nationally but most frequently in the South. "Don't fault me for that."

favor To resemble. "He favors his daddy."

federal building A humorous term, doubtless invented by unreconstructed Confederates, for an outhouse.

feel below the ford To feel under the weather.

feel like a stewed witch To have a bad hangover.

feels to me Seems to me. " 'I reckon I'll get me a mule somewhere and some seed-cotton and guano, and grow me a crop of cotton this year,' Dude said. 'It feels to me like it's going to be a good year for cotton. Maybe I could grow me a bale to the acre, like Pa was always talking about doing.' " [Erskine Caldwell, *Tobacco Road*, 1932]

feisty Conceited, bragging, acting with impudence beyond a person's stature. "Stop acting so feisty all the time."

fell off Lost weight. "He's fell off a lot—lost one hundred pounds."

fellow An old black term for a white man.

female daughter A redundancy recorded by Faulkner, among others. See usage example at FISH-BLOODED.

fence lifter A heavy rain, but one less heavy than a GOOSE DROWNDER.

Ferginny Virginia. " 'That's right,' Pettigrew said. 'Thomas Jefferson Pettigrew. I'm from old Ferginny.' " [William Faulkner, *Requiem for a Nun,* 1951]

ferrididdle A small ground squirrel; used mainly in Southern mountain regions.

fetching Very attractive. "She's a real fetchin' woman."

fetchy An old term for attractive, charming.

F.F. A member of a first family, especially of Virginia but of any state or country.

F.F.V. An abbreviation for First Families of (or in) Virginia. "The old things we could make out among the unknown writing were a set of letters that looked like a disorderly F.F.V." [*Knickerbocker Magazine,* volume 29, 1847] " 'Ah,' Benbow said. 'An F.F.V., or just an unfortunate sojourner here.' " [William Faulkner, *Sanctuary,* 1931]

fice; fiest; fyst; fyste; fyce; fist; fists; fise; feice; feist; faust; faus; fif; fouce A small dog; often a derogatory term. "You sell me your half of that trick overgrown fice." [William Faulkner, "Shingles for the Lord," 1943] "In Missouri or Mississippi he would have been labeled 'fice,' which is equivalent to saying that he was a terrier-like dog of no particular breed." [Christy Mathewson, *Second Base Sloan,* 1917]

Fiddle-dee-dee! An exclamation indicating that something is nonsense, made famous by Margaret Mitchell's heroine Scarlett O'Hara in *Gone with the Wind* (1936): "She said 'fiddle-dee-dee!' many times . . . and vowed that she'd never believe anything any man told her." *Fiddle-dee-dee* was popular long before Scarlett, being a corruption of the Italian *Fedido* (by the faith of God).

fidgets A creepy nervousness. "I've had the fidgets all day."

Figinny An old, obsolete pronunciation of Virginia or Virginny.

figures don't lie but liars sure can figure A saying from down Texas way, where they claim to be quickest on the drawl.

filé Powdered sassafras leaves. Filé is used to thicken GUMBO.

find To give birth to a child. "I'm a-goin' t' find another baby afore long. I found my ten babies all alone here in Georgia."

fine-haired Aristocratic; conceited. "He's a fine-haired son-of-a-bitch, ain't he?"

finer than frog's hair Very thin or fine. "That table's nearly perfect. The scratches are finer than frog's hair."

fire-eater An often violent, always uncompromising believer in the Southern cause before and during the Civil War, the term dating back to the 1840s. Anonymous doggerel of the day described the fire-eaters:

> Down in a small Palmetto State the curious ones may find
> A ripping, tearing gentleman, of an uncommon kind,
> A staggering, swaggering sort of chap who takes his whisky straight,
> And frequently condemns his eyes to that ultimate vengeance which a clergyman of high-standing has assured must be a sinner's fate;
> This South Carolina gentleman, one of the present time.

firehunt Hunting deer and other animals at night by jacklighting them (shining light in their eyes to stun them). "Now you know . . . you can't fire-hunt deer at night." [Marjorie Kinnan Rawlings, *Cross Creek,* 1942]

fire-time The end of November to the first warm days in spring. "Ma Baxter said, 'Don't seem possible fire-times here again.' " [Marjorie Kinnan Rawlings, *The Yearling,* 1938]

first-dark A Gullah term for "twilight."

first-folks Mainly black Southern usage for the best-bred people, people of quality.

first light Dawn.

fish-blooded Cold-blooded, cold, uncaring. "Look here, you old fish-blooded son of a bitch, are you going to just sit there and let your only female daughter . . . drive alone up

yonder . . ." [William Faulkner, *The Mansion,* 1959]

fish fry A picnic at which fish are fried and served; the event sometimes includes actually catching the fish. Free fish fries were long a favorite entertainment of Southern politicians.

fishing worm An earthworm; used in the coastal South.

fish muddle A fish stew; a gathering where fish stew is served.

fist and skull fight A fight with just fists, no weapons of any kind.

fittin' Fit, fitting, appropriate; pleasant. " 'If I'd of knowed you was comin',' she said, 'I'd of cooked somethin' fittin'.' " [Marjorie Kinnan Rawlings, *The Yearling,* 1938]

fixing Preparing. "He's fixing to leave real soon."

flang one's thang Exhibit one's genitals. "What would have to be wrong with a guy to make him flang his thang out in front of women?" [Larry Brown, "Waiting for the Ladies," 1990]

flash Stylish. "The hat was soiled now but still flash, the coat below it had been white once too, a little flash too . . ." [William Faulkner, *The Mansion,* 1959]

flat of the back Flat on one's back. "She was tired of laying flat of her back."

flat out To drive very fast, with the gas pedal flat to the floor. "He drove that truck flat out, till the tree stopped him."

fled Sped; left hastily. "He didn't answer. The car fled on." [William Faulkner, "Elly," 1934]

fleshen To put on weight, become fleshy. "I fleshened up again." [Marjorie Kinnan Rawlings, "Cocks Must Crow," 1939]

flinderation Being in the state of flinders or fragments. "That hurricane blew the house all to flinderation."

fling up To vomit. "He flung up his dinner."

flittercakes Pancakes, which are also called *fritters, corncakes* and *battercakes* in the South.

flittern An old Southern term for a pancake.

Florida The Sunshine State was the Florida Territory before being admitted to the Union as the 27th state in 1845. *Florida* means "land of flowers" in Spanish; Ponce de Leon named it in 1513 with "flowery Easter" in mind. See also FLY-UP-THE-CREEK.

Florida cooter The Florida terrapin *(Pseudemys concinna);* also called the *hard-backed cooter* and the *soft-shelled cooter.*

Florida cracker A CRACKER residing in Florida.

Florida room A term used in Florida and other Southern states for a living room with large windows to catch the sun.

Floridy Florida. "This right here . . . is the old Spanish trail clear across Floridy." [Marjorie Kinnan Rawlings, *The Yearling,* 1938]

flounty A flaunting action. " 'Ummm-mm,' said Mother, 'sounds flounty.' 'Yeah it was flounty. One of the flountist things I ever saw.' " [Calder Willingham, *Rambling Rose,* 1972]

flowing bitch A female dog in heat or season.

flugins Very cold, used mainly in the old expressions "It's cold as flugins" and "It's cold as blue flugins."

flutter mill A small waterwheel made for or by a child. "Up, over, down, up, over, down—the flutter mill was enchanting . . . Unless leaves fell, or squirrels cut sweet bay twigs to drop and block the fragile wheel, the flutter mill might turn forever." [Marjorie Kinnan Rawlings, *The Yearling,* 1938]

fly-up-the-creek Southerners don't use this expression today, but it is recorded as early as 1845 as the nickname for a resident of Florida. Floridians were so called because *fly up the creek* is a popular name of the small green heron common in the state. Walt Whitman used the expression in this sense, and it later meant "a giddy capricious person."

F.M.C.; F.W.C. There were a number of freed and escaped slaves in the United States long before the Civil War. By 1840 the terms F.M.C., "free man of color," and F.W.C., "free woman of color," were in common use, and blacks for many years proudly affixed the terms after their names.

fog-beaded Covered with droplets of condensed fog. "[She was] tall, lean, fog-beaded, in her tennis shoes and a long rat-colored cloak trimmed with what forty–fifty years ago would have been fur . . ." [William Faulkner, "Mule in the Yard," 1930]

Foggy Bottom The U.S. State Department in Washington, D.C. has been humorously called Foggy Bottom at least since the early 1960s, due to its location near the Potomac River on a piece of land long called "Foggy Bottom." The designation caught on because of the "foggy" gobbledygook emanating from the department.

fo' God Before God. " 'Fo' God I wuz jes dis minute huntin fer you,' she said." [William Faulkner, "Mule in the Yard," 1930]

folderol Falderal; nonsense, foolish talk. " 'Now, Puss, tell me true, do you understand his folderol about books and music and oil paintings and such foolishness?' " [Margaret Mitchell, *Gone With the Wind*, 1936]

fooling around Depending on the context, it can mean being involved in extramarital sex. "She caught him foolin' around and left him."

foolishment Foolishness. "Stop that silly noise right now. I've had enough of your foolishment."

fool thing Foolish thing. "Every fool thing happened to him."

foot! An exclamation of anger. " 'Foot! I'm mad at you for not getting the house,' old Mrs. Pease told Laurel." [Eudora Welty, *The Optimist's Daughter*, 1972] See also SHOOK HIS FOOT.

footwasher A foot-washing Baptist; member of a religious group, often Baptist, that practices the washing of each other's feet as part of certain religious services. "Each of the footwashers was unlacing the left shoe of the person he faced." [Carl Carmer, *Stars Fell on Alabama*, 1934]

for Sometimes added after verbs showing desire and before an infinitive, as in "I don't intend for him to go." ("I don't want him to go.")

force An old term for a group of slaves working on a plantation.

for certain Certainly, assuredly. "It's goin' to snow today for certain."

forched Fetched.

foreigner; furriner A nonresident of a Southern state. "He's some kind of furriner, maybe from New York City."

forenoon An synonym for morning rarely heard anymore.

for good and always An old-fashioned term meaning forever. "I'll love her for good and always."

for sure Certainly. "He is going to come for sure."

for to In order to. "I went down there for to see my gal."

for true Certainly, truly, really. "I'll be there for true."

40 acres and a mule A promise, with no basis in fact, made by dishonest politicians to newly freed slaves after the Civil War. Each freed slave, they said, would receive 40 acres of land and a mule to work it with. "When we were children we used to ridicule the slogan 'forty acres and a mule' as a stupid deception used by the Yankees to get the black men to vote for the Republicans." [Katherine Lumpkin, *The Making of a Southerner*, 1947]

for why? Often used as "why?" in Cajun. "For why you hit me?"

fowl-crow A chiefly Gullah term for the time when the cock crows dawn, cock-crow. "Every morning she got up at first fowl-crow."

fox-fire A fungi-caused phosphorescent glow on decayed wood. "They'd hunt in the wood-pile for the turquoise bits that were called fox-fire."

frail To flail, beat. "If you're going to whip him, you better whip the rest of us too and then one of us can frail hell out of you." [William Faulkner, *The Hamlet*, 1940]

frammed Spanked. " 'Now, mister Impudent Bigmouth, you'll git yourself frammed good with a brush.' " [Marjorie Kinnan Rawlings, *The Yearling*, 1938]

"Frankly, my dear, I don't give a damn." See GIVE A DAMN.

franzy Frenzy, madness, an excited state.

franzy house A whorehouse; an insane asylum.

frazzle To severely whip or beat. "He frazzled him near to death."

frazzlin'! Damned. "I don't like him one frazzlin' bit!"

freehearted Very generous. "He was too freehearted with his money, but his cousin was downright stingy."

French harp An old term for a harmonica; also called *mouth organ*.

French Quarter A well-known area in New Orleans famous for its restaurants and entertainment.

fresh New, just purchased. "She got them fresh from the store today."

freshen To give birth to a baby, applied to a cow dropping a calf.

"She slept by herself on a pallet on the floor, refusing even to let Lov kiss her or touch her in any way. Lov had told her that cows were not any good until they had been freshened . . . ." [Erskine Caldwell, *Tobacco Road*, 1932]

fret To worry. " 'I wrote another card and said at least tell his mother what had been fretting my son, if they knew so much, and they finally got around to answering that Roscoe didn't want me to know.' " [Eudora Welty, *The Optimist's Daughter*, 1972]

frisky as a flea on a flat dog Very frisky, lively. "I had a puppy down in Texas frisky as a flea on a flat dog."

fritter-minded Frivolous. "I felt ashamed at my fritter-minded carrying on."

fritters See FLITTERCAKES.

friz Froze. "I like to friz to death."

frog Often used to mean a toad.

frogmow stew A dish made not of frogs but of seafood; originally made on Frogmore, one of the Sea Islands off South Carolina.

frogsticker A pocketknife with a long blade; often called a *toadsticker* elsewhere.

frogstool A toadstool, a poisonous mushroom. "Be careful not to eat frogstools—they're poisonous."

frog-strangler A humorous name for a heavy flooding rain, a long downpour; also *toad-strangler*.

from Sometimes used to mean for: "I can't blame him from crying"; also used redundantly, as in "I can't help from crying."

from the jump From the very beginning. "I'll give you a history of Henry Clay, from the first jump of him." [*Maysville* (Kentucky) *Eagle*, July 12, 1831]

frozen words An old story from Texas tells of a winter so cold that spoken words froze in the air, fell entangled on the ground and had to be fried up in a skillet before the letters could reform and any sense could be made of them. But the idea is an ancient one, not Southern in origin, used by Rabelais and familiar to the Greek dramatist Antiphanes, who used it in praising the work of Plato: "As the cold of certain cities is so intense that it freezes the very words we utter, which remain congealed till the heat of summer thaws them, so the mind of youth is so thoughtless that the wisdom of Plato lies there frozen, as it were, till it is thawed by the refined judgment of mature age."

fry-meat A Gullah term for fried meat.

fuck up Get drunk and raise hell. " 'Let's go fuck up. You want to?' 'Fuck up? Where at?' 'Ah, hell. We can just go fuck up uptown if you want to. I don't care. Just anywhere.' " [Larry Brown, "92 Days," 1990]

fulled Became full (said of the moon). See usage example at CAUGHT.

full-up Completely full. "I'm full-up on coffee."

fun To tease, fool or joke with someone. "Don't take it so hard; he was only funning you."

funky Has a multitude of slang meanings, including repulsive, malodorous and stinking; earthy, simple yet compelling; excellent, effective; musically hard-edged and urban; old-fashioned, nostalgic; pleasantly eccentric; deviant, kinky; and highly emotional. Probably all derive ultimately from the Southern dialect word *funky,* meaning moldy, strong-smelling, malodorous.

funny-peculiar Strange. "He says, 'Funny—haha or funny-peculiar . . .'

And I says, 'Funny-peculiar.' " [Eudora Welty, "Petrified Man," 1941]

furnish A bill or account for supplies in a general store; from the verb *furnish* (to supply). "The storekeeper said he would put it on my furnish."

fur piece A long way, a long distance. "It's a fur piece to Grandma's house."

fuss To quarrel; scold.

fuss and feathers Nonsense over nothing at all. " 'It's a bunch of fuss and feathers,' she said. 'Ross just flirts, that's all.' " [Calder Willingham, *Rambling Rose,* 1972] The expression is used nationally, too, and *Old Fuss and Feathers* was the nickname of Union general Winfield Scott, a Virginian by birth.

fussbox The usual term for a fuss-budget in the South.

fuzzed up Excited, disturbed. "They were all fuzzed up about it."

G

gallery (1) A long porch, veranda; also called *piazza*. "He just spent the rest of his time sitting on the gallery in summer and in the library in winter with the bottle, reading Latin poetry." [William Faulkner, *The Town*, 1957] (2) A porch in front of a store. ". . . Houston ordered whoever was on the front gallery to step inside and fetch him out whatever he had come for like they were Negroes." [William Faulkner, *The Mansion*, 1959]

galloping fence Used in South Carolina to mean a straight rail fence.

galluses; gallowses Suspenders. "Bright red galluses held up his pants."

galvanized Yankee A term Southerners used to describe other Southerners sympathetic to the North during the Civil War; printed in many Southern newspapers of the day.

gang A group of animals of the same kind. "We were got half way, meeting great Gangs of Turkies . . ." [John Lawson, *A New Voyage to Carolina*, 1809]

gank-gutted Skinny, thin. "Look at that gank-gutted woman." [Marjorie Kinnan Rawlings, "Gal Young Un'," 1932]

gardenia "Mr. Miller has called it Basteria . . . I would call it Gardenia, from our worthy friend Dr. Alexander Garden of S. Carolina." "If Dr. Garden will send me a new genus, I shall be truly happy to name it after him, Gardenia." These quotations from an exchange of letters between a friend of the botanist Linnaeus and the great botanist himself, 1757–58, reveal the politicking that is sometimes involved even in naming something. Linnaeus did honor his promise to their mutual friend and two years later dedicated a newly discovered tropical shrub to Garden, even though the Southern amateur botanist did not discover the beautiful sweet-smelling *gardenia*. Alexander Garden (ca. 1730–1791), a Scottish-American physician, resided in Charleston, South Carolina, where he practiced medicine and also devoted much of his time to collecting plant and animal specimens. He discovered the Congo eel and a number of snakes and herbs. An ardent Tory, he returned to England during the Revolutionary War and later became vice-president of the Royal Society. Dr. Garden was by all accounts a difficult, headstrong man. When his American granddaughter was named Gardenia Garden in his honor, he still refused to see her. After all, her father had fought against the British!

garden sass Garden vegetables; *sass,* apparently a variation of *sauce,* was first applied to stewed fruit and is used in New England as well. "Her garden sass needed cultivating, and so I just hitched up Ida and came out here to plow it a little for her." [Erskine Caldwell, *Georgia Boy,* 1943]

garret Often used in Maryland to mean an attic.

Gate City A nickname now or in the past for several cities, including Atlanta and Louisville, because they are each situated at the entrance to a region. Atlanta is also called the *Gate City of the South.*

Gate City of the South See GATE CITY.

gator An alligator. The word *alligator* is seldom heard in the South.

gator-bit Bitten by an alligator.

gaum; gom; gorn (1) *v.* To smear. "The baby's all gaummed up with molasses." (2) As a noun, *gaum* means "a mess." "You're making a gaum out of the food, child."

gay Before its present use for a homosexual, *gay woman* or *gay* often meant a prostitute in the South, just as *gay house* meant a bordello. Both usages are found in William Faulkner's *The Reivers,* 1962.

gee Old slang and dialect for agree. "The figures didn't gee."

gee and haw Cries, meaning "turn right" and "turn left" respectively, used when working mules, horses and oxen. " 'I'll steer if that's all you needs,' Ned said. 'I been what you calls steering horses and mules and oxen all my life and I reckon gee and haw with that steering wheel ain't no different from gee and haw with a pair of lines or a good.' " [William Faulkner, *The Reivers,* 1962]

geechee A derogatory term, often used by both blacks and whites, describing Southern rural blacks, although it has also been applied to blacks in general. The term also refers to Gullah, a dialect of Southern seacoast or rural blacks, and can describe any low-country South Carolinian, especially from the Charleston area. *Geechee* may derive from northern Georgia's Ogeechee River or from the name of an African tribe in Liberia's Kissy region.

gemmen A pronounciation of gentlemen.

gempmuns A mostly black pronunciation of gentlemen. " 'That's something else about gempmuns you won't never know,' the groom said."

general See CAPTAIN.

Georgia Georgia is named for George II of England (1683–1760), who was not a particularly popular monarch. Discovered by Hernando de Soto in 1540, it became the last of the 13 original colonies in 1732 when a British charter was granted for the establishment of "the Colony of Georgia in America." It was the fourth state in the United States and is nicknamed the "Peach State" and the "Empire State of the South."

Georgia buggy A humorous term for a wheelbarrow.

Georgia button " 'Skewers,' in the South known as 'Georgia buttons,' are just crude forms (wooden pine, locust thorns) . . . and the bones and shell pins of primitive peoples served the same purpose." [*Montgomery Advertiser,* August 6, 1933]

Georgia chicken Humorous term for salt pork.

Georgia cracker A CRACKER living in Georgia.

Georgia credit card Slang for a short length of hose used to siphon gas out of another person's gas tank.

Georgia flower A nickname for fuchsia shrubs.

Georgia ice cream Grits.

Georgia Major A tongue-in-cheek term similar to KENTUCKY COLONEL, but it can also be a derogatory term for a pretentious, self-important person.

Georgia man A term slaves sometimes used for slave-dealers. "There I thought . . . that some Georgia man, as the negroes then called the slave-dealers—for to Georgia many of the negroes were then sold . . . would leap upon me from the woods."

[Frederick Thomas, *John Randolph of Roanoke,* 1853]

Georgia pen A log prison common in Georgia in the early 19th century and during the Civil War.

Georgia piercer A large mosquito. "The 'Georgia piercer' or 'Gallinipper', if curses could annihilate it, would be driven from off the earth." [*Harper's Magazine,* November 1862]

Georgia pitch pine A valuable abundant tree also known as the Southern pine and the red, brown, yellow or long-leaved pine.

get about To move around. "She can't hardly get about anymore."

get a holt of Get a hold of. "And besides, the main thing was to get a holt of Uncle Rodney and my twenty quarters . . ." [William Faulkner, "That Will Be Fine," 1935]

get-go The beginning. "I been here since the get-go."

get gone To depart, leave. "Give me my share so I can get gone."

get grown To grow up. "When I got grown, I moved out of there."

get in the wind of Get wind of, discover. "He was cheatin' on his expense account till his boss got in the wind of it—now he's lookin' for work."

get in behind To egg on, push, encourage. " 'And then De Spain come home at dinner time and I reckon maybe Miz de Spain got in behind him because about middle of the afternoon he rides up to house . . .' " [William Faulkner, *The Hamlet,* 1940]

get leave of   To get permission. " 'Is you going to get leave of the county to get married?' he asked doubtfully. 'Or is you just going to live along without it?' " [Erskine Caldwell, *Tobacco Road,* 1932]

get low for Jesus   To prostrate oneself in prayer to Jesus Christ. " 'I can get low for Jesus too. I can get low for Him too.' " [William Faulkner, *Requiem for a Nun,* 1951]

get me   To get for oneself. "I'm gonna get me some pie."

get one's ashes hauled   To be sexually satisfied, as in the black folk blues, "Well, you see that spider climbin' up the wall,/ Goin' up there to get her ashes hauled."

get oneself a boss   To get married. "He got him a new boss now."

get on the river   To find employment on the Mississippi, aboard a steamboat, etc. Mark Twain used this expression in *Old Times* (1875).

get shed of; get shut of   To get rid of. "Let's run that tire flat so we can git to town and git shed of him. I don't like to waste time around that smell." [Erskine Caldwell, "Savannah River Payday," *The Complete Stories of Erskine Caldwell,* 1953]

get the bulge on someone   To get the advantage over someone. "You don't watch it, he's gonna get the bulge on you."

getting fair   The weather is clearing up, getting good. "It's getting fair outside."

getting oneself up   Dressing up to go out, putting on makeup. " 'She's upstairs in her room,' said Doll, 'getting herself up.' " [Calder Willingham, *Rambling Rose,* 1972]

get up backwards   To get up on the wrong side of the bed, be irritable.

ghy   Going to; used principally by blacks. "A ghy tell um! I ghy do hit!" [William Faulkner, "Uncle Willy," 1936] See also GWINE

gift child   A term (recorded in no other dictionary, so far as can easily be determined) used principally among Southern blacks, particularly in Mississippi, for a child given to someone to raise by a relative or friend unable to raise the child.

giggle soup   A name for any alcoholic drink, especially in North Carolina.

gime   See GWINE.

gimme a dope   See DOPE.

gin   (1) Early on used for *if,* deriving from the pronunciation of the Scotch-Irish schoolteachers of the South, who were often indentured servants. (2) By; before. "I'll be there gin supper." (3) As a shortening of *cotton gin* and a corruption of the word *engine*, *gin* was first used in the South and had little use in other sections of the country.

gin rickey Rickeys can be made of any liquor combined with carbonated water and lime juice, but the most famous drink in the family is the *gin rickey*, invented about 1895 and named after "a distinguished Washington guzzler of the period," Colonel Rickey, according to H. L. Mencken. Just which Colonel Rickey is a matter of dispute, however. Several theories have been recorded by Mencken in his *American Language, Supplement I* and in other sources, but none is generally accepted.

gip; gyp A female dog, bitch.

gitar Common pronunciation of *guitar*.

give a damn This was originally "I don't give a damn," the expression probably brought back from India by military men in the mid-18th century. A *dam* was an Indian coin of little value. *I don't give a damn* is first recorded in America in the 1890s. Its most famous use was in the film *Gone With the Wind* (1939), in which Rhett Butler told Scarlett O'Hara: "Frankly, my dear, I don't give a damn."

give a little sugar To give a hug or kiss; said especially to a child. "Come over here and give me a little sugar."

give down the country To find fault with, upbraid, call to account.

give him the go-by Said in South Carolina of a woman who refuses a man's marriage proposal: "She gave him the go-by."

give in A Gullah phrase meaning "to tell." "She come for the job and give in her experience."

give it a lick and a promise Do something hurriedly, perfunctorily, quickly.

give-me-leif " '. . . likely you never hear of Give-me-lief. It was a game we played. You would pick out another boy about your own size and you would walk up to him with a switch or maybe a light stick or a hard green apple or maybe even a rock, depending on how hard a risk you wanted to take, and say to him, "Gimme leif," and if he agreed, he would stand still and you would take one cut or lick at him with the switch or stick, as hard as you picked out, or back off and throw at him once with the green apple or the rock. Then you would stand still and he would take the same switch or stick or apple or rock or anyways another one jist like it, and take one cut or throw at you.' " [William Faulkner, *The Mansion*, 1959]

give off To give away in a marriage ceremony. " 'I reckon you can,' said Rose. 'You're all comin' to the weddin', all of you, cause we want your Daddy to give me off.' " [Calder Willingham, *Rambling Rose*, 1972]

give one scissors To give someone a tongue-lashing. "He give him scissors, didn't he?"

give one the blacks To snub or ignore a person. "When I passed him on the street, he give me the blacks."

give out (1) Very tired, having no strength left. "I'm about give out." (2) give up, gave up. "I reckon you give out expecting me to come."

give up to be Generally conceded to be. "She's give up to be the prettiest girl in these parts."

give-way A giveaway. "It was a dead give-way."

givey Moist, muggy, soft. "The weather's givey today."

giving tongue A dog's cry when chasing game. ". . . he heard the bellike voice of old Julia, giving tongue in great excitement." [Marjorie Kinnan Rawlings, *The Yearling*, 1938]

giving tongue like a hound in the field Talking incessantly, especially gossiping. ". . . with Honey Wilkes giving tongue like a hound in the field, the entire County would know about it before six-o-clock." [Margaret Mitchell, *Gone With the Wind*, 1936]

gizzard-string Gullah for a supposed tendon in the stomach. "He laughed so hard he like to popped his gizzard-string."

glid Slid, glided. "The time just glid by."

glom Take, grab, swipe; apparently from the British dialect word *glaum* or an old Scottish word, although *glom* had early hobo use in America. "He glommed the whole bag of them."

Glorious Cause A Southern name for the Civil War. " 'Take a good look at them,' came Rhett's gibing voice, 'so you can tell your grandchildren you saw the rear guard of the Glorious Cause in retreat.' " [Margaret Mitchell, *Gone With the Wind*, 1936]

go Going. "I hope y'all [are] go [to] remember us."

goan See GWINE.

go away To lose weight or shrivel up. "When it's cooked up, the spinach will go away."

go by cow express To travel by foot (or shoe leather).

go chase cats Get lost, get out of here. ". . . he didn't like Horton a bit and once in trembling fury had told him to go chase cats, scram, go home . . ." [Calder Willingham, *Rambling Rose*, 1972]

God Almighty's overcoat wouldn't make him no vest Said of a very conceited person.

go down Gullah for "to take to childbed." "Her time to go down was near."

God's nightgown! An Southern exclamation of exasperation or surprise made famous by Margaret Mitchell's heroine Scarlett O'Hara, who uses it several times in *Gone With the Wind*, 1936: " 'God's nightgown,' cried Scarlett, leaping from the bed. 'Aren't things bad enough without you talking about dying?' "

goed Went. "Away we goed." [Marjorie Kinnan Rawlings, *The Yearling*, 1938]

gogo Used mainly in Louisiana for the buttocks. "He pinched her gogo, and she slapped his face."

go halvers To share equally. "I'll go halvers with you on it."

go hungry and ragged To be poor, have nothing. " 'I hear what you say, Miss Henny, but it makes no difference,' he told her determinedly. 'I'll just have to go hungry and ragged, if need be.' " [Erskine Caldwell, *Jenny By Nature*, 1961]

go in To begin, especially a church service or schooltime. "School goes in at 9 o'clock."

Gold Coast A name for that part of Louisiana on the banks of the Mississippi 30 miles or so upriver from New Orleans.

Gold Coast Negro A slave brought to America from the region so named in West Africa.

Golden Coast Same as GOLD COAST.

gollop To swallow greedily. "They golloped up that rabbit and left nothing but the bones."

gone where the woodbine twineth Woodbine is a honeysuckle (*Lonicera periclymenum*) that was often planted on graves in years past. An 1870 song written as a tribute to those who died in the bloody Civil War went "Then go where the woodbine turneth,/ When spring is bright and fair,/ And to the soldier's resting place/ Some little tribute bear." From this song by Septimus Winner the expression *gone where the woodbine twineth* came to refer to someone who had died or even someone who had gone someplace from where he would never return. It is currently used in the South and nationally as well.

gonna clean your clock Going to get even; going to beat you up. "I'm gonna clean your clock!"

goober (1) Goober, for "peanut," was not coined in the southern United States. It originated in Africa as the Bantu *nguba* (peanut) and was brought to the American South by African slaves in about 1834. A dialect term for many years, it has achieved wider usage over the past 50 years. PINDER, another word for peanut, comes from the Kongo *npinda* and is used chiefly in South Carolina. (2) During the Civil War a nickname for a resident of North Carolina.

goober digger An affectionate term for a Southern backwoodsman.

goober grabber; goober gabbler (1) Nickname for a native of Georgia. (2) A poor country person, one who digs for peanuts.

goober pea A peanut.

Goober State A nickname for Georgia.

gooch To dog; gouge. " 'What're you laughin' at, son?' said Mary, gooching him roughly in the ribs." [Thomas Wolfe, *Look Homeward, Angel,* 1929]

good (1) Fully, completely. "They'll dry pretty fast soon's the sun gits good up." (2) Well; primarily an East Texas expression. "I'm good, thank you, ma'am."

good and heavy To a considerable extent, in a big way. " 'God is got it in good and heavy for the poor [Jeeter said]. But I ain't complaining.' " [Erskine Caldwell, *Tobacco Road,* 1932]

gooder (1) Mostly a mountain term for a good one or a good thing. "That's a real gooder!" ("That's a good joke!") (2) Better. "Foxes love corn gooder'n I do." [Marjorie Kinnan Rawlings, *The Yearling,* 1938]

goodest The best. "That's the goodest yet."

good for the wholesome An old term meaning "good for the health."

good man A child's term for God; used mostly in the Southern mountains.

good ole boy A white Southern male exemplifying the masculine ideals of the region; any amiable Southerner, provided he likes guns, hunting, fishing, drinking, football and women, in roughly that order; a loyal Southerner, rich or poor, devoted to all things Southern. The term had popular use in the mid-1960s. Said the late Billy Carter, President Jimmy Carter's brother, of the good ole boy: "A good ole boy . . . is somebody that rides around in a pickup truck . . . and drinks beer and throws 'em out the window." [*Redneck Power: The Wit and Wisdom of Billy Carter,* 1977]

good ole rebel Perhaps older than GOOD OLE BOY is the little-heard *good ole rebel,* which derives from a song entitled "Good Old Rebel" written by Innes Randolph in the 1870s: "I am a good old rebel—/ Yes, that's just what I am—/And for this land of freedom/I do not give a damn./I'm glad I fit agin 'em/And I only wish we'd won;/And I don't ax no pardon/For anything I've done."

goody (1) A nut's kernel. "Her cake had goodies in it." (2) An egg yolk. "She broke open an egg with two goodies in it." (3) Jam or jelly. "Spread some goody on my bread."

gooey weather Muggy weather.

goofer A witch doctor; a spell performed by a witch doctor; derives from a word of African origin brought to the South by slaves.

goofer dust   A powder used in conjurations by witch doctors.

google   See GOOZLE.

go on   To carry on; show grief; make an outcry. "The widow was down on the grave cryin' and goin' on."

goose drownder   A very heavy rain. "We've had some real goose drownders this year."

goose hangs (honks) high   All's well, everything is looking good. "We made the deal. Everything is lovely, and the goose hangs high."

gooses   Sometimes used as the plural for *goose* instead of *geese*.

goot   An insane person.

goozle   The windpipe or throat of a human or an animal, especially a pig; also called *google, guzzle* and *gozzle*. " 'Why, that's his goozle. What's a goozle? Well, if he didn't have no goozle, he couldn't squeal.' " [Marjorie Kinnan Rawlings, *The Yearling*, 1938]

gopher wood   The southern yellow-wood, *Cladrastis lutea*, said to be one of the rarest and most beautiful trees of the American forest.

Gorilla   Derogatory nickname for Abraham Lincoln common in the South during the Civil War. "He was long detained in Washington, having interviews with Abe, the Gorilla; Seward, the Raven; and Feathers Scott." [*Richmond Dispatch*, November 13, 1861] Lincoln was also called the "Illinois Gorilla." His own Secretary of War, Edwin Stanton, called him the "Original Gorilla."

gorn   See GWINE.

gospel bird   Chicken, because the bird is so often served at Southern Sunday dinners. See also DINNER.

got   Sometimes omitted in speech, as in "I ain't no firewood."

got a low eye for a high fence   To think too much of oneself. " 'Now think o' that beat-down human aspirin' to Grandma,' Penny said. 'He's shore got a low eye for a high fence.' " [Marjorie Kinnan Rawlings, *The Yearling*, 1938]

go to hell in a bucket   To deteriorate rapidly; also *go to the hell in a handbasket*. "Neither of us could figure it out, all we knew for certain was that the marriage of Rose and Dave began to go to hell in a bucket . . ." [Calder Willingham, *Rambling Rose*, 1972]

go to ride   To go for a ride. "How would you like to go to ride?"

go to the bad   To spoil; deteriorate; become immoral. "She's praying her daughter won't go to the bad."

go to the bridge with   To stand by, support. "I'm your friend and I'll go to the bridge with you."

go to the well with To stick by someone to the end; the saying is now common throughout the U.S.

go to the whole coon An old, perhaps obsolete, Southern expression patterned on *go the whole hog* (go all out for something).

go up An obsolete Civil War expression for "to be hanged or finished." "Soon after the blocade many thought we Confederates should 'go up' on the salt question—couldn't salt our meat and should be starved into subjection." [*London Index,* June 2, 1864]

gourd An old term for the head, dating back to the early 19th century.

government Common Southern pronunciation of *government,* though it is also used nationally.

gower An old mispronunciation of *giaour,* a word, Turkish in origin, for an unbeliever.

graceful as the capital letter *S* Very graceful. " 'Well, Rosebud,' said Daddy, 'now you are here, darling, and I swear to God graceful as the capital letter S.' " [Calder Willingham, *Rambling Rose,* 1972]

gracious plenty More than enough. "We've got gracious plenty of it."

grain A little, a bit of; chiefly used in the Southern mountains. "You might o' been a grain warmer about hit."

gramy To vex, annoy. "Ain't any need to be gramied."

grand Tall; from the French and often used in the Louisiana-French dialects.

grand baby A common term for a grandchild that isn't recorded in any dictionaries so far as can be easily determined; heard recently (1991) from a Southern woman in the Empire State Building in New York City, of all places: "I got three grand babies down home."

grandboy Grandson. " 'I got just as much right to a trip as you and Lucius,' Ned said. 'I got more. This automobile belongs to Boss and Lucius ain't nothing but his grandboy and you ain't no kin to him at all.' " [William Faulkner, *The Reivers,* 1962]

Grand Creole See MAN OF SUMTER.

Grand Cyclops See CYCLOPS.

granddaddy Used more often in the South for grandfather than anywhere else.

granddaddy clause A variation on GRANDFATHER CLAUSE.

Grand Dragon A high-ranking official of the KU KLUX KLAN.

Grandfather A form of address once often applied to elderly male blacks. ". . . and there was a Negro family in a wagon in the road and Bayard said, 'Hold on, Grandfather,' and

turned the car off into a ditch . . ."
[William Faulkner, *The Town*, 1957]

grandfather clause A clause used by some Southern states in their constitutions after 1890 in which they disenfranchised blacks by stipulating that new literacy and property qualifications for voting applied only to those who did not have the right to vote before 1867. In other words, the clause exempted from the new literacy and property qualifications for voting all those men who were entitled to vote before 1867 or who had lineal ancestors who were entitled to vote before 1867. Since no blacks could vote or had ancestors who could vote before that time, this meant that no blacks were permitted to vote.

grandfather graybeard The Southern fringe tree *(Chionauthus Virginiana)*, which is also known as *gransy greybeard, old man's whiskers* and *grandfather's beard.*

grandfather's beard See GRANDFA-THER GRAYBEARD.

gransy greybeard See GRANDFA-THER GRAYBEARD.

Grand Wizard of the Empire The head of the KU KLUX KLAN; other "Grand" offices, in the Klan's heyday, were the Grand Dragon, Grand Ensign, Grand Exchequer, Grand Giant, Grand Gobling, Grand Klokard, Grand Kludd, Grand Magi, Grand Monk, Grand Scribe, Grand Sentinel, Grand Titan and Grand Turk.

grannies!; granny! A mild expletive. "Grannies! He went and did it again."

granny An old woman; a fussy woman-like man; a midwife; a senile man.

granny-woman A midwife. "If this fails to cure, send for an old granny-woman who will cross two sticks in his mouth." [Carl Carmer, *Stars Fell on Alabama*, 1934]

grass sack See CROCUS SACK.

grave-box A coffin.

gravel To annoy or embarrass someone. "She gravels me with all her airs."

graveyard cough A very bad cough from a cold or cigarettes.

graveyard rabbit A rabbit that is said to have magical powers because it lives in a graveyard. "You er one er deze yer graveyard rabbits, dat wat you is." [Joel Chandler Harris, *Uncle Remus and His Friends*, 1892]

graveyard stew Bread or toast in milk, sometimes with sugar sprinkled on; so named because invalids often eat it, or because it is poor people's fare and a long diet of it is unhealthy; used in other regions as well.

graveyard widow An actual widow, not a grass widow (an expression used nationwide and meaning "a woman divorced or separated from her husband").

gravy Can mean, in addition to its standard usage, grease rendered from salt pork.

gray A term, first coined in 1861, for the Confederacy or the Confederate Army, from the color of its official uniforms; also *boys in gray.*

grayback A Confederate soldier. "The gray-backs came through with a rush, and soon the musket balls and cannon shot began to reach the place, where we stood." [*McClure's Magazine,* October 1898]

graybacks Paper money issued by the Confederacy during the Civil War in place of the Union's greenbacks; also called BLUEBACKS and *graycoats.*

graybeard An old man. "That night the Board of Aldermen left—three graybeards and one younger man, a member of the rising generation." [William Faulkner, "A Rose for Emily," 1930]

graycoats See GRAYBACKS.

grayjacket A Confederate soldier. "A short-waisted, single breasted jacket usurped the place of the long tail coat . . . The enemy noticed this peculiarity, and called the Confederates gray jackets . . ." [*Southern Historical Society Proceedings,* volume 2, 1876]

Great American Mudhole An early 19th century nickname for Washington, D.C.; it was also called *The Capital of Miserable Huts.*

great balls of fire! A Southern exclamation made popular by rock-and-roll singer Jerry Lee Lewis' song "Great Balls of Fire."

great day in the morning! An exclamation of surprise. " 'Mah Johng!' gasped Miss Tennyson Bullock. 'Great Day in the Morning, I'd forgotten about it.' " [Eudora Welty, *The Optimist's Daughter,* 1972]

Great Dismal Swamp See DISMAL SWAMP.

Great Rebellion The Civil War. "Unexampled success has attended our agents in canvassing for the 'Great Rebellion.' " [Thomas Headley, *The Great Rebellion,* 1862]

Great Revival The religious revival begun in Kentucky and Tennessee near the beginning of the 19th century. "The Great Revival of 1800 and its attendant institution, the camp-meeting, were pure products of the frontier of the Old Southwest." [Everett Dick, *The Dixie Frontier,* 1948]

green beans Stringbeans.

green peach One of the many Southern synonyms for a clingstone peach; *pickle peach* is another one. See also CLINCH PEACH.

grigri; grisgris; greegree A charm or a magical formula used to bring bad luck to a rival; derives from an African word recorded as early as 1557.

Grinnich Village A Southern pronunciation of New York's Greenwich Village. " 'Because who knows,' I says, 'she may done already found that dream even in jist these . . . two days, ain't it? three? . . . That's possible in Grinnich Village, ain't it?' " [William Faulkner, *The Mansion*, 1959]

gripsack Republican A Reconstruction term for a CARPETBAGGER. "These gentlemen treat with contempt the charges of the gripsack Republicans." [*Congressional Record*, March 30, 1881]

gris-gris A term, used mainly in Louisiana, for a magic spell made by waving hands over someone.

grits Hominy grits. Coarsely ground hominy (made from corn) that is boiled and often then fried, especially as a breakfast dish or as a side dish to serve with meat.

grits mill Sometimes used for *grist mill* in Florida and nearby Southern states.

grocer store A grocery.

groom's cake The name of a cake served at weddings in addition to the traditional bridal cake; often a fruit cake or chocolate cake made of layers in graduated sizes.

groundhog case A last chance, a last resort, a do-or-die situation. "We got to win this one for Mississippi; it's a groundhog case with us."

ground pea A peanut.

ground worm An earthworm, in Virginia coastal areas.

growed Grown. "Ain't you never growed tomatoes?"

growing moon A waxing moon. "It's not a good time to plant on a growing moon."

grow like Topsy " 'Never was born, never had no father, nor mother, not nothin' . . . I 'spect I growed,' " the slave child Topsy replied when Aunt Ophelia, a white woman from the North, questioned her about her family. The scene in Harriet Beecher Stowe's antislavery novel *Uncle Tom's Cabin, or Life Among The Lowly* (1852), the most popular book of its day, had great impact, especially in unauthorized dramatic versions of the novel, and inspired the saying *to grow like Topsy*, describing any unplanned, often sudden growth.

growned Grown. " 'Did you notice how all Buddy had to do was to tell them boys of his it was time to go [to the Army], because the Government had sent them word? And how they told him good-bye? Growned men kissing one another without hiding and without shame. Maybe that's what I am trying to say . . .' " [William Faulkner, "The Tall Men," 1941]

grow off To grow up. "The chickens growed off big and fine." [Marjorie Kinnan Rawlings, "Cocks Must Crow," 1939]

grub up To dig out. "I been grubbing up a clump of willows outen my spring pasture for fifteen years." [William Faulkner, *The Hamlet,* 1940]

grumtion A term used mainly by blacks for "scrumptious." "We all had a grumtion fine dinner."

guano Often used to mean commercial fertilizer in several Southern states.

guardun An old-fashioned pronunciation of *guardian.*

guerillas See COPPERHEADS.

Guinea In pre-Civil War times, a black person recently transported from Africa's Guinea coast was called a Guinea. "It should also be noted that 'guinea Negro' used to be applied to any newly arrived Negro slave." [*American Speech,* April 1947]

guinea corn A species of millet brought from Africa by slaves.

Gullah (1) American dialect, spoken on the Sea Islands and along the South Carolina-Georgia coast. It contains some 5,000 African terms and takes its name either from Ngola (Angola) or from the West African Gola tribe. (2) A derogatory term used by whites. " 'Goddam your Gullah hide, Sam Moxley!' Judge Rainey shouted at him." [Erskine Caldwell, *Jenny By Nature,* 1961]

gully-washer A heavy rain. One old story has it that in the Ashland, Virginia *Herald-Progress* someone advertised: "Wanted: One good rain. No 10-minute gully-washers need apply."

gum! A mild expletive, *gum* here being a corruption of *God.*

gumball machine See BUBBLEGUM MACHINE.

gumbo (1) A stew usually made with chicken and/or seafood and tomatoes and often thickened with okra. (2) The okra plant or its pods. It derives from *Gombo,* an African Bantu name for okra. (3) A soil that becomes sticky and nonporous when wet. (4) The name given to a French patois spoken by blacks and Creoles in Louisiana. (5) Someone of mixed French and Indian blood; a black person.

gumbo box An obsolete term from slavery times meaning "an animal-skin drum."

gumbo filé "Gumbo [is now] applied to other kinds of gumbo thickened with a powder prepared from sassafras leaves. This powder goes by the name of *filé,* the past participle of French *filer,* 'to twist'; hence *gumbo filé* signifies properly, 'ropy or stringy gumbo.' " [William Read, *Louisiana-French,* 1931] See also GUMBO.

gumbo French See GUMBO.

gumbo town A contemptuous term for a small town.

gump A foolish, silly person.

gunja A sponge cake sweetened with molasses; from the African Hansa language *ganga,* meaning "ginger," which apparently became the Gullah *kanja,* a molasses bread.

gunshot house A term used in Louisiana for a long house with two or three rooms arranged in a row.

guv Gave. "I guv it to him yesterday."

gwin See GWINE.

gwine Going, going to. "I'm gwine call them boys." Also *gwyne, gine, goan, gorn, gwin, ghy.* It is a pronunciation the South's early aristocrats borrowed from upper-class English speech.

gwyne See GWINE.

H

hack To embarrass; annoy; rattle; confuse. "They kept calling him names till he was right hacked." The term may come from *hackle,* an instrument used to break flax.

hadn't ought Ought not, should not. "He said he hadn't ought to have done it."

hae Early on used for *have,* deriving from the pronunciation of Scotch-Irish schoolteachers of the early South, who were often indentured servants.

haint (1) Ain't. "I haint going." (2) A ghost or apparition.

hairy dick Heretic; also HARRY DICK. " 'Called us cow hunters around these parts [Florida] because we had to hunt so many mavericks—some of them older riders called 'em hairy dicks, cause they wouldn't stick with all the others—' 'Heretics,' Mama corrected him quickly, a rose-petal flush on her pale cheeks . . ." [Peter Matthiessen, *Killing Mr. Watson,* 1990]

half-leg high Measuring up to the knee. "My corn is only half-leg high."

half-strainer A middle-class person. someone halfway between quality folk and "poor white trash"; someone who pretends he's something he is not.

The term probably originated with black speakers.

hall A haw, the fruit of the Old World hawthorn, which can be red or yellow.

hamper basket A hamper.

hand A charm or amulet, especially one wrapped in red flannel; used mostly by Southern blacks.

hand-gallop A hurry. "He lit off at a hand-gallop."

handing down Helping down, as from a carriage. See usage example at DRESSED WITHIN AN INCH OF HER LIFE.

hand-running In a row, in succession. "You've won four days hand-runnin' now."

handwrite An old term among rural folk for handwriting. "I'm sure it's writ in his handwrite."

hang up To be intimate, to have sexual relations. " 'Lov ain't thinking about no turnips,' Dude said, in reply to his father. 'Lov's wanting to hang up with Ellie May. He don't care nothing about how her face looks now—he ain't aiming to kiss her.' "

[Erskine Caldwell, *Tobacco Road,* 1932]

hanker To crave or desire. "I been hankering to have some grits."

hant A haunt, a ghost; the usage isn't confined to the South. "The boy watched him in complete and rapt immobility. As if I might be an apparition he thought. A hant. Maybe I am." [William Faulkner, "Mountain Victory," 1940]

hantle A small crowd. "A hantle of men came out for the meeting."

happen-so An accidental occurrence. "Gittin' that buck was pure happen-so." [Marjorie Kinnan Rawlings, *The Yearling,* 1938]

happen to an accident To have or suffer an accident. "He happened to a right bad accident."

happen to a catastrophe See HAPPEN TO AN ACCIDENT.

happify To make happy; an old term not much used anymore.

happy as a pine borer in a fresh log Very happy; content. " 'He's living in Grandma's shed,' Boyle said, 'and happy as a pine borer in a fresh log.' " [Marjorie Kinnan Rawlings, *The Yearling,* 1938]

hard-backed cooter See FLORIDA COOTER.

hardshell A HARDSHELL BAPTIST or any severe, straight-laced, very conservative person.

hardshell Baptist A strict Baptist who proclaims hellfire; a member of the Primitive Baptist Church or an Old-School or Antimissionary Baptist; a Baptist who judges everyone very strictly by his beliefs and rules, even himself in many cases. "What I don't like about hardshells, they think everybody but them is goin' t' hell—even the dead little babies." [Carl Carmer, *Stars Fell on Alabama,* 1934] "Everytime she heard it, Bessie always said that the other people did not know any more about God's religion than the male preachers who talked about it knew. Most of them belonged to no sect at all, while the rest were hard-shell Baptists. Bessie hated hard-shell Baptists with the same intensity that she hated the devil." [Erskine Caldwell, *Tobacco Road,* 1932]

hardshell church A church made up of HARDSHELL BAPTISTS.

hardshell sermon A severe sermon by a HARDSHELL BAPTIST or any other clergyman.

hard-tail A mule. "Machines are replacing the 'hard-tail' or 'fur-head.' "

harm Harmful; mostly a Gullah expression. "I hate to say a harm word to him."

Harpers Ferry, West Virginia This beautiful little town in easternmost West Virginia on the bluffs at the

confluence of the Potomac and Shenandoah rivers is famous in American
history because the fanatic abolitionist John Brown was captured and
hung there just before the Civil War.
The town takes its name from one
Robert Harper, who established a
ferry at the site in 1747.

harry dick An old, once-popular
expression for "heretic" in the Florida Everglades, as was HAIRY DICK.

harrykin A pronunciation of *hurricane*. "We ain't really got anything
to worry about but Hall Creek bottom tomorrow [Boon said]. Harrykin Creek ain't anything.' " [William
Faulkner, *The Reivers*, 1962]

has Often substituted for *have*, as
in, "We has plenty time."

**hasn't sense enough to flag a freight
train** Is very stupid, can't do the
simplest things.

hassle Originally a Southern dialect
word meaning "to pant noisily like a
dog," *hassle* has come to be used
nationally as a synonym for quarrel
or trouble, perhaps because those involved might be breathing noisily.
Hessle is a variation often heard.

haul ass To leave with haste, depart
quickly. "Let's haul ass out of here."
The term originated in the South but
has some national use today.

have Sometimes omitted in speech,
as in "You don't seem to kept up
with these modern ideas." [William

Faulkner, "Shingles for the Lord,"
1943]

have a bloodrush To get angry.

have a burr in one's saddle To be
extremely irritated, agitated; also *have
a burr under one's saddle*. "He's got a
burr in his saddle."

have a chicken to pick To have a
quarrel to pick with someone. "I have
a chicken to pick with you."

have a crow See PICK A CROW.

have brass on one's face To be bold,
sassy, impudent. "She sure has a lot
of brass on her face."

have no time with one Chiefly a
Gullah term for "can't compare to
one." "In dancing he has no time
with you."

have off To remove, take off. "Have
off your coats, gentlemen."

have one over To reprimand. "My
old man comes in drunk again, I'm
going to have him over."

have out To have picked from a field
an indicated amount of cotton. "I
suppose I have out 10 or twelve bales
. . ." [*A Florida plantation record*,
1854]

Haviland Fine china. William
Faulkner writes in *Absalom, Absalom!*
(1936) of "the food, on the damask
before the Haviland beneath the can-
delabra . . ."

haw See GEE AND HAW.

hawg-killin' A hilarious celebration. "We had a hawg-killin' time."

he (1) Often used redundantly after a masculine singular subject. "John he did it first." (2) Sometimes used for *his*. "He best do he job."

headin; headen A pillow.

headish Headstrong. "He's a mighty headish man."

headkerchief A handkerchief wrapped around the head.

headmark A historical term for a merit mark given to the pupil who was at the head of his or her class in spelling at the end of the spelling lesson for the day.

heap A lot, a great deal, a large quantity. "He did it a heap o' times."

heapa folks A large crowd.

hear? Do you hear me, do you understand me? "When you get down to Georgia, give me a call, hear?" It is often pronounced *heah*.

hear tell To hear something said. "I hear tell you want a girl." [Marjorie Kinnan Rawlings, *Cross Creek*, 1942]

hearn An old-fashioned term for *heard*. "I've hearn you tell that story afore."

heart The juicy, tasty center part of a watermelon. ". . . he was always busy splitting open one of those big Senator Watsons. When he had got the heart cut out, and had passed it around, he would wipe the blade of his pearl-handled knife on his pants leg and shake hands all around." [Erskine Caldwell, "The People's Choice," *The Complete Stories of Erskine Caldwell*, 1953]

hearts-a-bustin'-with-love The burning bush *(Euonymous americanus)*, which has seed pods that burst open to reveal many scarlet seeds. It also goes by the names hearts-a-bustin', strawberry bush, swamp dogwood, arrowwood and spindle bush.

heavy case Chiefly Gullah for an extraordinary person. "She is a heavy case in dis world."

heel string Achilles tendon.

he (she) found the hole Said of a very unlucky or stupid person. A shortening of the one-line joke: "He's a guy that drowned in a river that was only six inches deep on the average— he found the hole."

hell A colorful name for a thick tangle of rhododendron or laurel, so vast that people have become lost in it; also called *Laurel hells*.

hell a mile An exclamation. "Hell a mile, he ain't been out of hearing long enough to done that." [William Faulkner, *The Hamlet*, 1940]

hell and sulphur Exclamation. "But fifty goats. Hell and sulfur." [William Faulkner, *The Hamlet*, 1940]

hellborn Born to a terrible fate. " 'I hellborn, child,' Nancy said. 'I won't be nothing soon. I going back where I come from soon.' " [William Faulkner, "That Evening Sun," 1931]

hell fire! An exclamation. " 'Hell fire,' Father said. 'You can't do that.' " [William Faulkner, *The Town*, 1957]

hell-totin' A colorful old curse. " 'You great infernal, racket-makin', smokin', snortin', hell-totin' sons of thunder,' cried the old man, cursing the steamboats."

help To put food on a plate. "Ma Baxter sat at the table waiting for them, helping their plates." [Marjorie Kinnan Rawlings, *The Yearling*, 1938]

helpless as a turtle on his back Completely helpless. " 'I never said he wasn't [a very fine man] but he's helpless as a turtle on his back.' " [Margaret Mitchell, *Gone With the Wind*, 1936]

helt Held. "I've helt back my shot." [Marjorie Kinnan Rawlings, *The Yearling*, 1938]

hem up To gather together, round up. " 'He's [God is] like a man that's got too many mules . . . And . . . when Monday morning comes, he can . . . hem some of them up and even catch them if he's careful about not never turning his back on the ones he ain't hemmed up.' " [William Faulkner, *Requiem for a Nun*, 1951]

hep Common pronunciation of *help*. "I cain't hep it." [Marjorie Kinnan Rawlings, *The Yearling*, 1938]

hé quoi What!; French, often used in the Louisiana-French dialects.

herb Herb; but it is sometimes pronounced and written *yerb* and *yarb*. "I'm gonna have me some yerb tea."

here Often used superfluously, as in, "This here girl is mine." Variously pronounced *hyar, heah, year, hyeh, yeah, hyer, yar, hyur, yer.* See also THERE.

hern Hers. " 'She's a right tall girl,' he said. 'With them skinny legs of hern.' " [William Faulkner, *Sanctuary*, 1931]

Heroes of America An secret organization, also called the *Red Strings,* formed in North and South Carolina after the Civil War. "The dislike of whites to the Union League was so great that the local bodies began to assume other names: Red Strings and Heroes of America in North and South Carolina." [Walter Fleming, *Documentary History of Reconstruction,* 1906] See also UNION LEAGUE.

hero of New Orleans A nickname of General Andrew Jackson, referring to his victory over the British at New Orleans in 1815.

her smile makes the old feel young and the poor feel rich Said of a charmin' woman.

hesh up Heard in Texas for "hush up."

Hessian An old term, not much used, for a loud, overbearing person.

hessle See HASSLE.

het Heated, angry, excited; used in New England and other areas as well. "He got all het up."

he-uns Himself. "He found him a new wife for he-uns."

hey A salutation, as in "Hey, John, how you been?"

hickernut Hickory nut.

hickory A switch that is made of any wood, not necessarily hickory wood. "I made me a peach-tree hickory."

Hidy Hi, hello. " 'Hidy. I see you got my cow there. Put this rope on her and I'll get her outen your way.' " [William Faulkner, *The Mansion,* 1959]

high as the hair on a cat's back Very expensive; also *higher than a cat's back.* "Gas is high as the hair on a cat's back this week."

high blood High blood pressure, *low blood* being low blood pressure. "He's got high blood."

higher than a Georgia pine An old term for someone very drunk. "He's higher than a Georgia pine, but not quite high as a kite."

high-headed (1) Proud, obstinate. "It may suit my neighbor to have one of them high-headed Roanoke planters to come here." [*Southern Literary Messenger,* volume 3, 1837] (2) Head held high, proudly. ". . . and Her sitting high-headed in the wagon for old Marse John to lift her down." [William Faulkner, "There Was a Queen," 1933]

high jamboree A once popular dance. "The dance of High Jamboree is evidently of remote mystical African origin." [Bret Harte, *Waif of the Plains,* 1890]

highlone An old, rare expression meaning "to go alone without any encumbrance." "Mulatto Jack returned home with the Mares he was sent for; but so poor were they, and so much abused had they been by my rascally overseer, Hardwick, that they were scarce able to highlone, much less to assist in the business of the plantations." [George Washington, quote from a 1760 letter, *George Washington's Writings* (Worthington Ford, ed.), 1889]

high lonesome A wild, drunken spree. "Old Dad and Jim Day got on a high lonesome and started to paint the town red." [J. M. Franks, *Seventy Years in Texas,* 1924]

high-minded Proud, touchy. "You have to walk on eggs with him, he's so high-minded."

high sheriff A humorous, disparaging term for a local sheriff; based on the old English *High Sheriff,* the supreme sheriff in the land.

high-tempered Very irritable; said of someone who loses his or her temper easily.

high yellow; high yaller A once-common term, now considered offensive by many, referring to a mulatto of light yellow complexion.

him Himself. "He aims to find him a new wife." It is sometimes pronounced *um* or *em*.

hind end The buttocks. "He kicked him in the hind end."

hiney Backside, buttocks; a word with widespread U.S. use. " 'She thinks flirtation is just fun, a kind of game . . . Whee-ee, I'm wearing silly clothes that show my hiney . . .' " [Calder Willingham, *Rambling Rose*, 1972]

hippen A diaper; used mainly in Tennessee.

hire it done To pay to have something done. "Snopes built a new blacksmith shop . . . He hired it done, to be sure." [William Faulkner, *The Hamlet*, 1940]

hire one's time An obsolete expression referring to a slave paying his master for the right to use his own (the slave's) time for his own profit. "I decided to hire my time, with a view of getting money with which to make my escape." [Frederick Douglass, *Narrative of the Life of Frederick Douglass*, 1845]

his Used for *her* in Gullah. "His [Mary's] soul might be clean, but his [Mary's] body ought to be baptized."

his comb's getting red A sexually aroused male; based on the belief that a rooster's comb turns red when he is sexually aroused. "His comb was getting red for her even before they was introduced."

his (her) generosity is longer than his (her) pocketbook He (she) has good generous intentions but usually can't carry them out, especially in financial matters. ". . . mamma said papa ought to be ashamed that it wasn't Uncle Rodney's fault if his generosity was longer than his pocketbook, and papa said yes, it certainly wasn't Uncle Rodney's fault, he never knew a man to try harder to get money than Uncle Rodney did, that Uncle Rodney had tried every known plan to get it save work . . ." [William Faulkner, "That Will Be Fine," 1935]

his (her) head ain't done He (she) is feeble-minded or dull-witted.

hisself Sometimes used for *himself*, mostly in uneducated speech. "Brer Rabbit fling out de bag o' goobers an' jump out hisself and run home." [Joel Chandler Harris, *Uncle Remus Tales*, 1881]

hisn A shortening of *his own;* heard in the South but common to other areas of the United States. It is not, as generally thought, a backwoods Americanism but a contraction of long and respectable lineage, dating back to the early 15th century and used by Samuel Richardson in his novel *Clarissa* (1747). An old English adage goes "Him as prigs what isn't his'n/When he's cotch'd he goes to prison."

hissy A fit. "She like to have a goddamned hissy." [Larry Brown, *Joe*, 1991]

hit (1) It; generally used when it is meant to be emphatic or when it comes at the beginning of a sentence. "Hit's a hard bargain and you know it." (2) To yield or produce fruit. "The cherry trees didn't hit this year."

hitch To fight. "Me and you gonna hitch if you don't look out." The national slang *hitch* meaning "to unite in marriage" is also used in the South.

hit for To head for. " 'Come up, rabbits,' he said. 'Let's hit for town.' " [William Faulkner, *The Hamlet*, 1940]

hit the grit To depart quickly, hit the road. "He threatened to jail me, and I hit the grit." *Grit* here apparently means "gravel" or "gravel road."

hit up Excited, heated up.

hobo egg See ALABAMA EGG.

hobsonize To kiss. Lt. Richmond Pearson Hobson (1870–1937) won fame during the Spanish-American War when he tried to sink the collier *Merrimac* and block Santiago harbor. The young naval engineer was honored with parades and dinners when he returned to his native Alabama in August 1898. Because of his good looks and popularity, women often flung their arms around him and showered him with kisses when he appeared in public. "Kissing-Bug Hobson," as he was called, resigned from the Navy and ran successfully for U.S. congressman in Alabama, a state that later gave us another osculatory politician, Governor "Kissin' Jim" Folson. An obsolete expression today, *hobsonize* remains in historical dictionaries as one of the more curious linguistic forms.

hoecake and sorghum syrup A dish, consisting of a cornmeal cake or bread and syrup, that has formed the basis of the diet of many rural poor in the South in hard times. "We didn't have nothin' to eat lots of times, nothin' at all, not even hoecake and sorgum syrup which is what we ate a lot." [Calder Willingham, *Rambling Rose*, 1972]

hog Pork, as in "I had me some hog and hominy [pork and hulled corn]."

hog and Hominy State A nickname for Tennessee.

hog fat Fat in the way a hog is fat. ". . . [the horse is] hog fat. That's just exactly how it was fat: not like a horse is fat but like a hog: fat right up to its ears and looking tight as a drum' it was so fat it couldn't hardly walk, putting its feet down like they didn't have no weight or feeling in them at all." [William Faulkner, *The Hamlet*, 1940]

hog-meat Pork.

hog-smelly Smelling of hog, smelling very bad. "Get off those hog-smelly clothes and get into that bath."

hogwild Berserk. "He went hog-wild."

hoicked Caught, pierced and thrown. ". . . it . . . wouldn't live even through the first hour set free, flung, hoicked on a pitchfork or a pair of long-handled tongs into a city street." [William Faulkner, *The Mansion*, 1959]

hold oneself too high To act like one belongs to a higher class or station in life. "People . . . believed that the Griersons held themselves a little too high for what they really were." [William Faulkner, "A Rose for Emily," 1931]

hold one's feet to the fire To force someone to do something. "He probably learned . . . that he could go to his mother and hold the lawyer's feet to the fire anytime . . ." [William Faulkner, *Absalom, Absalom!*, 1936].

holdover Leftovers saved from an earlier meal; also *coldover*.

hold your tater Be patient, wait a while. "Just hold your tater and I'll be right with you."

hollering "By far the finest of all musical gifts is the hollerin' (also called hollering for the Lord). This is yodeling at its best—no more to be lik-ened to what is heard on the vaude-ville stage than grand opera can be compared with the hurdy-gurdy. It is the grand opera of the Okefeno-kee, where it is a common possession of man, woman and child." [*National Geographic*, volume 65, 1934]

hollering for the Lord See HOLLER-ING.

holp Helped. Southerners still say such things as "She holp her sister when she was sick," the old preterit *holp* meaning "helped" in this case and being an archaic past tense of the verb *to help* that was used many times by Shakespeare and survives in speech only in eastern Mississippi. "Then I taken my slingshot and I would have liked to took all my bird eggs, too, because Pete had give me his collection and he holp me with mine . . ." [William Faulkner, "Two Soldiers," 1943]

holt Hold. " 'Take a-holt of this pole,' Boon said." [William Faulkner, *The Reivers*, 1962]

holy laugh The hysterical laughter of one or many caught up in religious fervor at a camp meeting or other religious gathering. "When it got started in an audience, everybody would be seized with natural hardy laughter. It would last for hours sometimes. This was known as the 'holy laugh.' " [Everett Dick, *The Dixie Frontier*, 1948]

holy roller A term used in the South and elsewhere for a member of any religious sect whose services are often characterized by ecstatic movements that may include rolling on the ground or floor; the term is also applied to any overbearingly religious person.

holy tone; holy whine The speaking of Primitive Baptist preachers who sound an audible "ah" at the end of each breath pause. "Often the preacher had no idea what he would say from one 'ah' to the next. This 'holy tone' had charms for the audience and they preferred such a sermon to that by a learned college president." [Everett Dick, *The Dixie Frontier*, 1948]

home folks People from one's home town; familiar people. " 'Now that's more like acting like home folks,' Verly said with satisfaction as he stooped over and picked up the two worn suitcases." [Erskine Caldwell, "Girl With Figurines," *Gulf Coast Stories*, 1956] *Home boy* is a similar term.

home-place A family home. "She managed the 1,000-acre homeplace in Jackson."

hominy bread Bread made from coarsely ground hominy, puffed corn without the hulls. Often broken into a coarse meal and boiled in water or milk.

hominy grits See GRITS.

hone To yearn or pine for. "I'm honin' after some grits."

honey A common Southern form of address to female children or young women.

hongry Hungry. "Going to Grahamsville allus do make me hongry." [Marjorie Kinnan Rawlings, *The Yearling*, 1938]

honky-tonk Any bar or tavern.

hoodoo Someone who practices voodooism; to bewitch or put under a spell. "I heard people say hoodoos was cannibals and used to eat babies." [Robert Tallant, *Voodoo in New Orleans*, 1946]

hooped-up with Bound together, as if in a circle or hoop. " 'That's what I've been saying at every local meeting since the shutdown,' Will said. 'The local is all hooped-up with the A.F.L.' " [Erskine Caldwell, *God's Little Acre*, 1933]

hooray A ruckus. "He raised a big hooray in the store 'cause they wouldn't sell him a jug."

hoose House. See also PAAMS.

hooters Southern slang for female breasts. "She's got some pair of hooters."

hootnanny A derogatory epithet. "You're a big old fat hootnanny." [Marjorie Kinnan Rawlings, "Cocks Must Crow," 1939]. *Hootnanny*, usually spoken as *hootenanny*, also means a lively gathering including or featuring musical entertainment.

hoppergrass An old term used in east Virginia and elsewhere in the South for a grasshopper. " '. . . she ain't got no mo' sense dan a hoppergrass.' " [Margaret Mitchell, *Gone With the Wind,* 1936]

hopping John An old favorite Southern dish made of black-eyed peas, rice, bacon or ham or pork knuckles and red pepper or other hot seasoning. It is traditionally served on New Year's Day because of the superstition that black-eyed peas eaten then bring good luck for the coming year. "Before me, though at the head of many delicacies provided by papa, was an immense field of hopping John." [Caroline Gilman, *Recollections of a Southern Maiden,* 1838]

hopping like peas on a hot shovel Very active, especially said of a group of people; the term was commonly used in the 19th century and may still be in use today.

hoppytoad An ordinary toad.

hornswoggle To cheat, bamboozle, deceive; a fanciful term, now widely used, that originated in Kentucky in the early 19th century.

horse-reek The sweaty smell of a horse. "So we were standing there, Lightning's muzzle buried to the nostrils in Ned's hand, though all I could smell now was horse-reek and all I could see was the handful of grass which Lightning was eating . . ." [William Faulkner, *The Reivers,* 1962]

horse's patoot A horse's rear. "She's a horse's patoot."

horsepittle A pronunciation of hospital. " 'Spec dey's at de horsepittle.' " [Margaret Mitchell, *Gone With the Wind,* 1936]

horsing Acting like a mare or stallion in heat, acting as if sexually aroused; also *horsing and studding.* "Look at that horsing Ellie May's doing! . . . That's horsing from way back yonder." [Erskine Caldwell, *God's Little Acre,* 1933]

horsing and studding See HORSING. ". . . that man horsing and studding at that gal, and her trying to get away from him." [William Faulkner, *The Reivers,* 1962]

hot as blue blazes Extremely hot. "It gets as hot as blue blazes down in Alabama."

hot as floogies Very hot, as hot as a very promiscuous woman or floogie (floozie). The expression is always in the plural.

hot damn! Exclamation of joy or happiness. "What was so important about today? I bolted up in bed. Hot damn! Summer vacation!" [Tim McLaurin, *Keeper of the Moon,* 1992]

hotel A dining hall for students. This obsolete meaning was in use early in the 19th century at the University of Virginia.

hot hot A term used in Louisiana when the weather is extremely hot. "It sure is hot hot today."

hotten To heat. "I kin hotten that soup." [Marjorie Kinnan Rawlings, *Golden Apples*, 1936]

hot-water tea Tea made in a kettle.

hound dog A dog bred for hunting; a derogatory term for a mongrel or even a person, as in Elvis Presley's "You Ain't Nothin' but a Hound Dog," which was a remake of a blues standard.

hour by sun Before sunset or after sunrise. "It's two hours by sun [either two hours since the sun set or rose, whichever was closer]"; "he quit plowin' two hours by sun."

house (1) Concerning the word's interesting pronunciation in Virginia, a Southern correspondent writes: "I [once] heard a little girl with a Virginia accent . . . get four syllables out of her pronunciation of 'house.' I've tried it, and although my mother was from the Byrds of Virginia, I couldn't get more than three syllables out of it, no matter how I tried." (2) A name for a small floating peat island in the Okefenokee Swamp of Georgia and Florida.

house Negro In pre-Civil War times, a black slave who worked in the master's house; the derogatory *house nigger* was also common.

house wine of the South Lemonade.

how come? Why?; how did it happen that way? The expression, probably originating in the South, is now common throughout the United States.

howdy A contraction of "how do you do?" Generally regarded as an expression born in the American West, *howdy* began as a Southern expression and was taken west by Confederate Civil War veterans.

however you does No matter how you do it. "However you does, she don't like it."

how many Often used to mean "the last name" or "family name" in a question. " 'What's your name, fellow?' 'Dave.' 'Dave-How-many?' 'Dave Dawson.' " [Erskine Caldwell, *God's Little Acre*, 1933]

howsomever Howsoever, however. "Howsomever may I say this to please the gals?"

hucky duck Fine, great. "Maybe he'd given up on ever finding me and had just gone back home. That'd be real hucky duck if that was the case." [Larry Brown, "Gold Nuggets," 1990]

hullabaloo and uproar Great commotion. "Hell and damnation, all this hullabaloo and uproar because one confounded running bitch finally fixed herself." [William Faulkner, *The Hamlet*, 1940] *Hullabaloo* is often used alone.

hull the goobers for An obsolete expression meaning "to defeat." "We hull the goobers for any team in the state." See also GOOBER.

hunk An older meaning than the current meaning of "an attractive male" is the now rarely used *hunk* for "a country fellow."

hunky-dory Fine, about as good as something can be. The origin is uncertain, but there may be a Southern connection, as proposed by Carl Whittke in *Tambo and Bones* (1930): " 'Josiphus Orange Blossom,' a popular song . . . in a reference to Civil War days, contained the phrase a 'red hot hunky-dory contraband.' The Christy's [a minstrel group] made the song so popular that the American people adopted 'hunky-dory' as part of their vocabulary."

hurt To suffer or have need. "I'm hurtin' for it."

hurted Hurt. "You hurted the leetle thing . . . Bad hurted." [Marjorie Kinnan Rawlings, *The Yearling,* 1938]

hurting A hardship, suffering. "When a division leaves with 25,000 troops, that puts a hurting on everybody." [*New York Times,* November 15, 1990]

hush my mouth! Often said in surprise, as is *shut my mouth.* "Well, hush my mouth!"

hush puppy A deep-fried cornmeal cake that is very popular in the South. The name is traceable only to the time of World War I. The most common explanation for the odd name is that hunters tossed bits of the cakes to their dogs, telling them to "hush, puppy." A perhaps more authentic version notes that the cakes were first made in Florida, where people often fried fish outdoors in large pans, attracting dogs who would whine and bark. To quiet the dogs, the cook would fry up some cornmeal cakes and throw them to the dogs, shouting "Hush, puppies!"

hush your mouth Be quiet. " 'You hush your mouth!' Haw said, crying. 'Nobody's talking to you!' " [William Faulkner, "Two Soldiers," 1943]

hwich? Which?; what? It is often used in reply to an unheard question.

hyar; heah Common pronunciations of *hear* or *here.*

hydrant A faucet. "Ever' house [in Mississippi] has got a hydrant to it. All you got to do for water is turn a tap." [John Faulkner, *Men Working,* 1941]

hysterical marker Pronunciation, often facetiously, of *historical marker* heard in Texas.

I

I be dawg I'll be dogged, dog-goned. " 'I be dawg if he ain't a case now,' he said." [William Faulkner, *Sanctuary*, 1931]

Ibo-shin Slang for a black person in pre-Civil War days, deriving from the name of the Ibo tribe in the African Niger delta from which many slaves were sent to America.

ice-cream supper A late afternoon social gathering to raise money for a church or school with ice cream as the principal refreshment; called an *ice-cream social* in other parts of the country.

I declare! See I DECLARE TO GOOD-NESS!

I declare to goodness! This old-fashioned but still common excla-mation and its variations, such as *I declare!*, is often spoken with the ac-cent on the first syllable of the second word: "I *de*clare to goodness!"

I didn't go to do it I didn't mean to do it. "Many of them [Southerners] say 'I didn't go to do it,' meaning, 'I didn't mean to do it.' " [Mark Twain, *Life on the Mississippi*, 1883]

I do believe! A common emphatic exclamation. " 'I do believe Ashley would rather read than hunt!' "

[Margaret Mitchell, *Gone With the Wind*, 1936]

idn't A pronunciation of *isn't*.

I don't chaw my tobacco but once I'm only going to tell (or warn) you one time.

I don't know him from Adam's housecat See ADAM'S HOUSECAT.

I'd tell a man! I'll say!; I'll tell the world!

idy Idea. "I had no idy he'd be here."

if Sometimes omitted in speech, as in "See has he come."

if it harelips the South No matter what happens. "I don't care if it hare-lips the South, I'll be home for Christmas."

ifn If. "Ifn you want to come, let me know."

if so be If. "If so be a time comes when yeh have to be kilt . . ." [Ste-phen Crane, *The Red Badge of Cour-age*, 1894]

if that don't beat all Common expression of surprise or wonder.

if wishes were horseflesh we'd all own thoroughbreds Found in William Faulkner's *The Hamlet* (1940); may be Faulkner's invention or possibly a Southern country saying.

if you can't listen, you can feel A common warning to a child that if he doesn't do what he's told, he's going to get a good spanking.

if you've got a rooster, he's going to crow People do what nature designed them to do, despite artificial restrictions. " 'It's only fair to set the boy straight at the start, seeing as he's a male and women are females.' Ty Ty said. 'I've had the side of my barn kicked off because I was careless enough to lead a stud horse into the wind when I should have led him with the wind.' 'Talking don't help much,' Will broke in. 'If you've got a rooster, he's going to crow.' " [Erskine Caldwell, *God's Little Acre,* 1933]

I Godfrey! Euphemism for "by God!" "I Godfrey, if him and all of them together think they can keep me from working on my own church like any other man, he better be a good man to try it . . . I Godfrey, what a day!" [William Faulkner, "Shingles for the Lord," 1943]

il dit He said; French, often used in the Louisiana-French dialects.

il est bon heur It is early; French, often used in the Louisiana-French dialects.

ill as a hornet Angry, very irritable. "The boss is ill as a hornet today."

I'll be bound. I swear, I'll bet. " 'It skeered him too, I'll be bound,' he said." [William Faulkner, *Sanctuary,* 1931]

I'll be dinged! Euphemism for "I'll be damned!"

I'll drink all the blood that is spilled in a war between North and South! A common quip heard among FIRE-EATERS during the Civil War, a war in which 620,000 men were killed, the casualties exceeding America's losses in all other wars.

I'll give you a box with five nails A humorous punning way to say "I'll give you a good slap [or blow]." Someone might say, "Give me all that candy you have." "What I'll give you is a box with five nails," might be the reply.

Illinois Baboon A derogatory nickname given to Abraham Lincoln in the South; sometimes shortened to *"the Baboon"* and sometimes changed to "Illinois Gorilla" and "Gorilla." "To have come to reside in Charleston (S.C.) with an exequatur under the signature of the 'Baboon' and that obtained after the war had actually begun, would have been, to say the least, a step of doubtful policy." [*Richmond* (Va.) *Examiner,* December 11, 1861]

Illinois Gorilla See ILLINOIS BABOON.

Ima Hogg One of the best known of humorous American names. Ima Hogg (her real name) was the daughter of a Texas governor and was a prominent socialite. In addition to her name, she is well known for her collection of American decorative arts, now displayed in Houston in Bayou Bend, her home there. Ima Hogg is not the only humorous American name, for there are hundreds of gems like the following to choose from: Virgin Muse, Lana Amorous, Etta Turnipseed, Fannie Bottom, Arsie Phalla and Dill L. Pickle (who was a pickle salesman). There was even someone named La Void.

I'm from Missouri During the Civil War, "an officer of the Northern army fell upon a body of Confederate troops commanded by a Missourian. The Northerner demanded a surrender, saying he had so many thousand men in his unit. The Confederate commander, game to the core, said he didn't believe the Northerner's boast of great numerical superiority and appended the now famous expression, 'I'm from Missouri; you'll have to show me.'" Dr. Walter B. Stevens recorded this proud derivation of the phrase in *A Colonial History of Missouri* (1921), but other authorities support the following derogatory origin: Miners from the lead district of southwest Missouri had been imported to work the mines in Leadville, Colorado sometime after the Civil War. They were unfamiliar with the mining procedures in Leadville, and fellow workers regarded them as slow to learn, their pit bosses constantly using the expression, "He's from Missouri, you'll have to show him." Residents of the Show Me State obviously favor the former the-

ory, and "I'm from Mizorra," as they say, is a badge of distinction, signifying native skepticism and shrewdness.

Imperial Wizard The highest officer in the KU KLUX KLAN. Similarly, the Klan's headquarters is called the *Imperial Palace*.

impotent (pronounced im-PŌT-'nt) A pronunciation of *important*.

I'm so mad I could spit nails Very mad indeed.

in Sometimes used for *on*. "A man stood in the floor his feet apart . . . McLendon stood in the floor and cursed the others." [William Faulkner, "Dry September," 1931]

in a dither In a state of excitement. "She's all in a dither."

in a great while In a long period of time. "I haven't seen him in a great while."

in a manner A common redundancy in Southern speech, as in "She acts like she's rarin' in a manner to go."

in a sull In a sulking, sullen mood. " 'He's been in a sull ever since you married Judge McKelva and didn't send him a special engraved invitation to the wedding;' said Bubba." [Eudora Welty, *The Optimist's Daughter,* 1972]

in a swivet In a hurry. "You're always in such a swivet."

in course Of course. "In course I'll go."

indigo planter A planter in the early South whose major crop on a great plantation was indigo.

infair An old term for a dinner party or reception celebrating a wedding.

in one's country The region one hails from. "Down in my country we don't do it that way."

in reason Logically; almost without a doubt. "I know in reason that I am right."

insides The viscera, everything inside one's body; common in other areas of the United States as well. "They work the insides outen a fella." [John Faulkner, *Men Working,* 1941]

intend for Want, mean, expect, plan. "He didn't intend for her to hear."

in the ground Buried. "They waited until Miss Emily was decently in the ground before they opened it." [William Faulkner, "A Rose for Emily," 1930]

Invisible Empire The KU KLUX KLAN.

ironclad oath A name given the stringent oath of office prescribed by Congress in 1862 and applied at the close of the Civil War for office holders in the reconstructed states, according to the *Cyclopedia of America* (1914). The oath aimed at the exclusion of all who had participated in the rebellion.

irrepressible A person who believed that the Civil War was inevitable was called an irrepressible.

irrepressible conflict The Civil War, a term coined by Secretary of State William Seward in 1858.

is (1) Gullah for *has.* "Is you forgot?" (2) Am (mostly among black speakers); are. "I is going to church."

is all Sometimes used as a shortened form of "that's all" at the end of sentences. "I just pushed him, is all."

I'se I am; used mostly among black speakers. "I knows when I'se whipped."

island cotton Cotton raised on lands near the sea, especially in South Carolina; this black-seeded cotton was preferred to the green seed variety.

islet An old Creole expression for a New Orleans street or square.

it There. "It is only one man here."

I-talian A pronunciation of *Italian.* ". . . Lawyer had enough to keep him occupied worrying the I-talian government." [William Faulkner, *The Town,* 1957]

it's a comin' up a cloud See COMING UP A CLOUD.

it's not the size of the dog in the fight, it's the size of the fight in the dog Texas proverb.

it's raining black cats It's raining very heavily.

I vow! I declare!

I wasn't done it I wasn't doing it.

I wouldn't trust him behind a dime I wouldn't trust him at all; also *behind a thin dime, a dime edgeways, a broomstraw, a pin, a needle, a corkscrew,* etc.

J

jack A jackass. "We done made the trade and I can't break it now. You'll just have to keep that jack." [Erskine Caldwell, "Meddlesome Jack," *The Complete Stories of Erskine Caldwell,* 1953]

jackleg Someone untrained for his work; someone self-taught; an unscrupulous worker; also *jakeleg.* It possibly derives from *Jack* + black*leg;* used chiefly in the South.

Jackson Day A legal holiday in Louisiana in honor of Andrew Jackson's victory at the Battle of New Orleans on January 8, 1815.

Jacksoniana Many things were named after President Andrew Jackson (1767–1845), ranging from *Jackson crackers* (firecrackers) to *Jacksonian democracy.* One of the most interesting is *Jacksonia,* the name of a new Southern state suggested by the Tennessee senate in 1841 that was to include parts of Tennessee, Kentucky and Mississippi. The proposal came to naught.

jake A name for cheap liquor or rotgut during Prohibition days, especially in the South, where *jake* was the old toper's sneaky Pete.

jake leg Southern generic term for the various shakes, paralysis, impaired gait, and seizures caused by delirium tremors.

jambalaya A New Orleans Creole dish made of rice cooked with ham, sausage, chicken, shellfish or a combination, with herbs, spices and vegetables, especially tomatoes, onions and peppers; hence, any diverse collection of things. "The show was a jambalaya of stunts."

James River The name of a once-famous tobacco grown in the James River region of Virginia. "He pulled out a plug of James River and began chawing (chewing)."

Jamestown lily A name used locally in Jamestown, Virginia for JIMSONWEED; this was, in fact, the original name for the plant.

jam it Stow it, stuff it. "She said: 'I've bout had it with your goddamn mouth.' 'Jam it,' I said. 'Kiss my ass,' she said." [Larry Brown, "Falling out of Love," 1990]

jam up In the sense of "fine, first rate, excellent" (*not* a tight crush of cars, etc.), *jam up* dates back at least to the mid-19th century. "[I] introduced him to the jam-up little company in his command." [*Southern Literary Messenger,* volume 8, 1841].

jarfly Any of a number of cicadas that make strident noises.

jarhead Mule; recorded in North Carolina but used elsewhere as well.

"Jawbone" An obsolete but once popular song among slaves in the South.

jaybird A bluejay; used in other regions as well.

jayhawkers See COPPERHEADS.

jazz Originally a Southern regional word of uncertain origin. In fact, enough Southern men to form a good jazz group are credited with lending their names to this word. One popular choice is Jasper, a dancing slave on a plantation near New Orleans in about 1825; Jasper reputedly was often stirred into a fast step by cries of "Come on, Jazz!" Another choice is Mr. Rass, a band conductor in New Orleans in 1904. Charles, or Chaz, Washington, a ragtime drummer of Vicksburg, Mississippi, circa 1895, is a third candidate. A variation on the first and third choices appears to be Charles Alexander, who, according to an early source, "down in Vicksburg around 1910, became world famous through the song asking everyone to 'come on and hear Alexander's Ragtime Band.' Alexander's first name was Charles, always abbreviated Chas. and pronounced Chazz; at the hot moments they called, 'Come on, Jazz,' whence the jazz music." Few scholars accept any of these etymologies, but no better theory has been offered. Attempts to

trace the word *jazz* to an African word meaning "hurry" have failed, and it is doubtful that it derives from the chasse dance step, the Arab *Jazib* (one who allures), the African *Jaiza* (the sound of distant drums) or the Hindu *jazba* (ardent desire). To complicate matters further, *jazz* was first a verb for sexual intercourse, as it still is today in slang. (1) A distinctly American form of music that originated in the South. (2) To have sexual intercourse. " 'Come on upstairs [Ty Ty said] and jazz a little.' Darling Jill giggled outright." [Erskine Caldwell, *God's Little Acre*, 1933] The word is often used in the sense of prostitution. " 'He got two medals and when it was over they put him back in Leavenworth until one lawyer got a Congressman to get him out. Then I could quit jazzing again,' " says a prostitute in William Faulkner's *Sanctuary* (1931).

jazz up To make fancy; enliven; cheer up. "We need to jazz up that dress."

Jeff Davis coffee Confederate troops named this coffee substitute made from parched wheat after the Confederacy's president. See also LINCOLN COFFEE.

Jeff Davis money Confederate money, so named after the president of the Confederacy.

Jeff Davis (musical) box A humorous name given by Confederate soldiers to "the lumbering ill-built armywagons, which were apt to creak horribly for the want of grease." It of course "honored" the president of the Confederacy.

Jeff Davis pie An old recipe for custard pie flavored with nutmeg. Named for the president of the Confederacy.

Jefferson Davis The president of the Confederate States of America; his birthday is celebrated as a legal holiday (June 3, or the first Monday in June) in some Southern states.

Jefferson Day Thomas Jefferson's birthday, April 13th; a legal holiday in Alabama.

Jeffersonian simplicity An expression honoring Thomas Jefferson's dislike of pomp and ceremony in political and social matters.

Jefferson Territory A proposed name for what was to become the Colorado Territory. It was rejected by Congress in 1861 because it suggested the slaveholding South.

jelly A sweetheart. " 'Gowan goes to Oxford a lot,' the boy said. 'He's got a jelly there. He takes her to the dances. Don't you, Gowan?' " [William Faulkner, *Sanctuary,* 1931]

Jenny-Johnny A loveseat. "You'll have the parlor all to yourself and can sit in the jenny-johnny loveseat with him and play records and so on. The jenny-johnny is a fine place for arm hugging and things—that's what it's made for." [Erskine Caldwell, *The Earnshaw Neighborhood,* 1971]

jessie A critter (creature); can be said of humans or animals. "I had me a good go-round with them jessies [the Forrester family]." [Marjorie Kinnan Rawlings, *The Yearling,* 1938]

jewlarky; jewlarker Lover, sweetheart; a person of fine dress and manners. "I'm going to see my jewlarky." The origin of the expression, first recorded in 1851, is obscure.

jig; jigaboo A contemptuous, offensive term for a black person that perhaps originated in the South but is widespread in use.

jigger A chigger or flea.

Jim Crow Blackface minstrel Thomas D. Rice, "the father of American minstrelsy," introduced the song "Jim Crow" in 1828, claiming to have patterned it on the song and dance of an old fieldhand named Jim Crow he had observed in Kentucky. Rice's routine became so familiar here and on tour in England that a few years later a British antislavery book was entitled *The History of Jim Crow.* It is from this book and similar uses of Jim Crow to signify a black that the racially discriminating laws and practices take their name, though the first *Jim Crow laws* weren't enacted until 1875 in Tennessee.

jimsonweed *Jamestown weed* was the original name of *jimsonweed,* or the thorn apple, a plant that can be deadly poisonous when its foliage is wilted. *Datura stramonium* was named Jamestown weed because it was first noticed growing in America near Jamestown, Virginia, where the Indians smoked it like tobacco; in fact, soldiers among the insurgents in Bacon's Rebellion of 1675 are said to have eaten this weed when defeated and driven into the wilderness, many almost dying of it. Over the years *Jamestown weed* was slurred to *jimsonweed* in pronunciation, and by the 19th century, jimsonweed was the common name for the plant. It is also called JAMESTOWN LILY.

jimswinger An old term for a Prince Albert or long-tailed coat.

jine A black and rural white pronunciation of *join*.

jint A pronunciation of *joint*.

jist A pronunciation of *just*.

jizzywitch A katydid, which is a large, green long-horned grasshopper, the males of which produce a characteristic song sounding like "Katydid, Katydid."

job To jab. "I jobbed a piece o' meat on a stick." [Marjorie Kinnan Rawlings, *The Yearling*, 1938]

Joe boat An obsolete term for a small rowboat once common in Kentucky.

Joe Brown's pets The Georgia militia during the Civil War; so named after Joseph E. Brown, then-governor of Georgia.

Joe-darter An old term for a Jim-dandy, someone or something unsurpassed. "He's a real Joe-darter."

John Brown An old term in the South for "to damn"; after the abolitionist John Brown. "Well, I'll be John Browned!"

John Brown pike A weapon the abolitionist John Brown had made for his band of followers in Kansas but which was later copied by Southerners; sometimes erroneously called *Joe Brown pike*. "Many carried bowie knives in their boots and bore in their hands long thick poles with iron-pointed tips known as 'Joe Brown pikes.'" [Margaret Mitchell, *Gone With the Wind*, 1936]

johnny house A toilet, bathroom.

johnny-jug A demijohn (a large bottle with a short, narrow neck). "I got aholt of this johnny-jug." [William Faulkner, "The Tall Men," 1941]

Johnny Reb A Civil War term for a Confederate soldier but used since then to describe Southerners in general.

johnny-walkers Stilts.

joogled up Mixed together, agitated. " 'And hot under there, too, mon,' Ned said. 'I don't see how I stood it. Not to mention having to hold off this here sheet-iron cheven from knocking my brains out every time you bounced, let alone waiting for that gasoline or whatever you calls it to get all joogled up to where it would decide to blow up too.'" [William Faulkner, *The Reivers*, 1962]

jook See JUKEBOX.

jookin' See JUKEBOX.

joree To make fun of; to jest. "Papa joried Woody about the way he asked for things." [James Street, *My Father's House*, 1941] The *joree* is also a bird elsewhere called the *Chewink*.

josh A perhaps obsolete nickname for any man from Arkansas; the term became popular during the Civil War.

jower To quarrel. "All they did was jower about it."

juba dance A noisy, jubilant dance popular among black slaves. The origin of *juba* is unknown.

juberous Dubious; also *jubious*. "He was juberous about crossing the stream."

judge See CAPTAIN.

jughead A mule; also JARHEAD.

the juice ain't worth the squeeze It's not worth doing, the effort isn't worth the result; Heard from a Maryland correspondent but may be used in other regions as well.

jukebox A *juke house*, or *juke*, is a house of ill repute, a whorehouse, taking its name from the black Gullah dialect spoken on the islands off the coast of South Carolina, Georgia and Florida. The Gullah word *juke*, or *jook*, in turn apparently derives from the Wolof West African word *dzug* or *dzog*, meaning "to misconduct oneself, to lead a disorderly life." *Juke* naturally came to be associated with anything connected with a *jukebox*, even the early *jook* or *juke organs*, coin-operated music boxes that sounded like hurdy-gurdies and were often found in *juke houses*. When coin-operated phonographs became very popular in the early 1940s they were called *jukeboxes* after these early counterparts, so the name of this electrically operated machine can be ascribed to a West African tribe. A *juke* or *jook* also means a bar or tavern in parts of the South, and *jookin'* means to barhop from *jook joint* to *jook joint*, drinking, dancing and often fighting.

jularker An expression used in North Carolina for a boyfriend. "Who's your new jularker, Kathy?"

jumping alligator A humorous term for a razorback hog.

june See ZOON.

just a hoot and a holler away Nearby. "The store's just a hoot and a holler away."

just as good Might just as well. "You-all jist as good to pray for the heathen." [Marjorie Kinnan Rawlings, *Cross Creek*, 1942]

K

kaffir corn A grain sorghum brought to the South by slaves from Africa.

kah!; ki!; k-k! Gullah exclamations meaning *Ha!* " 'Ki, Doll,' May said scornfully, 'your's a fool . . . Ki,' she laughed. Helen burst into a raucous angry laugh. 'k-k-k-k—k-k!' " [Thomas Wolfe, *Look Homeward, Angel,* 1929]

Kaintuck An old pronunciation for the territory and later state of Kentucky.

keep up To keep a mistress. ". . . Logan who's been keeping a woman up for years . . ." [Thomas Wolfe, *Look Homeward, Angel,* 1929]

keep your britches on; hold on to your britches Don't be so impatient.

Kentucky ark Flatboats that could carry about 150 tons of cargo were once called *Kentucky arks* or *Kentucky boats.*

Kentucky bluegrass A grass *(Poa pratensis)* that grows particularly well in Kentucky and is widely used as a lawn grass.

Kentucky boat See NEW ORLEANS BOAT.

Kentucky burgoo (1) A celebrated stew made of chicken or small game and corn, tomatoes and onions; traditionally served in Kentucky on Derby Day, among other occasions. (2) A picnic at which burgoo is served.

Kentucky coffee tree *Gynocladus dioica,* whose seeds were once used as a substitute for coffee.

Kentucky Colonel Someone upon whom the honorary title of "Colonel" is bestowed in Kentucky, though no one takes the title very seriously.

Kentucky corncracker A term for a Kentuckian that was used in Civil War times.

Kentucky Derby A horse race for 3-year-olds held annually since 1875 on the first Saturday in May at Churchill Downs in Louisville, Kentucky; it was named after the English Derby at Epsom Downs, first held in 1780.

Kentucky fried chicken A synonym for Southern fried chicken.

Kentucky Jonathan An old, obsolete term for a rural Kentuckian.

Kentucky oyster "There was hog jole and cold cabbage, ham and Kentucky oysters, more widely known as

chittlings [CHITTERLINGS]. [Paul
Lawrence Dunbar, *Folks from Dixie,*
1898]

Kentucky rifle Famous in American
history as the rifle of the pioneers,
the long, extremely accurate Kentucky rifle is recorded by this name
as early as 1838. The flintlock muzzle
loader should, however, be called the
Pennsylvania rifle, for it was first made
in that state by Swiss gunmakers in
the 1730s and was perfected there.
"The British bayonet was no match
for the Kentucky rifle," wrote one
early chronicler.

Kentucky right turn According to
William Safire's "On Language" column in the *New York Times* (January
27, 1991), this is a humorous term
meaning "the maneuver performed
when a driver, about to turn right,
first swings to the left."

Kentucky screamer A Kentuckian.
" 'I say, you Kentuck screamer, what
kind o' livin' had you while you were
up the stream?' " [Henry Wetson,
Nights in a Block House, 1852]

Kentucky windage A method of
correcting the sighting of a rifle by
aiming the weapon to one side of
the target instead of adjusting the
sights.

Kentucky yell "A still louder laugh
presently increased into a Kentucky
yell." [Solomon Smith, *The Theatrical Apprenticeship of Solomon Smith,*
1846]

kerflummix To fall; to fail. "He ker-
flummixed today."

kernel Colonel, based on the word's
pronunciation. See usage example at
YIT.

ketch Catch. ". . . all he needed to
do was jist to do what he probably
done: ketching her after she had give
up . . ." [William Faulkner, *The
Mansion,* 1959]

ketch hound "Everybody needs a
hound around the house that can go
out and catch pigs and rabbits when
you are in a hurry for them. A ketch
hound is a mighty respectable animal." [Erskine Caldwell, "Kneel to
the Rising Sun," *The Complete Stories
of Erskine Caldwell,* 1953]

Key lime pie Named for the tart
limes of the Florida Keys, this delicious pie has been part of the Conch
cuisine for well over a century.

Key West This Florida place name
derives from a mispronunciation of
the Spanish *Cayo Hueso.*

kick (1) To pick, cause. "He's tryin'
to kick a fight with you." (2) To
reject a suitor, dismiss, jilt. "If [a
man's] suit was rejected, it was said:
'She kicked him.' " [Everett Dick,
Dixie Frontier, 1948]

kick the cat To become angry. "She
kicked the cat when she lost."

kid-glove orange "The Mandarin or
Tangerine orange . . . is sometimes
called the 'kid-glove orange,' because

you can break the skin and peel it without using a knife or staining the fingers." [Thomas Barbour, *That Vanishing Eden, A Naturalist's Florida,* 1944]

kilt Killed. "You ain't never seed a bear kilt." [Marjorie Kinnan Rawlings, *The Yearling,* 1938]

kin Family, relations. "He ain't no kin of mine."

King The name of a famous variety of upland cotton developed in North Carolina.

King Cotton A term once much used to personify the economic supremacy of cotton in the South. "Ye slaves of curs forgotten/Hats off to great King Cotton!" [R. H. Stoddard, "King Cotton," 1861]

King Kleagle An officer of the KU KLUX KLAN, usually the head of a state organization.

king's cure-all A Southern plant, *Oenotheris biennis,* once thought to be a cure for many ailments.

king's ex (excuse); king's cross An expression used when, in playing tag or base (a variation on hide and seek), a child falls down and wants to keep from being caught.

king's gifts Black slaves given by agents of Great Britain to the Indians in payment for their services often called themselves *king's gifts.*

King's Mountain Day October 7, the anniversary of the day in 1780 when 900 "mountain men" defeated a much larger British force at King's Mountain, South Carolina.

king snake A large, harmless snake, *Lampropeltis getulus,* found in the Southern states.

kinry; kinnery Relatives. "All our kinry will be home for Christmas."

kin to Related to. "He's kin to me—he's my second cousin."

kissing cousins A Southern Americanism that dates back before the Civil War. The term first implied a distant blood relationship but today more often means a very close friend who is considered family. It still is used in its original sense, however, in the sense of a relative far enough removed to permit marriage, an "eighth cousin" in the North.

Kiss my grits! An exclamation of surprise made popular on the television series, "Alice." "Well, kiss my grits!"

kiver A cover or blanket in North Carolina and other Southern areas.

kiyodle To sing joyously. "He goes kiyoodling along." [Marjorie Kinnan Rawlings, "Cocks Must Crow," 1939]

K.K.K.; KKK An abbreviation for the KU KLUX KLAN, recorded almost as early as the organization's inception in 1865.

Kleagle See KING KLEAGLE.

kneewalkin' drunk Very drunk indeed. "He wasn't unconscious but he was kneewalkin' drunk."

Knight of the Ku Klux Klan A member of the KU KLUX KLAN.

Knights of the Golden Circle A secret Southern organization, founded in 1854, that supported the Southern cause during the Civil War.

Knights of the Invisible Empire An old name for the KU KLUX KLAN. "Here was a chance to dress up the village bigot and let him be a Knight of the Invisible Empire." [Frederick Lewis Allen, *Only Yesterday*, 1931]

Knights of the White Camellia An organization founded after the Civil War that espoused the supremacy of whites over blacks. For a time in the late 19th century, this was another name for the KU KLUX KLAN. Also called the *White Camellias*.

knock along To move on in a leisurely way; also *knock long*.

knock cat-west To knock out of the way, to destroy. "The train hit the car at the crossing and knocked it cat-west." A variation of *to knock galley-west*.

knock out To hit fly balls in baseball. " 'Come on,' he said, 'I'll knock you out some flies.' Then he said, 'All right, you knock out and I'll chase um.' " [William Faulkner, *The Town*, 1957]

knowed Knew. "I've knowed him for some distance." [Marjorie Kinnan Rawlings, *The Yearling*, 1938]

knows Sometimes substituted for *know*, as in, "I knows it's true."

Ku Klux Klan A secret organization that arose in the South after the Civil War to preserve white supremacy. From 1865 to 1877 the name was often applied to all secret political organizations with the same purpose.

kungu See CONJURE BAG.

L

L An obsolete term for a fifty dollar bill; fives were called *Vs*, tens *Xs* and one hundred dollar bills *Cs*.

la bas Down there; French, often used in the Louisiana-French dialect.

ladybird The name for a ladybug beetle in parts of the South; a common nickname, which explains why former first lady Claudia Taylor Johnson was called Ladybird Johnson.

lagniappe A bonus gift often given by merchants to customers; derives from the American Indian *yapa* (a present to a customer), which came into Spanish first as *la napa* (the gift); pronounced "lanyap."

landgrave A term used in the Carolina colonies dating back to 1669 for a country nobleman, one who presided over a county.

Land of Abstractions An old nickname, dating back to at least 1845, for the state of Virginia, due to its abundance of political thinkers.

Land of Blood A nickname for Kentucky since the early 19th century, when it was famous for its Indian wars.

land o' cotton A nickname for the South since at least 1859: "I wish I was in the land o' cotton . . ."

Land of Flowers An old nickname for Florida.

Land of Legree A derogatory name given to the South by abolitionists five years or so before the Civil War, in allusion to the brutal planter Simon Legree in Harriet Beecher Stowe's *Uncle Tom's Cabin*. Sometimes the term was "Land of Legree and Home of the Slave."

Land of Magnolias A nickname for the South.

Land of Perpetual Youth A nickname for Florida, in allusion to Ponce de Leon's quest for the mythical Fountain of Youth.

Land of the Sky A nickname, since at least the turn of the century, for the Great Smoky Mountain region in North Carolina.

land pike A humorous term, referring to the little-valued fish, for a hog of an inferior breed or a razorback hog.

larrupin' truck A Texan's way of saying "good food." The word *larrupin'* is sometimes used alone to

149

mean "delicious," as in "That pie was larrupin'."

The Late Unpleasantness See UNPLEASANTNESS.

latitudes of lovely langour, the New England poet, novelist and travel writer Nathaniel P. Willis so described the South back in the mid-19th century.

laurel The general Southern term for a rhododendron.

lavish Plenty. "He'll see trouble and a lavish of it, too."

law To sue. "I'm going to law him in court."

Lawdy Mussy!; La!: Law!; Laud!; Law Sakes!; La Messy!; Lawsy Mussy!; Law me!; Lord how mercy! Exclamations meaning *"Lord!"* or *"Lord have mercy!"*

lay around the house like a rug Do nothing. " 'All Fred does is lay around the house like a rug. I wouldn't be surprised if he woke up some day and couldn't move.' " [Eudora Welty, "Petrified Man," 1941]

lay by To cultivate a crop for the last time in a growing season; to harvest; to set aside. "After the crop's laid by, we'll have nothing to do."

laying-by-time The period after harvest when there is less to do.

lay it to Attribute it to. " 'The only thing I can lay it to,' my old man said, 'is that calf just naturally likes to be around me . . .' " [Erskine Caldwell, *Georgia Boy,* 1943]

lay off To mark off a field with furrows before planting. "Brought anouther of the Muddy hole-plows home . . . and set it to laying off the 20-acre cut designed for carrots." [George Washington, *Diaries,* 1787]

lay (put) on the cooling board To kill. "I'll lay you on the COOLING BOARD!"

lay up To rest, hibernate. "He's layin' up for the big game Sunday."

leader A term used in slavery times to describe a slave who exercised some authority, though always under an overseer. "The overseer is expected to have . . . as many leaders as there are divisions of work." [Hugh Davies, (Alabama) *Farm Book,* 1862]

lean Meat, as opposed to the fat in meat. "He ate his supper when they brought it—the same sidemeat and molasses and undercooked biscuits he would have had at home; this in fact a little better since the meat had more lean in it than he could afford to eat." [William Faulkner, *The Mansion,* 1959]

learn Teach. " 'We can try him both ways and let him learn us which he likes [Ned said].' " [William Faulkner, *The Reivers,* 1962]

least one The smallest or youngest child in a family.

leastways At least. "Leastways, he can pay half of it."

leave To let, allow. "Leave him do it, leave her rest." [Marjorie Kinnan Rawlings, *The Yearling,* 1938]

Lee's Miserables A joking name given by Southerners to Victor Hugo's novel *Les Miserables* during the Civil War. "It was a ragged copy of *Les Miserables,* that book which caught the fancy of the Confederate soldiers. They had read it by camp-fire light and took some grim pleasure in calling it 'Lee's Miserables'." [Margaret Mitchell, *Gone With the Wind,* 1936]

leetle Little. "A leetle old light doc." [Marjorie Kinnan Rawlings, *The Yearling,* 1938]

left an orphan at the mercy of the Christians Abandoned in an alien place, said especially of someone from a different culture or environment. "'The pore child's an orphan . . . Left an orphan at the mercy of the Christians.'" [Marjorie Kinnan Rawlings, *The Yearling,* 1938]

leg down with To have sex with. "I still hadn't legged down with anybody and I knew that my sperm was backed up pretty deep. I didn't want the heartbreak of prostrate trouble." [Larry Brown, "92 Days," 1990]

lept Leapt. "My heart lept." [Marjorie Kinnan Rawlings, "Cocks Must Crow," 1939]

les oreilles de cochon Literally "pigs' ears"; a Cajun recipe for a deep-fried pastry.

less Let us. "'Less git going'." [Marjorie Kinnan Rawlings, *The Yearling,* 1938]

levee An embankment to protect lowlands during high water periods. The word that dates back to the early 18th century in America, coming from the French, and has special reference to the Mississippi River.

level down on Gullah for "to cause the level of a fluid to recede." "Do looka how Emma duh level down on de milk."

lick A blow. "He gave him a good lick."

lickblock A block of salt left out for horses and other stock to lick.

lick-log "Small troughs were cut in the trunk of a fallen tree and occasionally salt was placed there, making what was known as a lick-log." [Everett Dick, *The Dixie Frontier,* 1948]

lie A liar. "Don't call me a lie or I'll knock you down!"

Lie-all League After the Civil War, a benevolent organization called the Loyal League aided freed slaves. Some Southerners contemptuously called this the *Lie-all League.*

lief Leave; let. "I just as lief let them stay out here, if that's what they want to do." [William Faulkner, *The Hamlet,* 1940]

life does get daily An old saying meaning life gets wearisome or tiresome at times.

light To leave in a hurry; also *light a rag* and *light a shuck*. "He lit off for home."

light a rag See LIGHT.

light a shuck See LIGHT.

light bread Raised wheat bread, leavened with yeast and often store-bought, as opposed to CORN BREAD.

lighterd knots Kindling wood.

light in To begin. "I got to light in and fix a bed." [Marjorie Kinnan Rawlings, "Cocks Must Crow," 1939]

lightning wood Kindling wood.

light out To depart hastily. "He lit out for the river."

lights (1) Consciousness, senses. "What consolation is it trying to knock a bully's lights out and having your own dimmed in the process?" [William A. Percy, *Lanterns on the Levee,* 1941] (2) Viscera, bowels. (3) Eyes.

lightwood Resinous pine or other wood that is often used for kindling.

like a chicken-eating dog in a hen house With driven, unrelenting enthusiasm. "All they do is play ball with a bunch of schoolboys all day, and when night comes, they'll chase one woman after another like a chicken-eating dog in a hen house." [Erskine Caldwell, *Jenny By Nature,* 1961]

like a sick kitten on a hot rock Very cuddly. "She's like a sick kitten on a hot rock."

like for To like, to desire, to wish. "I would like for you to do it."

like to Almost. A common Southern expression that originated in Victorian Ireland. "I like to broke my back carrying it."

like trying to find flea shit in a pile of pepper Almost impossible to find, harder than finding a needle in a haystack. The phrase is used by a Southern U.S. senator in the movie *J.F.K.* (1991).

like wildfire in the wind Very fast. "The least little thing [of gossip] can start and then spread from one end of Sallisaw to the other like wildfire in the wind." [Erskine Caldwell, *Jenny By Nature,* 1961]

Likker'll make you not know your mama. Liquor will make you not know your mother. This Gullah proverb, which dates back to at least the 18th century and probably before then, was possibly adapted from an African proverb brought to America by South Carolina slaves.

limping Susan No one has found a satisfactory explanation for the name of this Southern dish of okra and rice.

Lincoln Brotherhood A political association of freed slaves formed after the Civil War to help protect their voting rights.

Lincoln coffee A Southern name for a coffee substitute made of various ingredients and used during the Civil War. See also JEFF DAVIS COFFEE.

Lincoln flag U.S. flag. "He it was who cut down the Lincoln flag at Occoqua, in spite of threats that he would be shot if he did." [*Charleston* (S.C.) *Mercury,* June 4, 1861]

Lincolnite A follower of Abraham Lincoln; a Northern soldier; a Northern sympathizer during the Civil War. "Woe to the Lincolnites when they meet those chivalrous sons of Carolina in battle array." [*Daily Dispatch* (Richmond, Va.), July 22, 1861]

Lincoln navy A Confederate term for the U.S. Navy during the Civil War.

Lincoln skins A name for fractional paper currency in South Carolina after the Civil War.

Lincoln spy A spy working for the U.S. government during the Civil War. "A Lincoln spy, named Lambert, was arrested at Manassas Junction." [*Charleston* (S.C.) *Mercury,* June 4, 1861]

lint-head A cotton-mill worker. " 'I'd rather be a God-forsaken lint-head

and live in a yellow company house than be what she and Jim Leslie are.' " [Erskine Caldwell, *God's Little Acre,* 1933]

lip To dip or rub snuff. "Ma Forester lipped a little snuff." [Marjorie Kinnan Rawlings, *The Yearling,* 1938]

lit a shuck Ran out, ran off quickly. "He lit a shuck as soon as he saw you." See also LIGHT.

Little Alec A common nickname for Alexander Stephens, vice-president of the Confederacy, because of his small slight stature.

Little bitty Little. "She is a little bitty woman."

little miss A term much used in the past by older black servants in reference to their white employer's daughter, regardless of the daughter's age or physique.

little old Little. "Listen at that little old cricket!"

Little Peacock See MAN OF SUMTER.

The Little Unpleasantness See UNPLEASANTNESS.

live along with To get along with. See usage example at GET LEAVE OF.

livestock A term used by slave-traders for the slaves they sold in pre-Civil War days. "The trader waked up bright and early, and come out to see his livestock." [Harriet Beecher Stowe, *Uncle Tom's Cabin,* 1852]

living on the lucky side of the road Having good luck. " 'But so far I've been spared that misery. Darling Jill acts crazy as hell sometimes, and about nothing. But we've been living on the lucky side of the road so far.' " [Erskine Caldwell, *God's Little Acre,* 1933]

Loafer's Hall An obsolete term for prison. "He was compelled to retire for awhile from the gaities of society into the retirement of 'Loafer's Hall.' " [*Daily Richmond* (Va.) *Enquirer,* July 3, 1861]

lobberheaded Stupid. "A pretty mother she would be, lobberheaded as a sow, to smother her baby." [Caroline Miller, *Lamb in His Bosom,* 1933]

loblolly Mud, ooze; a mess.

locker A closet. "He put it in the locker."

loft An Arkansas term for an attic.

lone star flag Usually applied to the flag of the Texas Republic but applied to the flags of several Southern states in Civil War times, including the flags of Virginia, South Carolina and Louisiana. "The Lone Star Flag was raised here [in Va.] today amid the exultant shouts of a tremendous multitude." [*Charleston* (S.C.) *Mercury,* December 25, 1860]

Lone Star State A nickname for Texas, deriving from the lone star on the Texas state flag.

long green A variety of homegrown tobacco with very large, long leaves.

long hunters An old name for the pioneer explorers from Virginia and North Carolina who first reached Kentucky and points west; they were so named because of the long time they were absent from home.

long sugar An old name once used in Carolina for a ropy kind of molasses.

long sweetnin' Molasses and other syrupy, fluid sweeteners. "Long sweetin' is to stick the finger in the molasses to the second joint; short sweetenin' to the first joint." See also SHORT SWEETENIN'.

long-tailed blue A black minstrel comedian dressed in a long-tailed coat.

look-a-here Look here. "Look-a-here what I found." The intrusive *a* in *look-a-here* is probably a survival of the pronoun *ye* or *you:* "Look ye here." It occurs in other expressions such as *look-a-yonder, look-a-there* and *look-a-hush,* which means "I am greatly surprised at what you say."

look-a-hush See LOOK-A-HERE.

looked up like a flash Looked up quickly. "He looked up like a flash and then turned his head."

looks like the back end of bad luck Looks terrible. "Now don't he look like the back end o' bad luck?" [Marjorie Kinnan Rawlings, *The Yearling*, 1938]

look without let Look without interruption, as long as one wants to. ". . . so that all the people . . . could . . . look without let at the pictures of men and women and children who were the same people that we were even if their houses and barns were different . . ." [William Faulkner, "Shall Not Perish," 1943]

loose-titted prostitute and a bare-assed whore A worthless disreputable woman. "He got worked up all over again and said never mind what I wanted to call her––she was a loose-titted prostitute and a bare-assed whore as far as he was concerned . . . I haven't heard such language since they closed the army camp down near Summer Glade after the war was over." [Erskine Caldwell, *Jenny By Nature*, 1961]

loost Loose. "Who turned him loost?"

Lord-a mercy! Common exclamation. "Lord-a-mercy! It was enough to make me cry." See also LAWDY MUSSY.

Lord-God The pileated woodpecker (*Dryocopus pileatus*), a large black and white American woodpecker with a prominent red crest. "At the Creek the pileated woodpecker is known as the Lord-God."

[Marjorie Kinnan Rawlings, *Cross Creek*, 1942]

lord of the jaybirds A mild expletive. "'Lord of the jaybirds, if we weren't all out of whiskey I'd make you sweat.'" [Marjorie Kinnan Rawlings, *The Yearling*, 1938]

lose one's britches Lose a lot of money.

losing one's lunch Vomiting, throwing up.

lost bread A mainly New Orleans term for French toast sprinkled with powdered sugar.

Lost Cause The cause of the South in the Civil War, first recorded as the title of a book in 1866.

Louisiana bit An obsolete term for a small coin, probably a picayune.

Louisiana flag A kind of iris found in the New Orleans area that grows in the water and blooms around the beginning of April.

love bubbles A woman's breasts.

low (1) Very seriously. "The sister of a friend of his was low sick." [William A. Percy, *Lanterns on the Levee*, 1941]

low blood Low blood pressure.

low cotton A mainly black expression for a state of depression. "I was in what Ford would call 'low cotton.' " [William A. Percy, *Lanterns on the Levee,* 1941]

low-downer A poor person; a poor white.

lower'n a doodle-bug Low-down, vermin. " 'Ever one of 'em's lower'n a doodle-bug. And black-hearted to boot.' " [Marjorie Kinnan Rawlings, *The Yearling,* 1938]

low man; low woman A short man or woman. "He's a low, fat feller."

low quarters An old term for oxford shoes.

low-rate To deprecate, put down. "Papa went to the man and began low-rating the dog." [James Street, *In My Father's House,* 1941]

lub A pronunciation, mainly by blacks, of *love.*

luck Short for "a piece of luck"; heard mostly in Gullah speech. "I never had a luck in my life."

"Lucy Long" The title of a minstrel song once popular with blacks in the South, a song that inspired a dance called the *Lucy Long walkaround.*

Lum The proper name, as in the old radio program "Lum and Abner," is a corruption of *Columbus.*

lynch This verb for extralegal hanging comes from the name of a Southerner, but who was the real Judge Lynch? At least a dozen men have been suggested as candidates for the dubious distinction. Scholarly opinion leans toward Virginia's Captain William Lynch (1742–1820), who was brought to light by Edgar Allan Poe in an editorial on "lynching" that he wrote in 1836 when he edited the *Southern Literary Messenger.* Poe claimed that the first lynch law originated in 1780 when Captain Lynch and his followers organized to rid Pittsylvania County, Virginia of a band of ruffians threatening the neighborhood. Poe even affixed to the editorial a compact drawn up by Lynch and his men. William Lynch's identity was further verified by Richard Venables, an old resident of the county, in the May 1859 issue of *Harper's Magazine.* But without evidence of any actual hanging, there was still room for doubt. Finally, additional proof was found in the diary of the famous surveyor Andrew Ellicott, who visited Captain Lynch in 1811 and gained his friendship. According to Ellicott's diary, William Lynch related how his lynch men, as they were called, were sworn to secrecy and loyalty to the band. On receiving information accusing someone of a crime, they seized the accused and questioned him before a court of sorts. If he did not confess immediately, he was horsewhipped until he did and was sometimes hanged whether he confessed or not.

M

machine Car; an old expression heard in the South and other regions. "He got in his machine and headed off down the road."

macock A melon similar to a muskmelon, the word probably derived from an Indian dialect of the Maryland-Virginia area.

mad Anger, fit of anger. "I got my mad up again."

madam Long used as a title for the woman in charge of a house or to distinguish a woman from her daughter-in-law, who is called "Mrs."

Magnolia City An old nickname for Houston, Texas first recorded in the late 19th century.

Magnolia State A nickname of Mississippi because of the great number of magnolia trees growing in the state.

mahogany tree Another name for the Kentucky coffee tree common in Kentucky and other parts of the South.

main strength The strength of the human body. See usage example at TARPOLLYON.

mais But; French, often used in the Louisiana-French dialects.

mais non! No!; French, often used in the Louisiana-French dialects.

make To produce a crop. " 'Look at that [pear] tree [in bloom],' Varner said. 'It ought to make this year, sho.' " [William Faulkner, *The Hamlet*, 1940]

make a blue fist of An old term meaning "to make an utter failure of." "[He] would make a blue fist of takin' a dead aim through double sights . . ." [William Caruthers, *The Kentuckian in New York*, 1834]

make accustomed To make one used to something. " 'This is the durndest automobile I ever saw,' Jeeter said. 'It don't do the same thing long enough to make me accustomed.' " [Erskine Caldwell, *Tobacco Road*, 1932]

make a crop To raise a crop. "Did you make a good crop?"

make a die of it To die. "Doc said, 'I can't take much credit for savin' you. Your time just hadn't come to make a die of it.' " [Marjorie Kinnan Rawlings, *The Yearling*, 1938]

make it up To plan, agree. "They was a bunch of us made it up to go yestiddy." [John Faulkner, *Men Working*, 1941]

make like To pretend. "He made like he neither had seen nor heard." [Sidney Lanier, "9 From 8," *Dialect Poems,* 1884]

make one's manners To act politely; to bow or curtsy; to say "How do you do." " 'Watch now,' Miss Reba said. 'Lucius, this is Miss Corrie.' I [Lucius] made my manners. 'See what I mean?' Miss Reba said. 'You brought that nephew of yours over here hunting refinement. Here it is, waiting for him.' " [William Faulkner, *The Reivers,* 1962] "I got out of the car and made my best Southern manners." [Jonathan Daniels, *A Southerner Discovers the South,* 1938]

make out; make out like To pretend. "He made out like he didn't know."

makes me so mad I could spit 10 feet Makes me furious. ". . . now they turn on me and act so pious and try to make me leave town. It makes me so mad I could spit ten feet." [Erskine Caldwell, *Jenny By Nature,* 1961]

make out your supper Finish your supper (dinner), don't leave anything on your plate.

make the riffle To make the grade, succeed. "He couldn't make the riffle."

male cow A euphemism for a bull.

male hog Euphemism for a boar.

mam; ma'am A respectful form of address to female elders. "Good afternoon, mam."

mamma A mother is more often called "mamma" than "mom" in the South.

mammy A term formerly used frequently in the South for a black woman hired as a white child's nurse or as a white family's servant.

mammy; maumer; maum; muh; muddah Mother.

Man Above God. "It all depends on the Man Above."

Manassas The Southern name for the Civil War battle known as Bull Run in the North.

man-fever A woman's sexual lust for a man; a woman's lust for marriage to a man. "Now that she's got man-fever, she's got no more shame than a naked whore on a bedquilt with a big spender on a binge." [Erskine Caldwell, *Jenny By Nature,* 1961]

man horse Stallion. "The Negro man had warned her: 'He's a horse, missy. But he's a man horse. You keep out of there.' " [William Faulkner, *The Hamlet,* 1940]

mannerable Polite. "Course she's too mannerable to go around braggin' about it." [James Street, "Old Gordon Place," 1943]

manniporchia Only in Northern Maryland does this word (deriving from the Latin *mania a patu* [craziness from drink]) mean the D.T.'s (delirium tremens).

Man of Sumter   General Pierre Gustave Toutant-Beauregard, the Louisiana Creole general who commanded the attacking Southern forces at Fort Sumter, South Carolina in the first battle of the Civil War. He was also known as the "Grand Creole" and, being a vain man, the "Little Peacock." One story has him throwing a victory party where champagne was piped into his garden fountain and flowed all night. Much heralded at the time of Sumter, the worthy "Grand Creole," or "Old Bory" to his troops, was soon eclipsed by greater Southern generals.

marais   A swamp or bayou; used chiefly in Louisiana and other Gulf States. It derives from a French word meaning "marsh" or "pool."

Mardi Gras   The day before Lent, Shrove Tuesday, long celebrated in New Orleans (and other cities around the world) as a day of carnival and merrymaking. Mardi Gras, literally "fat Tuesday" in French, takes its name from the fat ox *(boeuf gras)* paraded through Parisian streets in ancient times by mock priests at the head of the carnival procession on the day before the beginning of Lent. The fat ox was a reminder of the required abstinence from meat during the coming Lenten season of fasting and prayer. Called *Shrove Tuesday* in England and previously *Pancake Tuesday* because pancakes were traditionally served on the day before Ash Wednesday, the festival of *Mardi Gras* may have its origins in the old Roman fertility festival of Lupercalia once held at the same time of the year.

Mark Twain!   A slurred Southern mispronunciation of *mark on the twine, six fathoms!,* called out when riverboat leadsmen sounded the Mississippi River with weighted twine. It is generally thought that former riverboat pilot Samuel Langhorne Clemens took his pen name from the leadsman's call *"mark twain!,"* but he actually took it from another pilot, Isaiah Sellers, who had first used it as a pseudonym.

maroon   (1) An old term for "to camp out" or "to picnic." (2) A historical term for a fugitive slave; also *marooner*. The word probably derives from the French *marron,* thought to be an adaptation of the Spanish *cimarron* (wild). *Maroon* also meant "a domestic animal that has run wild," for slaves were so regarded.

marr   A Louisiana hunter's term for a shallow, slushy, grassy pool in a swamp; possibly derives from *mire*.

marry together   Gullah for marry. "Dey done and got married togedder."

marster   An old, mainly black pronunciation of *master*. "There was even a fool who tried to interfere once, whereupon the negro turned upon him with the stick lifted and his teeth showing a little and said, 'Marster

mighty nigh Very nearly, almost; sometimes shortened to *might nigh*. "It's mighty nigh the end of the game."

mighty right Correct, right. "You were mighty right about that man— he's a damned liar."

mighty shouting right Darned right. "You're mighty shouting right I'm going to come."

mikal Mica. " 'We calls it mikal,' said the dirty old man. 'It's same as iron glass.' " [Jonathan Daniels, *A Southerner Discovers the South*, 1938]

mile Often used for the plural *miles*. "We done cut down ever'thing in two mile." [John Faulkner, *Men Working*, 1941]

Mimphis Some older citizens of Memphis, Tennessee will tell you they are from Mimphis, Tinnissee, though the pronunciation is no longer heard among the great majority of Memphians.

mind To remind; remember. "You mind what I say."

mind off To ward off (flies), shoo away. "Mind the flies off the food."

minners A pronunciation of *minnows*.

minor A small, shrill, singing voice. "The shrill, melancholy minor of Prissy was raised . . ." [Margaret Mitchell, *Gone With the Wind*, 1936]

minorest Smallest, least significant. ". . . the best he could possibly hope would be to lose it quick, since any semblance or intimation of the most minorest victory woulda destroyed him like a lightning bolt . . ." [William Faulkner, *The Mansion*, 1959]

mint julip An alcoholic drink, associated with Kentucky and the South since the early 19th century, made with bourbon, sugar and finely cracked ice and garnished with sprigs of mint, all served in a tall, frosted glass.

mirate To wonder, admire. "I suspect that Mr. Wiggins died mirating over the powers of evaporation in his climate." [Jonathan Daniels, *Tar Heels*, 1941]

miscegenation Marriage or cohabitation between a man and woman of different races, especially between blacks and whites. The term did not arise in the South; deriving from the Latin words for "to mix" and "race," it is said to have been coined in a pamphlet entitled *Miscegenation: the Theory of the Blending of the Races, Applied to the American White Man and Negro*, published anonymously by New York journalist David Goodman Croly (1829–1889) in 1863.

mischiefs Mischievious children. " 'Little mischiefs! Wull you look at them showing off,' said Miss Adele." [Eudora Welty, *The Optimist's Daughter*, 1972]

miserable Old term for *miserably.* "Eggs is miserable scarce."

misery An ache or pain. "I got me a misery in my stomach." [Marjorie Kinnan Rawlings, *Cross Creek,* 1942]

mislick An awkward slash that cuts oneself. "He was making wild slashes with a knife when he made a mislick and slashed his own thigh."

miss A Southern courtesy title used with a woman's first name only, whether she is married or not, as in Miss Scarlett of *Gone With The Wind. Miz* is used before a married woman's last name, as when Scarlett became Miz Hamilton. To complicate matters, however, *Miss* often sounds like *Miz* in Southern pronunciation.

Miss Elizabeth A term used by blacks to describe any white female employer, the female counterpart of *Mr. Charlie* (q.v.).

Missippi; Missip; Massassip Common pronunciations of *Mississippi* by black and white Mississippians and other Southerners. " 'I seen the Missippi River at Memphis once,' Ned said." [William Faulkner, *The Reivers,* 1962]

missis; missus Wife; the term is common outside the South as well. "The missis is out."

Mississippi One theory holds that the Chippewas named the river for which this Southern state is named the *mice sipi* (the big river), which white men spelled *Mississippi.* The

Magnolia State, at one time called the Bayou State, was admitted to the Union in 1817 as our 20th state. For another possible derivation of *Mississippi,* see FATHER OF WATERS.

Mississippi bottom Any bottomland situated along the Mississippi River.

Mississippi Bubble A disastrous financial scheme devised by Englishman John Law in France in 1717, in which he issued currency based on what he predicted would be great gains through trade in Louisiana and other parts of the Mississippi region.

Mississippi butternut A Confederate soldier from Mississippi, because of the color of his uniform.

Mississippi canebrake See CANEBRAKE.

Mississippi coondom "During the early 1840s the Whig party was frequently denounced as the aristocratic party of the slaveholders, the democracy of Mississippi designating the local organization as 'the empire of Mississippi coondom." [Arthur Cole, *The Whig Party in the South,* 1913]

Mississippi jager A famous longbarreled, muzzle-loading rifle used by American hunters of big game; also called a *yager.*

Mississippi River See FATHER OF WATERS.

Mississippi roarer Once a disparaging term for a violent, rowdy type of person common along the Mississippi.

Mississippi state   An old term for any one of the states in the Mississippi Valley.

missy   An old, mostly black pronunciation of *Mrs*.

mistis   A common pronunciation among black slaves for *mistress*. "I'll take it to the mistis and tell her the truth."

Missouri   *Missouri* is either the name of a Sioux tribe, "people of the big canoes," living in the region, or comes from an Algonquian word adopted by the French meaning "muddy water," in reference to the Missouri River. The Show Me State was admitted to the Union in 1821 as our 24th state, having previously been the Missouri Territory.

Missouri toothpick   A bowie knife. See also ARKANSAS TOOTHPICK.

Mr. Charlie   Originally the term for a boss or overseer, *Mr. Charlie* is now black slang in the South and elsewhere for a white man or white people in general; also *Charlie, Charles, Chuck*.

Mr. Lincoln's War   The Civil War.

misuse   To abuse, hurt. " 'Fore God!' Het hollered. 'He [the mule] fixing to misuse the cow!' " [William Faulkner, *The Town*, 1957]

mite   A bit, a little; also, someone or something that is very small. "In a mite of time." [Marjorie Kinnan Rawlings, *The Yearling*, 1938]

mite of trouble   A little trouble. "In all the time I've lived here, I've never had a mite of trouble with the neighbors." [Erskine Caldwell, *Jenny By Nature*, 1961]

Miz   Mrs.; a title of respect for a married woman in the South since long before *Ms.*, which is pronounced the same way. " 'They all got married sooner or later, somehow. That's right, because whoever heard of an old-maid whore? There ain't no such thing Miz Jones—Miz Brown—Miz Smith—Miz Hotrocks—Miz Biggerbottom.' She giggled again. 'That's what I want—a last name . . . I've got to get me one soon because I'm sure-God on my way to growing old.' " [Erskine Caldwell, *Love and Money*, 1954] See also MISS.

mizzling   Drizzling, raining fine drops. ". . . and why He should turn around for the poor, mizzling souls of men that can't even borrow tools in time to replace the shingles on His church, I don't know either." [William Faulkner, "Shingles for the Lord," 1943]

Mockingbird State   A nickname for Florida.

mommocked up   Damaged or defaced.

monkey nigger A contemptuous, offensive expression for a black houseservant dressed in fancy clothes; the term was used in pre-Civil War times by whites, especially poor whites, and some blacks. "He knew it without being aware that he did; he told Grandfather how, before the monkey nigger who came to the door had finished saying what he said, he seemed to kind of dissolve . . ." [William Faulkner, *Absalom, Absalom!*, 1936]

moodie An old, perhaps obsolete term for a sweet potato; it takes its name from *Bermuda*, from where it was first brought to the American South.

moondown The time when the moon appears to go down.

moon pie A round pastry with marshmallow filling sold in many parts of the South.

moonshine Liquor made illicitly by individuals with no distilling license; in this sense, *moonshine* dates back to the late 19th century. The name reflects the fact that the liquor was made surreptitiously, at night under the light of the moon. It was first used in this sense in the American South, although the British previously used the term to mean any smuggled liquor.

more Sometimes heard in constructions like *more better, more lonesomer, more messier, more righter, more worser, more tireder,* etc.

more better Better, in Cajun speech. "My horse more better as (than) that."

more rain, more rest A saying once popular among black workers in the South.

mortgage-raiser A lazy or do-nothing farmer. "All Starnes had ever raised was a mortgage, so Stribling paid for the funeral." [William Faulkner, "Hair," 1931]

mornglom; mornglown Morning twilight, an hour before dawn. "They left at mornglom."

mosey To stroll or saunter about in a leisurely manner, an expression used in the South, West and, to a lesser degree, in the rest of the country. According to *Webster's* and most authorities, the Spanish *vamos* (let's go) became *vamoose* in American English, which begot the word *mosey* as defined above. " 'Well I just thought I'd mosey down the street and look around.' " [Calder Willingham, *Rambling Rose*, 1972]

mosquito hawk Dragonfly; darning needle.

mossback A reactionary, a person living in the backwoods; used in other regions as well. "We thought of course that he and his new aldermen would have repealed it for no other reason than that one old mossback like Colonel Sartoris had to convince another old mossback like Mayor Adams to pass it." [William Faulkner, *The Town*, 1957]

mostest Most. "He got there fustest with the mostest drinks."

Mother of Commonwealths The state of Virginia, a term used since the 19th century.

Mother of Presidents The state of Virginia.

Mother of States Another nickname for Virginia, because it was the first settled of the original states.

mought Might. " 'They mought have kilt us, but they ain't whupped us yit, air they?' " [William Faulkner, *Absalom, Absalom!,* 1936]

Mount Vernon George Washington's home, a national shrine, was named after Vice Admiral Sir Edward Vernon by George Washington's half-brother Lawrence, who served under Vernon during the War of Jenkin's Ear (1739). Vernon also gives his name, or nickname, to *grog.* He was called Old Grog by his men after the impressive grogram coat he often wore on deck. But when he cut down on his men's rum rations and ordered that the rum be watered down, his men defiantly named the adulterated rum *grog* after the admiral.

mouth organ Harmonica; also called *French harp.*

moves like dead lice are falling off Moves very slowly. "He moves like dead lice are falling off him."

m'sieu Mister; French, often used in the Louisiana-French dialects.

mucha Gullah for many. "Ben is gwine to stop sayin' so mucha sinful words."

much oblige (Pronounced muchablige) Thank you, thanks; also much obliged. "Muchablige for the drink, ma'am."

muda grass Bermuda grass.

mudcat A Mississippian. See also MUDCAT STATE.

Mudcat State "Mississippi is occasionally spoken of humorously as the Mudcat State, the inhabitants being quite generally known as Mud-cats, a name given to the large catfish abounding in the swamps and the mud of the rivers." [Maximillian Schele De Vere, *Americanisms,* 1871]

muddy enough to bog the shadow of a buzzard Muddy enough to mire down the slightest thing. "Pa said that mud would bog a buzzard's shadow."

mud lark See SLOW BEAR.

mud lump "Small islands of bluish clay suddenly emerge from the [shallow] water . . . These are the famous mud lumps of the Mississippi." [*Putnams' Magazine,* May 1868]

mudsill An old opprobrious term first applied to members of the white laboring class in South Carolina and then applied by Southerners to all

Northerners during the Civil War period and after. "White niggers, mudsills, Northern scum, Base hirelings, hear me, and be dumb." [James Stoddard, *Vanity Fair*, March 1860]

muley Stubborn. "He sure is a muley fella."

mumble peg Mumblety-peg, a game played with a pocketknife in which the object is to stick the knife in the ground in a number of prescribed ways. *Mumblety-peg* is more common, but the old Southern *mumble peg* is more correct as the name comes from the phrase *mumble the peg,* which refers to an old rule calling for the losing player in the game to pull a peg from the ground with his teeth.

Murfreesboro The Southern name for the Tennessee Civil War battle called Stone River in the North.

muscadine See SCUPPERNONG.

muss A mess or disorder. "Things are all in a muss."

mussy Mostly black pronunciation of *mercy.* "Mussy on us!"

mutton corn An old term in parts of South Carolina for early *(matin)* corn.

my Sometimes omitted in speech, as in "I never in life hear Pa sing so hard before."

my heavenly day! A common exclamation. " 'My heavenly day!' Ma screamed. 'Handsome's gone!' " [Erskine Caldwell, *Georgia Boy,* 1943]

my mama didn't raise a (or no) stupid child (or fool) Don't take me for stupid.

N

nairn Not any, not a one. "Ah don't have nairn."

naked as a boiled chicken Stark naked. " 'I'll jerk every yellow hair out of your head! I'll rip off every piece of your clothes till you're naked as a boiled chicken!' " [Erskine Caldwell, *Jenny By Nature,* 1961]

narrow-asted; narrow-headed Epithets defined in the quotation following. " 'He insulted me,' Boon said. 'He told Son Thomas I was a narrow-asted son of a bitch.' Now Mr. Hampton looked at Ludus 'All right,' he said. 'I never said he was narrow-asted,' Ludus said. 'I said he was narrer-headed;' 'What?' Boon said. 'That's worse,' Judge Stevens said. 'Of course it's worse,' Boon said, 'Can't you see? And I ain't even got any choice. Me, a white man, have got to stand here and let a damn mule-wrestling nigger either criticize my private tail, or state before five public witnesses that I ain't got any sense." [William Faulkner, *The Reivers,* 1962]

nary Not. "Ain't nary a one come last night."

nary red An old expression meaning "not a (red) cent." "I ain't got nary red."

Natchez Trace An old, once-popular route that began as a series of buffalo trails; it stretched over a total of 700 miles: from New Orleans to Natchez, Mississippi and then on to Nashville, Tennessee.

natural sorry Stupid, very slow. "That ol' boy is natural sorry."

nature Often used to mean "libido" or "sex drive."

naw'lins Persistent Louisiana pronunciation of *New Orleans,* heard in other Southern states as well.

nearabout Nearly. "We can make twelve bales of cotton, near 'bout every year." [John Faulkner, *Men Working,* 1941]

nebber A mostly black pronunciation of *never.*

needcessity Necessity. "Bring all your needcessities." [James Still, "On Double Creek," 1940]

needful Necessary.

Negrah A common Southern pronunciation of *Negro.*

Negro breakdown See BREAKDOWN.

Negro English An offensive term for black dialect.

Negro quarter The housing for blacks on plantations in slavery times; often called the *Quarters*.

nekkid; nekked Naked. See usage example at COMPLICATE UP.

nervous as a long-tailed cat in a room full of rocking chairs Very nervous indeed, often with eyes darting around.

neutral ground (1) The dividing area between the two sides of a highway; used primarily in Mississippi. (2) In New Orleans, a term for a traffic circle.

never hit a lick Made no effort, didn't lift a finger.

nevermore A word associated with the South from Poe to Faulkner. "Quentin didn't answer. He lay still and rigid on his back . . . breathing hard but slow, his eyes wide open upon the window, thinking 'Nevermore of peace. Nevermore of peace. Nevermore Nevermore Nevermore.'" [William Faulkner, *Absalom, Absalom!*, 1936]

neversomeless A black term for *nevertheless*.

never turned a tap Made no effort, never lifted a finger.

new ground Land that has recently been cleared of trees for farming.

New Orleanian A resident of New Orleans.

New Orleans boat A 19th-century flat boat, with sides boarded like a house, about six feet high, and with a roof covering it; also called a *Kentucky boat*. It was used in both Southern and Western waters.

New Orleans oven "The graves [in New Orleans] are also elevated. The dead are buried in [oval] sepulchral houses, which are termed here 'ovens.' These often contain three or four tiers. Those belonging to the wealthy are frequently very handsome, and built with marble walls." [John Wortley, *Travels . . .*, 1851]

New Orleans salt Poison. "'He got off the steamboat with the six black people.' Herman Basket said, and a big box in which something was alive, and the gold box of *New Orleans salt* about the size of a gold watch. And Herman Basket told how Doom took a puppy out of the box in which something was alive, and how he made a bullet of bread and a pinch of the salt in the gold box and put the bullet into the puppy and the puppy died." [William Faulkner, "A Justice," 1950]

nick A Louisiana term for a pile of wood.

nickel A nickel's worth. "Gimme a nickel of candy."

nig An obsolete, offensive term meaning "Negro" or "nigger."

nigger An offensive term for an African-American, and often any dark-skinned person, first recorded in about 1640. The word derives from the Spanish *negro* (black). The derogatory term *nigger* has been used in many expressions, including *nigger drunk* (extremely drunk), *nigger worshiper* (one who favored emancipation or one who now supports black political causes), *nigger killer* (a slingshot), *nigger crib* (a segregated railroad car), *nigger breaker* (an overseer especially severe in his treatment of slaves), *nigger hound* (a person who caught fugitive slaves) and *nigger dog* (a dog trained to catch slaves), among many others.

nigger baby "Among the cant words produced by the late Civil War, *nigger babies* also became very popular; the term originated with the veterans serving under the Confederate General Hardee, who gave that name to the enormous projectiles thrown into the city of Charleston by the Swamp Angel of General Gillmore, as his monstergun in the swamps was ironically called." [Maximilian Schele De Vere, *Americanisms*, 1871]

niggerly A perhaps obsolete term for *niggardly*, a folk etymology.

nigger out An obsolete, offensive term once meaning "in Southern phraseology," according to *Bartlett*, "to exhaust land by the mode of tilling without fertilization pursued in the slave states."

Niggra Common Southern pronunciation of Negro. " 'Now wait a minute! I never said a word about the niggras [Daddy said], and you misrepresent me constantly on that point. Damn you, darlin', I am not antiniggra!' " [Calder Willingham, *Rambling Rose*, 1972]

night on to Almost; also *nigh on to*. "It was night on to sunrise when he got home."

night rider One of a band of mounted men in the South during Reconstruction who rode at night, terrifying blacks and black sympathizers.

ninny Breast milk or a breast.

no-count No good, worthless, good-for-nothing; of no account. " 'All birds got to fly, even them no-count dirty ones,' said Missouri from the porch." [Eudora Welty, *The Optimist's Daughter*, 1972]

no ham and all hominy An old term meaning "all work and no pay."

nohow In no manner, no way. "I can't do it nohow."

Noisette rose The beautiful blush noisette rose variety was crossed from two other plants in Charleston, South Carolina by plantsman Philip Noisette in 1816.

nome Pronunciation of *no, ma'am*. " 'Nome,' I said, 'I ain't hungry, I'll eat when I git home.' " [William Faulkner, "Two Soldiers," 1943]

no more chance than a kerosene cat in hell with gasoline drawers on No chance at all. "He thinks he'll beat me, but he ain't got more chance than a kerosene cat in hell with gasoline drawers on."

no more chance than a mouse has of drinking milk out of a saucer with a cat Almost no chance. "I've heard it said over and over that an older woman like me has no more chance to marry a worthwhile man in this day and age than a mouse has of drinking milk out of a saucer with a cat." [Erskine Caldwell, *Jenny By Nature,* 1961]

no more chance than a pig in a dog race No chance at all.

no more shame than a naked whore on a bedquilt No shame at all. See usage example at MAN-FEVER.

non compos mentis time of the month Time of a woman's period, menstruation. "Daddy . . . muttered something to the effect that it must be the non compos mentis time of the month for Rose . . ." [Calder Willingham, *Rambling Rose,* 1972]

none Sometimes used for "at all" as a form of double negative in sentences like "It shouldn't hurt you none." ("It shouldn't hurt you at all.")

noon Eat lunch with, or gather together with, at noon. "I'd not insult my neighbors that-a-way. We'll noon with them." [Marjorie Kinnan Rawlings, *The Yearling,* 1938]

North Carolina; South Carolina Both states really honor three kings. *Carolina* derives from the Latin *Carolus* or *Carolana* (Charles). Originally dedicated to France's Charles XI in the 16th century, the territory now comprising North and South Carolina was next named for England's Charles I. Charles I granted the patent for the Carolinas to Sir Robert Heath in 1629, and Heath called the territory *Carolana* in his honor. This it remained until 1663 when Charles II granted a new patent and the colony was called *Carolina* in his honor.

North Carolina Yankee An obsolete term for any industrious South Carolinian farmer newly arrived from North Carolina.

Northern coffee See SOUTHERN COFFEE.

nose like a preacher for sin and fried chicken A knack for finding or discovering something. "Flem [Snopes] his-self, with his pure and simple nose for money like a preacher's for sin and fried chicken." [William Faulkner, *The Mansion,* 1959]

no slow fuckin'! Work faster, no malingering. A guard to chain gang convicts in the movie *J.F.K.* (1991): "Move it along. No slow fuckin'!"

no such of a thing No such thing. "You'll do no such of a thing." [Marjorie Kinnan Rawlings, "Cocks Must Crow," 1939]

not about to To have no intention at all of doing something.

not a circumstance to Can't be compared with. "He's not a circumstance to Henry."

notionate Peevish, impulsive. "She's mighty notionate when she's sick."

not one tittle Not one bit, not one iota. "Now, what it produced or failed to produce . . . would make not one tittle of difference in this present life." [William Faulkner, *The Mansion*, 1959]

not to know beef from bull's foot A phrase used in the South and elsewhere meaning to be exceedingly dumb; also *not to know B from bull's foot, not to know bees from bulls foot* and *not to know beeswax from bull's foot*.

noway Anyway. " 'I ain't none too pleased to have you around, noway [Jeeter said]' " [Erskine Caldwell, *Tobacco Road*, 1932]

noways In no way. "I can't no-ways recollect." [Marjorie Kinnan Rawlings, "Cocks Must Crow," 1939]

nowheres Nowhere. "It won't get you nowheres."

now I lay me Prayer, short for the common prayer beginning "Now I lay me down to sleep . . ." "Do you say your 'Now I lay me' in bed or kneeling down?"

N'Yawlins A common pronunciation of *New Orleans*.

outfavor To be better looking than someone. "She outfavors any girl in Louisiana."

outgrowed Outgrown. " 'I done outgrowed that too' [Reba said]." [William Faulkner, *The Mansion,* 1959]

outlander A foreigner; someone who lives in another place. "Don't get no ideee we're goin' to look at no outlander." [Marjorie Kinnan Rawlings, *The Yearling,* 1938]

out'n Out of. "Take it out'n the box."

out of snuff Very upset. "As we say in Texas, he's out of snuff."

outten the light Used by South Carolinians for *turn off the light;* also *cut off the light.*

outward Adam An obsolete term for one's body. "I had no sooner elongated my outward Adam, than they [had] at it again." [Davy Crockett, *The Adventures of Davy Crockett,* 1836]

overplus A surplus. "We have an overplus of supplies." [John Faulkner, *Men Working,* 1941]

over-topped Outbid at an auction. " 'I just start the bidding,' Eck said. 'I don't have to buy it lessen I ain't overtopped.' " [William Faulkner, *The Hamlet,* 1940]

over yonder In heaven; in the afterlife. "Dey don't sell po' niggers down the river over yonder." [Mark Twain, *Pudd'nhead Wilson,* 1893]

ox Used as plural instead of *oxen,* especially in poor rural areas. " 'I didn't know there was that many ox in the whole country' [Dude said]." [Erskine Caldwell, *Tobacco Road,* 1932]

oxen Sometimes used as singular. "He is a mighty good oxen."

P

paams Palms. "Accustomed to the brisk voices of upland Georgia, the drawling flat voices of the low country [Charleston] seemed affected to her. She thought if she ever again heard voices that said 'paams' for 'palms' and 'hoose' for 'house' and 'woon't' for 'won't' . . . she would scream." [Margaret Mitchell, *Gone With the Wind*, 1936]

paddlefish A fish, *Polyodon spathula*, found in the streams of the Mississippi; also called *bullfish, billdown* and *Biblefish*.

pain de babeurre A buttermilk bread of New Orleans.

pain perdu Pain perdu (lost bread) is usually called *French toast* outside of New Orleans.

paintless Unpainted. ". . . and he saw the weathered paintless store with its tattered tobacco and patent-medicine posters . . ." [William Faulkner, "Barn Burning," 1939]

pairsaul Pronunciation of *parasol*. "You can tote this pairsaul a while." [William Faulkner, "Raid," 1934]

palamity; palmity Without substance; highfalutin. "He's makin' palmity talk, fancy words, no substance."

Palm Beach suit A traditional suit made of a light fabric named after the city where the fabric originated.

palmeeter Palmetto tree.

palmetto A South Carolinian. See also PALMETTO STATE.

palmetto banner flag The state flag of South Carolina.

palmetto button A small button worn by nullifiers in South Carolina to distinguish them from Unionists.

Palmetto Chivalry An old term for the aristocrats of South Carolina.

Palmetto City A nickname of Charleston, South Carolina.

Palmetto Coast An old name for the coastal area around Charleston, South Carolina.

Palmetto Republic A nickname for South Carolina after the state seceded from the Union in 1860. "A salute of 100 guns was immediately fired in honor of the Palmetto Republic." [*Charleston Mercury*, December 25, 1860]

Palmetto State A nickname for South Carolina, whose state seal consists of a palmetto tree supported by twelve spears and a fallen English oak at the foot of the palmetto tree.

pamelas A confection made from grapefruit peel, sugar and water. This name is perhaps a corruption of the French *pamplemousse* (grapefruit).

Pamunkey Indians Once the leading tribe of the Powhatan confederacy of Virginian Algonquian tribes.

Panhandle State A nickname for West Virginia because of its shape on the map.

panne meat A New Orleans dish of breaded veal cutlet browned with onions.

parcel A bunch, a small group. "A parcel of men came up the path."

parch To roast. "Parch the pindars (peanuts)."

pardon Pardon me; French, often used in the Louisiana-French dialects.

parish The designation for a county in Louisiana.

passage Reservations, tickets. " 'I've got my passage,' Laurel said. 'The afternoon flight from Jackson on Monday.' " [Eudora Welty, *The Optimist's Daughter*, 1972]

passel A group, many; a corruption of "parcel." " 'Well, good-day,' he said. 'I just hope for the sake of the Confedricy that Bed Forrest don't never tangle with you with all the horses he's got.' Then he said it again, maybe worse this time because now he was already on a horse pointed toward the gate: 'Or you'll damn shore leave him just one more passel of infantry before he can spit twice.' " [William Faulkner, "My Grandmother Millard," 1943]

pass the biscuit The singular is used in this case to mean biscuits; that is, pass the platter or basket of biscuits.

pavement Used for *sidewalk* in parts of Maryland.

pawing Sexually molesting or feeling with the hands. " 'Stop pawing me,' she said. 'You old headless horseman Ichabod Crane.' " [William Faulkner, *The Hamlet*, 1940]

pay (one) no mind To pay no attention, pay no heed; also *pay no never mind*. "But she never paid no mind to that neither." [William Faulkner, "Shingles for the Lord," 1943]

peach and cane land An old term in Texas to describe land good for cultivation, from land with wild peach trees growing on it.

peach-orchard coal A term used in 19th-century Kentucky for a superior variety of coal.

peart Pert. "You look right peart." [Marjorie Kinnan Rawlings, *The Yearling*, 1938]

peckerwood (1) A poor white (though its earliest meaning was "woodpecker"). "The gentlemen and the Negroes are afraid of the red-necks, the peckerwoods who are pressing down upon the rich flat Delta from the hard, eroded hills . . ." [Jonathan Daniels, *A Southerner Discovers the South,* 1938] (2) A joking term. "His name for me was 'Peckerwood,' a shortened Dixie version of redheaded woodpecker . . . he'd beckon me over . . . and sing softly in his tenor voice: 'Heah a dime for you, Peckerwood. Brang me a nice cold dope [Coke] 'fo ah melt and run all ovah the flo'.'" [Calder Willingham, *Rambling Rose,* 1972]

peeled out Accelerated, pulled away from other cars in traffic, drove off at high speed. "He peeled out of the parking lot, and a police car took off after him."

peert Very fast, quick. "Buck called, 'Light me a smudge, boy, be peert.'" [Marjorie Kinnan Rawlings, *The Yearling,* 1938]

pelican flag The state flag of Louisiana, which consists of a red star upon a white field and the Louisiana emblem of a pelican feeding her young.

Pelican State A nickname for Louisiana, because the pelican is seen so often along its waters.

penny one Nothing at all. "He ain't got penny one."

penny-piece Short, small, frail. "Lem Forrester looked down at him and said, 'Why, you lettle ol' penny-piece,

you.'" [Marjorie Kinnan Rawlings, *The Yearling,* 1938]

perambulator Baby carriage; used in other regions as well. "Girls are born weaned and boys don't ever get weaned. You see one sixty years old, and be damned if he won't go back to the perambulator at the bat of an eye." [William Faulkner, "Hair," 1931]

perked up To have gained weight. "Sara Jane sure has perked up."

persimmon skin An offensive term for a light-complexioned black man or woman.

pet A boil, carbuncle, pimple, wart, etc. "I got a big pet on my cheek."

piazza A large porch; also called *veranda* or *gallery.* "Come on out on the piazza."

picayune An old term for a nickel, used in New Orleans and other areas.

picayunish Picky. "She sure is picayunish."

pick a crow To find fault with; to have a bone to pick; also *have a crow.* "I have a crow to pick with him."

pickaninny An old offensive word for a black child that appears to have derived from African slaves' pronunciation of the Portuguese *pequenino* (small child).

pick at Annoy, pester, aggravate. "Don't pick at your sister like that!"

picked before ripe Said of a short or very puny person. "He was picked before he was ripe."

pickle peach See GREEN PEACH.

piddle-diddle A North Carolinian term meaning "to delay or procrastinate." "Stop your piddle-diddlen'."

piddling around Fooling around, wasting time. "I'm o' no mind to set around waitin' breakfast and you two piddlin' around in the woods." [Marjorie Kinnan Rawlings, *The Yearling,* 1938]

pie Any baked dish that resembles a pie, such as macaroni pie, potato pie, etc.

piece A short way. "He lives a piece up the road."

Piedmont rice An old story holds that Thomas Jefferson stole seeds of this rice while traveling in Italy and smuggled them home in his pockets, despite the fact that Italy wanted to continue its monopoly on this type of rice and had made the crime of stealing the seeds punishable by death. Jefferson's introduction of the rice was important because *Piedmont rice* can be grown without irrigation.

pigeon-tailed coat An old-fashioned coat with tails. " 'You never bought a garment of clothes or shoes or a hat neither in your life,' Boon said. 'You got one pigeon-tailed coat I know of that old Lucius McCaslin himself wore.' " [William Faulkner, *The Reivers,* 1962]

piggin A small wooden bucket with one extended stave serving as the handle.

pigs' ears See LES OREILLES DE CO-CHON.

pilau A much-loved dish of the lower South consisting of rice cooked in poultry or meat broth.

pile on the agony An old phrase, not much used anymore, that was once fairly common in the South and other regions and means "theatrical or extremely exaggerated emotional behavior." "No one piles on the agony like she does, she belongs on the stage." Also *pile up the agony.*

piller Pillow; a pronunciation bordering on a new word that early Southern aristocrats borrowed from upper-class English speech.

pin A common pronunciation of *pen.*

pinder; pindar; pender Another word for peanut that was brought to the American South by slaves. It derives from the Kongo *npinda* and is used mostly in South Carolina. See also GOOBER.

pine straw Fallen needles of pine trees.

piney woods Woods abounding with pine trees, especially a rural backwoods area. " 'What is he—a locally renowned turpentine-and-rosing man up there in those Alabamy piney woods?' " [Erskine Caldwell, "Kathy," *Gulf Coast Stories,* 1956]

piney woods Georgian A derogatory term similar to POOR WHITE.

piney woods rooter A humorous term for a razorback hog.

pisen See PIZEN.

pissant; pisant A small, foul-smelling ant; a despicable person or thing.

pitch out To leave abruptly. "He pitched out for Alabama."

pity on us Common exclamation. " 'Well, pity on us, we got to have our meat. Who'll git it if you don't.' " [Marjorie Kinnan Rawlings, *The Yearling,* 1938]

pizen Poison; *pizen* or *pisen* is a pronunciation that the South's early aristocrats borrowed from upper-class English speech. " 'He shot a doe-deer and used the liver to draw out the pizen.' " [Marjorie Kinnan Rawlings, *The Yearling,* 1938]

pizzle-grease An ointment used for medical purposes made from fat boiled from a hog's pizzle (penis).

pizzlesprung Slang for tired, worn out, pooped; heard in Kentucky.

plague take it! An old oath or exclamation.

plantation Negro An old term for a slave working on a plantation. "His speech was a blend of the softly blurred speech of the Southerner, some of which is frankly borrowed from the liquid vernacular of the plantation negro." [Ripley Saunders, *Colonel Todhunter of Missouri,* 1911]

plat-eye Gullah for an evil spirit that lives in the woods.

play like To pretend. "Let's play like we have some money."

play pretty A toy; used mostly among mountain speakers, though it is recorded in Florida and other areas.

play the dozens To insult one another in a rapid exchange of insults, a phrase used by both whites and blacks. An example is found in a sequence in Erskine Caldwell's *God's Little Acre* (1933) where one character says to another: "If you want to play the dozens, you're at the right homestead." See also DOZENS.

pleased as a basketful of possumheads Very pleased indeed. This uncommon expression capitalizes on the possum's proverbial grin, or what seems to us a grin.

plug ugly *Plug ugly* describes "a city ruffian or rowdy" or any such disreputable character. First recorded as an Americanism in 1856, the word is of unknown origin, although one early source says it derived in Baltimore ". . . from a short spike fastened in the toe of [such rowdies'] boots, with which they kicked their opponents in a dense crowd, or as they elegantly expressed it, 'plugged them ugly.' "

plumb; plum Very, completely, squarely, quite. "I plumb forgot about it." According to an old joke: "There's a town [near Bluefield, West Virginia] called Plumbnearly—plumb down in West Virginia and nearly in Virginia."

plumb curdled Completely sour, mean, nasty. "And Pat eliminated him from horse-trading. And so he just went plumb curdled." [William Faulkner, *The Hamlet,* 1940]

plumb stark naked Naked.

plummy Rich, very desirable. "That's plummy soil."

plunder Junk, rubbish; any stored personal property. "Bessie jerked back the quilts on Dude's bed, and ran into the next room where the roof had fallen in. It was the other bedroom, the room where most of the children had formerly slept, and it had been deserted because one section of the roof had rotted away. It was filled with plunder." [Erskine Caldwell, *Tobacco Road,* 1932]

plunder room An attic; used in South Carolina.

po' Common pronunciation of *poor.*

pocasin; pocoson; poquoson An American Indian word for *swamp,* once more commonly used.

poh' boy; poor boy; po' boy A hero or submarine sandwich in Texas and other Southern states.

poke A small paper bag for groceries, etc.

poke a dead cat at To insult someone.

poke-easy A slowpoke, a lazy or slow person or animal.

Poke stalk In the presidential campaign of 1844, Southern supporters of James Polk carried tall stalks from the pokeweed plant through the streets as their standard. In Tennessee, ox drivers who favored Henry Clay covered the horns of their oxen with clay, and the Polk supporters gathered pokeberries and stained the horns of their own oxen with them.

pole fence A straight rail fence; used in Texas.

police Often pronounced *po*-leese.

poltroon Though standard English meaning "a wretched coward," the word is not heard much anymore save in the South. "It is a fact, I never lie, or not often. The writer who lies to his reader is not only a poltroon, but a bad writer besides." [Calder Willingham, *Rambling Rose,* 1972]

pompano A tasty fish of the genus *Trachinus* found along the Atlantic and Gulf coasts of America and especially common on the Florida coasts.

pone (1) The *pone* of the famous Southern *pone bread* and *corn pone* is from the Powhatan Indian word *apan* (something baked). Corn pone is baked in large, flat, oval, hand-shaped cakes. A variation of the word *pone* is recorded by Captain John Smith as early as 1612. (2) A lump, a swelling, a callous. "Marilyn had . . . pones on her feet." [Larry Brown "92 Days," 1990]

pony bread   PONE bread.

poontang   Thomas Wolfe used this word for the vagina or "a piece" in *Look Homeward, Angel,* and Calder Willingham used it more graphically in *End as a Man.* The expression, first referring to black women and now to both blacks and whites, might be expected to have a diverting story behind it, as unusual as *poontang* sounds, but it probably comes from the French *putain* (prostitute) by way of New Orleans.

poor   Often pronounced *po'* or *pore.*

poor boy   See POH' BOY.

poor buckra; po' buckra   POOR WHITE TRASH. " 'Poor buckra,' 'poor white trash,' or 'white trash,' are the terms by which the Negro designates them, and *poor* means a great deal in this connection. It includes not simply pecuniary poverty, but ignorance, boorishness and general social degradation. The Southern Negro never applies the term *poor* to anyone who has the manners and breeding of a gentleman, however light his purse . . . Sometimes they [the children] would have a falling-out, and the white children would say 'nigger,' and the colored ones would say

'po' buckra, po' buckra.' " [*Dollar Times,* December 11, 1856] See also BUCKRA.

poor colored trash   A white rejoinder to POOR WHITE TRASH.

poor-do   Scrapple; a term used mostly in the Southern mountains.

poor Joe   The *poor Joe* or *po' Joe,* as it is called, is another name for the great blue heron, especially in the American South. No "Joe" is honored by the name. It is doubtless from the Vai language of Liberia and Sierra Leone, where *pojo* means "heron," and was introduced to America by Vai-speaking slaves.

poorly; po'ly   Sick, ill. "I'm feelin' poorly."

poor white   "In discriminating Southern speech, it [poor white] was not used to include all white persons who were poor . . . The 'poor whites' were those who were both poor and conspicuously lacking in the common social virtues and especially fell short of the standard in certain economic qualities." [W. T. Couch, *Culture in the South,* 1941] An old black Southern rhyme goes

> My name is Sam,
> I don't give a damn.
> I'd ruther be black
> Than a poor white man.

poor white folksy   Of or pertaining to POOR WHITE TRASH. "I wouldn't do my hair in a three strand braid on no account; it is too poor-white-folksy fer me." [*Harper's Magazine,* August 1864]

poor white trash Lower-class white people. "There were white people who were poor and there were poor white people. The difference was absolute." [Jonathan Daniels, *Tar Heels,* 1941] The offensive term goes back at least to the early 19th century. "The slaves themselves entertain the very highest contempt for white servants, whom they designate as 'poor white trash.'" [Frances Kimble, *Journal,* 1833] Terms like POOR WHITE, *poor white trash,* REDNECK and PECKERWOOD are often slur names in about the same class as NIGGER.

pop A peanut shell that has grown without a nut in it and "pops" when pressed.

popskull Bad or illegal whiskey that can produce violent headaches.

porch baby A child too young to let run free.

pore Common pronunciation of *poor.*

possum To pretend, fake. "He closed his eyes and possumed sleep."

possum fat and hominy "'Possum fat and hominy' is a favorite dish with Western and Southern negroes." [William Blane, *An Excursion Through the U.S. and Canada. . . ,* 1824]

possum toddy A drink made from the fruit of the persimmon tree; once a favorite drink in the South.

post-bellum After the Civil War, a term that appears to have first been recorded in the South in about 1874.

potato hill A field of potatoes.

potato stomper; tater stomper A potato masher utensil.

pot likker The rich liquid left after boiling vegetables with fatty meat.

pounding A POUND-PARTY.

pound party An old custom of bringing food to a new minister's home, each donor giving a pound of preserves, groceries, etc. The custom is still practiced today but has been modernized. Donors give any nonperishable food, often canned foods, with no emphasis on the pound measurement.

powerful Very. "That was a powerful good meal."

powerfully Deeply. "A-studyin' and musin' powerfully." [Sidney Lanier, "9 from 8," 1884]

powerful much A lot; very much. "'When you see Tom [Ada said], tell him that his old Ma would like powerful much to see him.'" [Erskine Caldwell, *Tobacco Road,* 1932]

powerful way A considerable, imposing, sexual way; great sex appeal. "She'd marry quick enough then, because she's got a powerful way with her, woman-like." [Erskine Caldwell, *Tobacco Road,* 1932] It can also be used in a nonsexual way to mean simply "considerable," "imposing" or "impressive."

praise the Lord! Common exclamation. " 'Praise the Lord,' Jeeter said, 'what went and done that?' " [Erskine Caldwell, *Tobacco Road,* 1932]

praline The nut candy associated with New Orleans and the South is actually a 17th-century French invention. The Marechal du Plessis-Praslin got heartburn from eating almonds, one story goes, so his servant suggested that he have his chef brown the almonds in boiling sugar to make them more digestible and voila!—the praline. They were first called *Praslins* and then the spelling was altered to *pralines.* In the American South, of course, the readily available pecans replaced the almonds in the pralines.

pranking Fooling around; causing a commotion. "I wasn't pranking, officer, I was just standing here."

precious thang A term of endearment to any child or loved one.

prespire A common pronunciation of *perspire.*

pretty (1) Any pretty thing—a toy, ribbon, jewel, etc. " 'I done everything I can think of to make her satisfied and content [Lov said]. Every week I go to Fuller on pay day and buy her a pretty.' " [Erskine Cald-

well, *Tobacco Road,* 1932] (2) The vagina. "Miss Willie's been sitting there on that high step showing her pretty and he's been looking at her a right long time . . . Miss Willie is bare as a plucked chicken, except for one little place I saw . . . and he's got his pecker up." [Erskine Caldwell, "August Afternoon," *The Complete Stories of Erskine Caldwell,* 1953]

prize open To pry open. "Do you mean he took that damned screwdriver and prized open your mother's desk, too?" [William Faulkner, "That Will Be Fine," 1935]

process See CONK.

prone To impress deeply from an early age. "It just warn't proned into that dog to ketch rabbits."

prong To dig, poke. "They burst into loud idiot laughter, pronging each other in the ribs." [Thomas Wolfe, *Look Homeward, Angel,* 1929]

proud Glad, pleased, happy. "I'm proud you remembered . . . Proud to see you." [Marjorie Kinnan Rawlings, *The Yearling,* 1938]

prove up To prove. "If your hen proves up false to you . . ." [Marjorie Kinnan Rawlings, *Cross Creek,* 1942]

prowlin' Wandering about, hanging out. " '. . . he ain't a thing but a boy. Got his mind on nothin' but prowlin' and playin'.' " [Marjorie Kinnan Rawlings, *The Yearling,* 1938]

public woman A prostitute. "But he knew what his father's reaction to his marriage with a once-public woman would be . . ." [William Faulkner, *The Hamlet,* 1940]

pugnuckling Feeding horses. " 'What's pugnuckling?' I said. 'Try can you put your mind on knuckling up some feed for that horse,' Ned said to me, still louder." [William Faulkner, *The Reivers,* 1962]

puke A low, contemptible person. "He, sir, is a puke of the first order."

puke-stomached Weak-stomached, without courage. "All right. If you are too puke-stomached to do it yourself, tell me where it is." [William Faulkner, *The Hamlet,* 1940]

pukish Nauseated.

pulleybone Wishbone. "Who got the pulleybone last Thanksgiving?"

pullikins An old term for pincers or forceps.

pummy An old term for pulp, especially cane pulp.

pumpkin yam A yellow yam potato, so called because of its color.

pure Good, perfect; downright. "I cain't raise young uns in a pure thicket . . . I'm in a pure fix." [Marjorie Kinnan Rawlings, *The Yearling,* 1938]

purely Exceedingly. "They're purely friendly folk." [Marjorie Kinnan Rawlings, *The Yearling,* 1938]

purty Pretty. "She's real purty, the purtiest girl I ever seen."

pushencry A humorous old term for emergency. "In case of pushencry, you can depend on me."

puss Vagina, pussy; expertise at sex. "Lord love her, she had trouble keeping me home; her puss was just not that good." [Larry Brown, "Big Bad Love," 1990]

pussel-gutted; pussle-gutted; puzzle-gutted Big, protuberant-bellied; also *pus-gutted, pussy-gutted, pustle-gutted;* perhaps derives from *purse* or from the dialect term *puscle,* suggesting a swollen gut. "You durned fool, I sent word to you two days ago to get away from there before that pussel-gutted Hampton come prowling around here with that surrey full of deputies." [William Faulkner, *The Hamlet,* 1940]

pussy-gutted Potbellied or PUSSEL-GUTTED.

put a mouth on To cast a spell upon, put a curse upon.

put at To talk to someone persistently. "He'd put at Pop to wed me."

put down the laundry Do the wash or laundry; heard in New Orleans.

put him under the jail Said of one so bad they shouldn't just imprison him, they should bury him, put him under the jail.

put him up Put the dog outside, in another room, etc. "Put Rover up, will you, he's giving me a headache."

put on the cooling board See LAY ON THE COOLING BOARD.

put out Said of a tree, to make leaves in spring. "Gum is the first tree to put out." [William Faulkner, *The Hamlet*, 1940]

puts him on the funny side Said in Kentucky of a woman who turns down a man's marriage proposal. "She put him on the funny side."

puttened Put. "He puttened the cub in it . . ." [Marjorie Kinnan Rawlings, *The Yearling*, 1938]

put the bee on someone A phrase used in the South and other regions meaning "to exert pressure on someone."

put the cat on one To get the better of someone. "He sure put the cat on him."

put the rug To die. "He's about ready to put the rug."

puzzlement A puzzle, a mystery. "Hit's been a puzzlement to me all these years since it happened." [Marjorie Kinnan Rawlings, *The Yearling*, 1938]

Q

quadroon ball A fancy ball once held in New Orleans that, according to one old account, was "attended by part-Negro women and white men, often to enable the latter to choose mistresses." The term is first recorded in 1805.

quarter One-fourth mile. "I walked a quarter to the store."

quartering An old term meaning "diagonally." "I walked quartering across the street."

Quarters A group of houses or cabins for blacks on a plantation in the days of slavery and after; also *Negro quarter*. "The black people live down in the Quarters."

Queen City of the Mississippi St. Louis, Missouri; also called *Queen City of the Mississippi Valley*.

Queen of Floods An old name for the Mississippi River. "Through a vast uncultivated territory coursed the Queen of Floods and her many tributaries" began a newspaper article in 1832.

qu'est-ce c'est? What is it?; French, often used in the Louisiana-French dialects.

quick as a dog can lick a dish Very quickly. "There's not a female alive who can be trusted when they've got man-fever—they'll take a man away from you as quick as a dog can lick a dish." [Erskine Caldwell, *Jenny By Nature*, 1961]

quid A political party of pro-John Randolph men that stood against Jefferson and Madison in the early 19th century.

quietus To put an abrupt halt to. "His wife put the quietus to that flirting of his."

quile down Mostly Southern mountain talk for quiet down. "Get her quiled down."

quill An old rural term meaning "to move at a rapid pace." "He was really quillin' along."

quills A simple musical instrument made by slaves from pieces of reed.

quilting Gullah term for a quilting bee. "He never said a word when she stayed all day at a quilting."

quince drink An alcoholic drink made from quinces in the early South; often used as a purgative.

189

quiring An archaic word for choiring. "He went on down the hill, toward the dark woods within which the liquid silver voices of the birds called unceasing—the rapid and urgent beating of the urgent and quiring heart of the late spring night." [William Faulkner, "Barn Burning," 1939]

quituate An old humorous word meaning "to leave school before graduating," deriving from *quit* and *graduate*.

quiver bug An insect apparently common in Georgia but very rarely mentioned in print. " 'What you see, nigger?' Jimson asked, trembling like a quiver bug. 'You see something scary?' " [Erskine Caldwell, "Big Buck," *The Complete Stories of Erskine Caldwell*, 1953]

R

rabbiteye blueberry A blueberry bush native to the Southern United States and widely grown there. It is so called because to some the berries on the tall (up to 20-foot-high) plants resemble rabbit eyes.

rabbit tobacco *Rabbit tobacco,* or "rabbit terbaker," as Uncle Remus called it, is balsamweed, a plant used as a tobacco substitute by youngsters, despite its taste. It takes the name "rabbit" because it grows wild in fields where rabbits run.

racket store A store similar to a five and dime store. "I bought him a cheap pair at the Racket store." [Thomas Wolfe, *Look Homeward, Angel,* 1929]

raft A lot, a considerable amount of. " 'I expect he's got a wife and a raft of children to provide for.' [Jeeter said]." [Erskine Caldwell, *Tobacco Road,* 1932]

rag-baby A rag doll.

raggety; raggedy Ragged. "Get that raggedy thing out of here."

(a) rag on every bush A lot of women on a string. "That Don Juan has a rag on every bush."

rag-tag and bob-ends Mixed diverse elements; Perhaps related to *ragtag and bobtail,* meaning "riffraff, rabble." (The ragtag and bobtail of every nation poured into the frontier in search of gold.) ". . . the two of them creating out of the rag-tag and bob-ends of old tales and talking, people who perhaps had never existed any where . . ." [William Faulkner, *Absalom, Absalom!,* 1936]

rain bullfrogs To rain heavily.

rain bull yearlings To rain very hard.

raise To rear or bring up. " 'I'd have loved to ketched him leetle, Pa, and raised him.' " [Marjorie Kinnan Rawlings, *The Yearling,* 1938]

raising Rearing or breeding. "Folks around here don't got no raisin'."

raising more hell than a pig caught under a gate Vigorously protesting.

raise it A Gullah expression meaning "to begin singing a song." "Brer Dee raised it [a hymn], and all the people joined in."

raise sand; raise some sand To make a great disturbance. "If we don't go, the teacher will raise sand."

Ral Syphilis. "He thought he had the Old Ral."

rampageous Rowdy. "The whole rampageous bunch of them broke up the town."

ramrod rolls "The men added as dessert some 'ramrod rolls' from their knapsacks, and this was the first time Scarlett had ever seen this Confederate article of diet about which there were almost as many jokes as about lice. They were charred spirals of what appeared to be wood. The men dared her to take a bite and, when she did, she discovered that beneath the smoke-blackened surface was unsalted corn bread. The soldiers mixed their ration of corn meal with water, and salt too when they could get it, wrapped the thick paste about their ramrods and roasted the mess over camp fires. It was as hard as rock candy and tasteless as sawdust . . ." [Margaret Mitchell, *Gone With the Wind*, 1936]

ramshackle A ramshackle house. "They live in a ramshackle down by the tracks."

ramshagging Destroying; trashing. "But that door leads back into the house and he don't aim to have none of us master carpenter candidates maybe ramshagging the joint as a farewell gesture on the way out." [William Faulkner, *The Mansion*, 1959]

ramstudious; ramstugionus Rambunctious, full of high spirits.

'ramus An ignoramus. "The Gordons were Mississippi swamp folk, often called . . . peckerwoods, or 'ramuses, taken from *ignoramuses*, which is what everybody thought they were." [James Street, *In My Father's House*, 1941]

rantankerous Unruly, mean, bad.

rare (1) To rear or raise. "She rared him and his sister." (2) To rave, yell. " 'His Ma'll rare,' Penny said." [Marjorie Kinnan Rawlings, *The Yearling*, 1938] (3) To rear up.

rare as a virgin in a cathouse Very rare, almost nonexistent.

rascals Slang for female breasts. "She's got cute little rascals."

rather To prefer. "I rather that restaurant outside New Orleans."

rations Prepared food. "I had hot rations on the stove." [Marjorie Kinnan Rawlings, "Cocks Must Crow," 1939]

rat-killing A Texas term for busy work or what one is doing. "I got to get back to my rat-killing."

rattlesnake colonel A humorous title of respect. "Had it been a rattlesnake I should have been entitled to a colonel's commission, for it is a common saying here that a man has no title to that dignity until he has killed a rattlesnake." [Alexander Hamilton, *Works*, 1885]

raven Gullah for enthusiastic. "He was raven about his Daddy."

razee An old, perhaps obsolete Southern term for a drunken spree.

R.C. Royal Crown Cola, a favorite soft drink in the South. "I'm gonna get me an R.C. and a MOON PIE." See also COKE and DOPE.

reach To move something after reaching for it and obtaining it. "He reached our dinner bucket down from the limb and handed it to me." [William Faulkner, "Shingles for the Lord," 1943]

realm A Ku Klux Klan term for a state or region under the control of a *Grand Dragon*.

rearing plantation A historical term for a worn-out plantation used mainly for breeding and raising slaves for sale.

reb A Confederate soldier or sympathizer, this contraction of *rebel* arising at about the same time as the longer word in 1861.

rebel See REB.

rebel brigadier See CONFEDERATE BRIGADIER.

rebel yell; rebel yale All Southerners are capable of a *rebel yell,* an untranslatable, peculiarly wordless cry that has been with us at least since the Civil War and may be a corruption of the English fox-hunting *"tallyho"* but is always "a prolonged, high-pitched, bloodcurdling cross between a yell (yale) and scream." One expert believes that the rebel yell originally used in combat in the Civil War and intended to strike terror into the hearts of the enemy, came from the Creek Indians, loosely combining "the turkey gobbler's cry with a series of yelps." The high-pitched, blood-chilling yell was then (according to this theory) borrowed by Texans and adopted for their *Texas yell,* which eventually became the *rebel yell.* Others, however, say the Texans got their yell from the Comanchee Indians. In any case, everyone agrees that the "yah-hoo" or "yaaaaaheee" of fiction writers sounds nothing like the rebel yell.

reckon In *Life on the Mississippi,* Mark Twain wrote that "the Northern word 'guess' . . . is but little used among Southerners. They say 'reckon.' "

recollection This word had use in times past as a noun, as in "He has the most recollection for remembering names that I ever heard tell of."

reconstructed rebel An old term for a Southerner forced to accept the U.S. reconstruction plan for the South after the Civil War. See also UNRECONSTRUCTED SOUTHERNER.

reconstructionist A RECONSTRUCTED REBEL.

redbugs Another name for chiggers, the larva of a mite of the family Trombiculidae, which cause severe itching.

Red Cross Banner The Confederate battle flag is the most familiar symbol of the South but was not the official flag of the Confederacy, an honor that goes to the STARS AND BARS. The familiar Red Cross Banner was designed by General P. G. T. Beauregard following the first battle of Bull Run, after Southern troops in the confusion of battle mistook the Stars and Bars for the Union flag, which it resembled. The flag that most Southerners fly today is this Red Cross Banner or battle flag, not the Stars and Bars.

redeye A cheap, potent whiskey, the term dating back to the early 19th century.

redeye dish gravy A favorite Southern gravy made from the frying pan juice of country ham, thickened with flour and frequently containing a little coffee for color and flavor; also called *redeye gravy*. "I'll cook you a nice meal, Milo. You can have fried chicken and yams, or ham and redeye dish gravy, or country steak." [Erskine Caldwell, *Jenny By Nature*, 1961]

redeye gravy See REDEYE DISH GRAVY.

redneck A poor, white, often rowdy Southerner, usually one from a rural area. The word, which is sometimes derogatory, has its origins in the sunburned necks of farmers and outdoor laborers and originally meant a poor farmer. "A redneck is by no means to be confused with po' whites. Poor white men in the South are by no

means all po' white even in the hills. Lincoln and Jackson come from a Southern folk the back of whose necks were ridged and red from labor in the sun." [Jonathan Daniels, *A Southerner Discovers the South,* 1938] See also POOR WHITE, RAMUS.

red Republican A post-Civil War term used by Southerners for someone with violent radical Republican views.

Red Strings See HEROES OF AMERICA.

red-tail An old, derogatory term for a Native American.

red worm An earthworm; used in North Carolina

reeceet Recipe. "You got the reeceet for that gravy?"

refugee A term used in the South during the Civil War meaning "to leave a dangerous area for a safer place." " 'But Miss Honey and Miss India . . . refugeed to Macon, so we did not worry about them.' " [Margaret Mitchell, *Gone With the Wind,* 1936]

regulator Various illegal or extralegal organizations in the Carolinas were called regulators after their intention to purge the area of horse thieves and other criminals.

relish To enjoy; enjoy waiting. " 'We'll dress and cook hit now,' she said. 'We'll relish hit together right now.' " [William Faulkner, *The Mansion*, 1959]

retch A pronunciation of REACH. "Retch me that cup."

rice bird A nickname for an inhabitant of a rice-growing area, especially a South Carolinian.

Rice Coast Charleston and the South Carolina low country, where rice has been planted since Captain John Thurber, a Yankee shipmaster, presented a packet of it to an early settler on putting into Charleston harbor late in the 1680s. The only crops that rivaled rice in the region until after The Civil War were cotton and indigo.

rice rat A rat, *Hesperomys palustris,* abundant in Southern rice fields.

rid Rode. "Pap caught the mule and rid on down to Killegrow's." [William Faulkner, "Shingles for the Lord," 1943]

ride someone bug-hunting This century-old expression means "to punish someone by beating or whipping him severely or mercilessly ridiculing him." "Mind your manners, or he'll ride you bug-hunting. He'll rub your nose in the dirt."

ridge-runner A contemptuous term for a mountaineer.

right Very. "She's a right pretty girl and right nice, too."

right addled Very confused, lost. "She's right addled about the whole thing."

right by Alone, all by. "I'll go down to Augusta right by myself."

rightly (1) Really. "I don't rightly know the answer." (2) Very. "Your eyes are rightly blue."

right much Very much. "It upset her, as we say in North Carolina, right much." [Jonathan Daniels, *Tar Heels,* 1941]

right on Certainly, nevertheless, anyway. "He's a 'thievin' varmint, right on." [Marjorie Kinnan Rawlings, *The Yearling,* 1938]

right sharp A large quantity. "He picked a right sharp of beans from his garden."

right smart (1) A great deal or large number; very large or great; very much or many. "There was right smart of water in the ditch." "He is right smart of a man." (2) A good idea; also *right smart idea.* " 'What was hit? Remember, I got a right smart I can tell Mr. Provine and Major both now.' " [William Faulkner, "A Bear Hunt," 1934]

right smart of A great deal of. "He's got a right smart of work there, but he's making a right smart of money."

rings him off Said in Georgia of a woman who turns down a man's marriage proposal: "She rang him off."

rippit A fight, a fist fight.

rip-roodle An obsolete term meaning "to romp or go tearing about."

risin A boil; also *rising*. "Penny said, 'Well, Job takened worse punishment than this. Leastways, none of us ain't got risins.'" [Marjorie Kinnan Rawlings, *The Yearling*, 1938]

rising See RISIN.

rising beauties Big beautiful firm breasts, the expression made famous in American literature by this passage beginning: "'I ain't ashamed of nothing,' Ty Ty said heatedly. 'I reckon Griselda is just about the prettiest girl I ever did see. There ain't a man alive who's ever seen a finer-looking pair of rising beauties as she's got . . .'" [Erskine Caldwell, *God's Little Acre*, 1933]

Roanoke An Indian wampum once used in what is now Virginia, named after Roanoke, Virginia.

roasting ears Sweet corn, usually meant to be roasted or eaten on the cob.

Robert E. Lee cake A kind of coconut cream cake that was a favorite of General Robert E. Lee.

robustous An old, humorous term for *robust*.

rode hard and put up wet To have been treated badly, abused. "I feel like I been rode hard and put up wet, like a mistreated horse."

room-keep "The new word to room-keep, arising from the exigency which forces impoverished Southern families to content themselves with renting a few rooms and keeping house in them, has not yet obtained currency." [Maximilian Schele De Vere, *Americanisms*, 1871]

root, hog or die To get down to work and shift for oneself; originally a Southern expression, first recorded by Davy Crockett and based on the hog's unfailing ability to provide for itself by rooting the ground with its snout, which yields it everything from trash to truffles.

rough and easy A way of living comparable to living off the land without doing much farming. "We'll do the clarin,' we'll plow a field now and agin, but it's our nature to make a livin' what I reckon you'd call rough and easy." [Marjorie Kinnan Rawlings, *The Yearling*, 1938]

rove Look or glance all around. "He poised on the balls of his feet, roving his gaze." [William Faulkner, "Dry September," 1931]

rubber-nosed woodpecker in a petrified forest Someone completely incompetent for a job.

ruction A quarrel or fight.

rud To redden.

rue back To attempt to back out of a trade. "We swapped knives, and then he wanted to rue back."

ruint Ruined. " 'It's already ruint, sister,' the man said, 'but you'll have to put oil in it if you're going in to Augusta and back to Fuller again.' " [Erskine Caldwell, *Tobacco Road*, 1932] "When my clothes gets ruint or wore out [Ned said], I has to buy new ones myself.' " [William Faulkner, *The Reivers*, 1962]

run A small creek. "He's down by the run."

run a Mick "Running a Mick was to get an Irishman drunk; induce him to enlist for two or three hundred dollars; and obtain five times the sum from citizens desirous of procuring a substitute." [Junius Browne, *Four Years in Secessia*, 1865]

run around in the dark of the moon To lead a wild life. " 'Now you understand [Daddy said] we have three immature children here and don't be offended, but the question frankly and candidly is this: do you run around in the dark of the moon, are you a wild hotcha character or do you behave yourself?' " [Calder Willingham, *Rambling Rose*, 1972]

run haunts An old term meaning "to chase after something really not there." "When the dogs would rush in there was not a thing up there in the tree, and the darkies would immediately say, 'Let's go home; that dog was running haunts.' " [*Congressional Record*, January 11, 1900]

run-mad Used to describe someone who has gone mad. "He kept babbling like a run-mad man."

running one's mouth Talking too much. " 'All right [Boon said]. Jump out. You want to visit Alabama. You done already made yourself fifteen minutes late running your mouth.' " [William Faulkner, *The Reivers*, 1962]

rutting A euphemism for sexual intercourse. See usage example at WHY IN PLUPERFECT HELL.

S

sack   Small bag; a bag for groceries. "He got a paper sack of peanuts." "I've got two sacks of food in the car."

safe   A kitchen cupboard for storing food. "They's rations in the safe . . . You hongry?" [Marjorie Kinnan Rawlings, *The Yearling*, 1938]

sagaciate; segashuate   ". . . among Southern negroes *segashuate* means to associate with." [*American Speech*, February 1933] Generally, however, *sagaciate* or *segashuate* means "to get along with, endure" and is always used in a jocular fashion: "How does your corporosity sagaciate the inclemancy of the weather?"

salad tomatoes   A synonym for small cherry tomatoes in the Southern plains area.

Saltzburgher   A historical term for a member of a group of colonists from Salzburg, Austria who settled in Georgia early in the 18th century.

salubration   An old term for "celebration" or "rejoicing."

the same dog bit me   I feel the same way about it, I share your sentiments exactly. " 'I'd ruther eat cold bread in the woods than hot puddin' in the house.' 'Now you know,' Penny said,

'the same dog bit me.' " [Marjorie Kinnan Rawlings, *The Yearling*, 1938]

same like   Gullah for "just like." "He barked same like a dog."

Sambo   Blacks have probably been vilified with more slurnames than any other group in U.S. history. All are, of course, disparaging and offensive, and this includes *sambo,* a nickname for a black in the South and elsewhere. Ironically, the Little Black Sambo of the children's story who helped give the term widespread currency is really an East Indian, but *Sambo* was with us long before the boy who melted the tiger to butter. Possibly of Southern American origin, the term was introduced via the slave trade. The word, some believe, derives from the Kongo *nzambu* (monkey), which became *zambo* (bolegged) in Spanish. Alternate choices are the Foulah *sambo* (uncle) or the Hausan *sambo* (second son). It may be that *sambo* simply comes from the name of a West African tribe called the Samboses, mentioned in European literature as early as 1564.

sand buggers   A food made of vegetables in patty- or burger-like shape. "There were poke greens with bits of white bacon buried in them; sand buggers made of potato and onion

198

and the cooter [turtle] he had found crawling yesterday . . ." [Marjorie Kinnan Rawlings, *The Yearling*, 1938]

sand-hiller A country CRACKER in Georgia and South Carolina sandy areas.

sand-lapper Someone from the Southern swamps or lowlands as opposed to the mountains.

sandy Claus A pronunciation of *Santa Claus.*

sang A shortening of *ginseng.* "In Alleghany Co., Maryland, is Sang Run, which is a well-known sanging ground." [John Bartlett, *Americanisms*, 1877]

sass (1) Most garden vegetables, including lettuce, radishes, potatoes, onions, etc.; often *garden sass.* The word probably derives from *sauce.* (2) Talk back to. The word is an old English one used in other parts of the United States as well. "Don't sass me, young man!"

sassafac Pronunciation of *sassafras.*

sassinger An old, humorous term for sausage.

sattisfactual; sattafactual Satisfactory. "Everything is sattisfactual." The word is best known for its use in the song "Zippedy-do-da."

Save us from the devil and make a place for us in heaven. Amen. A mostly Southern prayer quoted in Erskine Caldwell's *Tobacco Road* (1932).

saw See SO.

saw gourds An old term meaning "to snore, to saw wood."

sawyer A log or tree caught in a river so that it hinders navigation; Mark Twain used the now-historical term in *Life on the Mississippi* (1883).

says which? What?; often used in reply to a question that was not clearly heard. *Say what?*, often heard in black speech, serves the same purpose.

say what? See SAYS WHICH?

scalawag Undersized, lean, undeveloped cattle of little use to American ranchers and farmers in the West; used toward the middle of the 19th century. The term came to be applied to disreputable people, rogues, scoundrels, rascals and those who refused to work and had a special use in the South after the Civil War to describe anyone willing to accept Yankee Reconstruction. As for *scalawag* itself, the word remains something of a mystery. It may derive from the Gaelic *sgalag,* one of the Shetland Islands that is known for its dwarf ponies and cattle, which could have been considered worthless. Other suggestions are the Scottish *scurrvaig* (a vagabond), the Latin *scurra vagas* (a wandering buffoon) and the English dialect *scall* (skin diseases). No one seems to know why the word, with so many possible British ancestors, is first recorded in

America. In 1862 the *Charleston* (South Carolina) *Mercury* wrote of a group "composed of ten parts of Andy Johnson Union men, ten of good lord and devil-ites, five of spuss, and seventy-five of scallawags."

scamp A Southern fish, *Mycterspercca falcata,* so called because of its ability to steal bait off lines successfully.

scaper A rascal. "You sly old scaper." [Marjorie Kinnan Rawlings, *The Yearling,* 1938]

scare-cat Scaredy-cat, one who is afraid of the slightest things. " 'Go on in yonder, scare-cat,' ordered the mother." [Eudora Welty, *The Optimist's Daughter,* 1972]

scare the puddin' out of Humorous term for "to cause a bad fright." "He scared the puddin' out of me."

scarify To scare or frighten.

scat *Gesundheit!* or *God bless* you! after someone sneezes; *scat* is common throughout the South and is especially much preferred in Arkansas over the other terms.

scatter-gun A shotgun.

schiese A German term for a paddle for handling loaves of bread; the word was once common in the Shenandoah Valley area.

scissortail flycatcher A Southern bird, *Milyulus forficatus,* also called the *bird of paradise.*

scotch To help out in a small way.

Scovilite One of a band of Carolina thieves put down by the REGULATORS. "The culprits . . . appealed to the royal governor for protection, and he sent a commissioner among them to adjust their differences. This was Colonel Schovel, who, instead of redressing the grievances on both sides, armed the depredators and paraded them for battle; they were, consequently, called Schofilites." [Joseph Johnson, *Traditions . . . in the South,* 1851]

scrape cotton To hoe weeds from around cotton plants.

scratch A bit, very little. " 'Sometimes I think it's just the old devil in her,' Lov had said several times. 'To my way of thinking, she ain't got a scratch of religion in her.' " [Erskine Caldwell, *Tobacco Road,* 1932]

scratchback Corn bread.

screamer Someone or something of great size, strength, abilities, etc. *Alabama screamer* and *Kentuck screamer* are synonyms.

scrimped and saved An expression used mostly in the South, though it did not originate there and is used nationally. " 'God damn it, listen,' " Miss Reba said. 'Missie had that tooth made, so she could put it in and take it out—worked and scrimped and saved for [it] . . .' " [William Faulkner, *The Reivers,* 1962]

scringe To cringe. "She scringed away from him."

scrouge over To squeeze over. "Scrouge over and give me some room."

scrouging Moving one's body around restlessly, energetically. See usage example at CAUGHT.

scuppernong The muscadine grape —a Southern grape, *Vitis rotundifolia,* with large sweet fruit. The name derives from the Scuppernong river and lake in Tyrrell Company, North Carolina where the grape was discovered in the 18th century.

scuppernong arbor An arbor made of native SCUPPERNONG grape vines. ". . . I knew at once that he was absent without knowing that he would now be in the scuppernong arbor drinking with Wash Jones." [William Faulkner, *Absalom, Absalom!,* 1934]

scuppernong claret A homemade wine of the native SCUPPERNONG grapes. ". . . as one man to another above the suave powdered shoulders of women, above the two raised glasses of scuppernong claret or bought champagne." [William Faulkner, *Absalom, Absalom!,* 1936]

scuppernong wine Wine made from the SCUPPERNONG. There are also scuppernong ice cream and sherbert.

scutter Rascal. "That frazzling old scutter jumped three feet high." It can also mean an expert.

Sea Island cotton A long silky cotton, *Gossypium barbadense,* once grown extensively on the sea islands of South Carolina, Georgia and Florida.

secede In the sense of "to secede from the United States," *secede* appears to have first been used by Thomas Jefferson in 1825: "Possibly their colonies might secede from the Union."

secesh A humorous, disparaging term used by Northerners for Southerners during the Civil War.

secesh colonel A humorous term for a COLONEL.

secessia A Northern term for the Southern Confederacy during the Civil War. See also SECESH.

"Secession Two-step" A popular dance song written by a Georgian at the start of the Civil War.

Second American Revolution The Civil War.

second settin' A child born to a woman near menopause. "He's the second settin' and he ain't to blame fer hatchin' out peculiar." [Marjorie Kinnan Rawlings, *The Yearling,* 1938]

Second War of Independence The Civil War.

see Gullah for *seen.* "Dey ain't never see one annudder."

seed Saw. "I've seed a bear." [Marjorie Kinnan Rawlings, *The Yearling*, 1938]

seed-tick coffee Any of several coffee substitutes (rye, okra seed, parched wheat, sweet potato, etc.) used in the South during the Civil War. "With seed-tick coffee and ordinary brown sugar costing fabulous sums and almost impossible to be obtained, it is small matter of wonder that the unsatisfied appetite of the rebel sharpshooter . . . often impelled him . . . to call a parley with the Yankee across the line." [*Century Magazine*, September 1888]

seein' pleasure Gullah for "having pleasure." "When I git old an tired seein' pleasure . . ."

seeing of Seeing. " 'Sister Bessie and Dude is married,' she said. 'Now you go away and stop trying to see inside. You ain't got no business seeing of them.' " [Erskine Caldwell, *Tobacco Road*, 1932]

sell down the river A universal phrase that has as its source the punishment of a slave by his owner by selling him to a sugar-cane plantation on the lower Mississippi, where work conditions were at their worst. The expression appears to have been first recorded in Harriet Beecher Stowe's *Uncle Tom's Cabin* (1852).

send to hell and the devil To punish severely. "When I catch him, I'll send him to hell and the devil."

serious as a jackass in a graveyard Very serious, often foolishly so. "Down in Texas we'd say he's serious as a jackass in a graveyard."

settee Often used for "couch" or "divan" in the South.

settin' up A wake for a dead person.

settled ". . . and the grey-headed bachelor, avuncular and what old Negroes called 'settled,' incapable now of harm, slowed the blood and untroubled now the flesh by turn of wrist or ankle, faint and dusty-dry as memory now the hopes and anguishes of youth . . ." [William Faulkner, *The Town*, 1957]

shack An old term meaning "to live like a bachelor in a shack." "They sent their wives away and shacked for a time."

shadetail A squirrel.

shame Gullah for *ashamed*. "You ought to be shame."

sharecropper A tenant farmer who in exchange for his labor receives certain necessities, such as lodging, and a share of the crop he raises. The sharecrop system dates back to the end of the Civil War in the South; the first sharecroppers were freed slaves.

sharp enough to hew his (her) own coffin Gaunt and sharp-featured from the hard living and hunger that relatively few Americans are familiar with today. "He knew then how true it was what Clem had said about Arch's sharecroppers' faces becoming sharp enough to hew their own coffins. His hands went to his chain before he knew what he was doing. His hand dropped when he had felt the bones of jaw and the exposed tendons of his cheeks." [Erskine Caldwell, "Kneel to the Rising Sun," *The Complete Stories of Erskine Caldwell*, 1953]

Sharpsburg The Southern name for the Civil War battle known as Antietam in the North.

shatters Pine needles that have fallen to the ground.

she-crab soup A creamy soup made with crabmeat; also called *crab soup*.

shavings Kindling wood, in Maryland.

shed A shed snakeskin. "The shed stretches . . ." [Marjorie Kinnan Rawlings, *Cross Creek*, 1942]

shed of; shut of Rid of. "She couldn't get shed of him."

shed (cut) one's baby teeth To acquire sophistication, to not be easily duped.

shell out To suddenly run away. "We shelled out from there."

shenanigin' around An old term meaning "fooling around."

Sherman's bummers During the Civil War, Southern civilians were, as one historian puts it, "in mortal terror of the lawless crew known as 'Sherman's bummers,' who rode on the flanks of [the Union general's] army, accounts of whose fiendish outrages were on every tongue." See also BUMMERS; YANKEE BUMMERS.

Sherman's hairpins Southerners invented the term *Sherman's hairpins* for the mutilated railroad tracks that General Sherman's troops in their march through the South heated with fires of railroad ties and twisted into grotesque shapes so that they could not be repaired.

Sherman's monuments General Sherman's troops burned many civilian homes to the ground in their march through the South. Often chimneys were the only part of the houses left standing, and Southerners bitterly dubbed them *Sherman's monuments*.

she (he) thinks he (she) hung the moon and stars Someone who loves another madly and blindly, as if that person were a god. *She (he) thinks she (he) hung the moon* means that one is conceited or arrogant.

shin An old euphemism for *damn*. "Well, I'll be dad-shin'd!"

shine Moonshine, corn whiskey.

shinnery A term, meaning "a dense growth of small trees, especially scrub oaks," that derives from the Louisiana French *chênière*, meaning the same, and is heard principally in Texas and the Southwestern United States.

shiplap A term widely used in the South for wooden siding on a house. See also BOXING.

shipoke A euphemistic pronunciation of *shitepoke,* a species of heron.

shirttail Small piece. "He can sholy take care of this little shirttail of a farm while me and you are whupping them Japanese." [William Faulkner, "Two Soldiers," 1943] *Shirt-tail* can also mean "a distant relation," as in "He's a shirt-tail cousin I've never met."

shirt-tail boy A young boy. " 'Nobody but your folks'll bother with a little ol' shirt-tail boy like you.' " [Marjorie Kinnan Rawlings, *The Yearling,* 1938]

shirt-tail lads Youngsters. " 'Clint and me used to take off as shirt-tail lads with both our dogs and be gone all day up in the woods.' " [Eudora Welty, *The Optimist's Daughter,* 1972]

shirt-tail run An old, probably obsolete term meaning "a fast run," one in which one's shirttail flutters out behind one. "It was your intention to make a straight 'shirt-tail' from old Kentuck for your village." [*Spirit of the Times,* August 7, 1841]

shirt-tail woodpecker A woodpecker found in Georgia, so named for its white tail. "The shirt-tail woodpecker had been bothering us for a long time . . . The peckers lived in the old dead sycamore tree in our yard, and Ma said the sensible thing to do was to chop it down.

My old man said he would rather see the Republicans win every election in the county for the rest of time than lose the sycamore." [Erskine Caldwell, *Georgia Boy,* 1943]

shivaree A mock serenade with kettles, pans, horns, etc., especially for newlyweds; any elaborate noisy celebration; from the Mississippi Valley French *charivari,* meaning the same.

shivering owl The screech owl; used mostly in the South Atlantic states.

sho' Sure. "I sho' is hot."

shoemake A pronunciation of *sumac.*

sholy A pronunciation, often but not always black, of *surely.* " 'Where's that tobacco sack I give you to keep yestiddy?' he said. 'You sholy ain't lost it?' " [William Faulkner, *The Reivers,* 1962]

sho' nuff (1) Sure enough, a pronunciation known to millions nationally from thousands of comedy routines. (2) Really, actually (in a question). "Are you that old, sho' nuff?"

shook his foot Had sexual intercourse. " 'Why you ever let him get on the bed without the money in your hand first, I don't know [Minnie said]. I bet he never even took his britches off. A man won't take his britches off, don't never have no truck with him a-tall; he done already shook his foot, no matter what his mouth still saying.' " [William Faulkner, *The Mansion*, 1959]

shore Sure. "You shore kin figger." [Marjorie Kinnan Rawlings, *The Yearling*, 1938]

shore don't; sure don't According to Fayetteville, Arkansas author Ervin Lewin: "One [Southernism] that I have encountered here and nowhere else is this: When I phone a store, such as a hardware, asking about some tool or other product, the response is nearly always, if it's not available, an almost invariably cheerful, 'Shore don't.' Why the basic 'sure' I don't know, but you can just about count on it."

shorely; sholy Surely.

short-commons A scanty allowance of food. "These short-commons aren't fit for a dog."

short sweetenin' Sugar; also used in Midland United States. See also LONG SWEETENIN'.

short talk Cursing, vilification.

short-weight Light, weak, unsubstantial. " 'When I get set and ready for a man, I'm going to get me a good one,' she said, inspecting him disdainfully. 'I ain't aiming to waste my good self on no short-weight plowboy.' " [Erskine Caldwell, "The Courting of Susie Brown," *The Complete Stories of Erskine Caldwell*, 1953]

shouldn't ought to Shouldn't. "You shouldn't oughta go to that jook joint."

shout To clap hands, tap feet, sway the body while singing spirituals.

shovelful of chicken tracks Very little; something inconsequential or next to nothing. "I wouldn't give you a shovelful of chicken tracks in trade for that, Tubby." [Erskine Caldwell, *The Earnshaw Neighborhood*, 1971]

Show Me State A nickname for the state of MISSOURI.

shuck Shook or shaken. "He shuck down the apples from the tree."

shuck out To leave. "He shucked out for parts unknown."

shucks. See BLUEBACKS.

shut my mouth! A Southern expression of surprise that has become a national cliché because it has been used so often in comic routines. Another similar expression is *"Hush my mouth!"*

sich A pronunciation of *such*. "It was no sich thing."

sick at (to) the stomach To be nauseous; to throw up, vomit. "He knew he was going to be sick at the stomach." [William Faulkner, "Dry September," 1931]

side meat Bacon or salt pork. ". . . and maybe he tried to pursuade her to eat too—the side meat he had probably brought home from the store Saturday night . . ." [William Faulkner, *Absalom, Absalom!*, 1936] ". . . the plate of fried sidemeat and canned corn and tomatoes stewed together . . ." [William Faulkner, *The Mansion*, 1959]

side pork   See SIDE MEAT.

sight   A lot, a large amount. "That bear moves a sight faster." [Marjorie Kinnan Rawlings, *The Yearling*, 1938]

signify   A black expression meaning to try to make a big impression on someone, to be pretentious. "Stop your signifying, man."

sigogglin   (pronounced *sy-gog-line*) Crooked, out of plumb or line. "You sawed that board off a little sigogglin."

silver gray   An elderly member of the home guard in several Southern states prior to the Civil War.

silver gray squirrel   A hunter's name for the Southern gray or Carolina squirrel, *Sciurus carolininsis*.

simblin   A variety of gourd or squash.

'simmon   A shortening of persimmon. " 'That's why you see me cakewalking with the ex-rebs to the illegitimate tune about 'simmon seeds and cotton.' " [O. Henry, *Roads of Destiny*, 1904] *'Simmon* and *persimmon* figure in many old Southern proverbs: "The longest pole takes the 'simmons"; "we all come down like 'simmons after frost"; "to be a huckleberry over someone's persimmon" (to be beyond someone's capacity); "to bring down the persimmons" (to win the prize); "to be a jump above someone's tallest persimmons"; "to walk off with, or rake up, the persimmons" (to win the prize); and "a huckleberry to a persimmon" (nothing in comparison with something else).

Simon Legree   Any hard boss; after the cruel planter and slave dealer in Harriet Beecher Stowe's *Uncle Tom's Cabin* (1852).

since the hogs et grandma (my little brother)   A long time ago. "I haven't had so much fun since the hogs et grandma."

singing   A gathering of people for the singing of songs. "I ain't seen her since the singing down by the river."

sinning shame   A terrible shame; an act contrary to religious standards. " 'They [the church congregation] always do their best to make me think everything I do is a sinning shame.' " [Erskine Caldwell, *Jenny By Nature*, 1961]

sippin' whiskey   The best quality bourbon.

sister   (1) A form of address to a woman, especially in poorer rural areas. See usage example at RUINT. (2) Used as a form of address by parents to female children in many

Southern families, as it is indeed in other areas. See also BROTHER.

sistern Sisters. "We are brethren and sistern here."

sivving Sifting. " 'Sifting,' he said. 'Sivving. Like flour. Straining folks through the back yard . . .' " [William Faulkner, *The Mansion*, 1959]

skeered Scared. "Ahead of him Tommy guffawed. It skeered him too, I'll be bound." [William Faulkner, *Sanctuary*, 1931]

skeet To spew water out the mouth from between the teeth.

skipper Old term for a meat maggot.

skin the bear at once An old term meaning "to quickly get down to brass tacks, or business." "But now, to skin the bar at once, can you give me and five other gentlemen employment?" [*New Orleans Picayune*, 1844]

sky-winding Helpless or senseless. "I knocked him sky-winding."

slack An old term for "impudence." "Don't give me none of your slack, young man."

slam-bang Exactly, smack dab. "He was slam-bang in the middle of it."

slash pine Any pine tree that grows in slashes, that is, low coastal areas. In North Carolina the slash pine, *Pinus taeda,* is also called the *swamp pine*.

slat A stick of chewing gum; mostly a Southern mountain term.

slaunch An angle. "I guess I've got the right slaunch on that point."

slave auction An auction at which slaves were sold in the "internal and infernal trade."

slave catcher A person, usually white but sometimes an American Indian, or even black man, who captured fugitive slaves for the reward.

slave depot A public area from where slaves were sold and shipped. "Along the streets you saw the sign, 'Slave Depot—Negroes bought and sold.' " [Albert Richardson, *The Secret Service . . .* , 1865]

slave driver One who supervised working slaves. "There was a dreadful slave-driver . . . carrying a wand with an iron tip heated red-hot." [Frances Baylor, *On Both Sides,* 1885]

slave melodies See SLAVE SONGS.

slave pen A holding area for slaves. "It was at Washington we first saw the slave pen. It is usually a sort of wooden shed, whitewashed, and attached to the residence of a slave-dealer." [Andrew Reed and James Matheson, *A Narrative of the Visit to the American Churches,* 1835]

slave songs A synonym, in slavery times, for what are today generally called "spirituals." "The plaintive slave songs have won popularity wherever the English language is spoken." [*Harper's Magazine,* May 1881] These spirituals were also called *slave melodies.*

slave quarters The area on a plantation occupied by the dwellings of slaves.

sleazy Flimsy. "She wore a sleazy red dress."

slip A wheelbarrow; used in Louisiana.

slipe An old term for a slice. "Cut me a slipe of lemon."

slipper An old term for any low-cut shoe or oxford.

slipperslide A colorful North Carolina term for a shoehorn.

slit-lip A harelip. " 'I bet he don't even know she's got a slit-lip on her [Dude said].' " [Erskine Caldwell, *Tobacco Road,* 1932]

slop Garbage, swill. "His pigs was eatin' the slop."

sloppin' good Very good; used in reference to foods. "That sure is sloppin' good Texas gravy."

slopsided Lop-sided, leaning to one side.

slorate An old term meaning "to destroy or kill large numbers of, slaughter."

slouch hat A soft, floppy hat of British origins made popular by Confederate troops.

slow bear A term foraging Southern troops used during the Civil War for farmers' pigs that they killed and ate. *Mud lark* meant the same.

slut An old term for a light made of a saucer of grease with a rag as a wick.

smack Squarely, completely. "We come up with him right smack at the edge o' Juniper Creek." [Marjorie Kinnan Rawlings, *The Yearling,* 1938]

smack dab Squarely, exactly. "It hit him smack dab in the eye."

smarter than a hooty owl Very smart, wise.

smart up To spruce up. "She's right pretty when she's smarted up."

smile like a basket of chips An old, perhaps obsolete expression for someone smiling widely in great happiness. "She smiled like a basket of chips."

smithers Fragments, smithereens. "He broke it up into smithers."

Smithfield ham "Almost due south from Suffolk . . . is Smithfield, the home of the famous Virginia Smithfield hams, grown on a peanut diet and cured with smoke of the burning shells." [*Concrete Highway Magazine,* September 1924]

smoked Yankee A derogatory term, now historical, applied in the South and other areas of the country, to black people, especially black Union soldiers. In 1864 a newspaper reported: "In Baltimore they call the negro soldiers, who are abundant here, 'smoked Yankees.'"

smooth Comb, brush; straighten. "'I must run upstairs and smooth my hair,' she told Stuart and Brent . . ." [Margaret Mitchell, *Gone With the Wind*, 1936]

s'mores A Southern treat made of toasted marshmallows and chocolate sandwiched between graham crackers and sometimes wrapped in tin foil, then heated over a campfire; so named because they are so delicious you always want "s'more"; now packaged nationally as a sandwich cookie to be heated in a microwave oven.

smothered pork chops Pork chops "smothered" with a thick sauce or gravy. The term probably derived from the Cajun use of the French word *etouffee* (smothered). Smothered dishes are genuine Southern cuisine.

snake An old nickname for a West Virginian.

snap bean String bean. "He has become rooted in . . . the exacting business of being a Virginian. He has learned to call string beans 'snaps.'" [*Saturday Evening Post*, July 24, 1943]

snap in her tits and power in her behind (ass) An attractive, sexy young woman. ". . . there is snap in her tits, all right, snap aplenty . . . there is snap in her tits and power in her behind." [Calder Willingham, *Rambling Rose*, 1972]

snapped An obsolete term meaning drunk. "You're about two-thirds snapped."

snapping turtle An old term for a mean-tempered, unpleasant person. "I am a Mississippi snapping turtle: have bear's claws, alligator's teeth, and the devil's tail; can whip any man, by G–d." [Christian Schultz Jr., *Travels on an Inland Voyage*, 1807–08]

snatch To treat angrily, verbally or physically; to snap at. "'Why you got to snatch a man just for passing the day with you?' Ned said." [William Faulkner, *The Reivers*, 1962]

snatching An old term meaning "charming, fetching." "That's a snatching dress you're wearing."

sniptious Smart, spruced up, neat, attractive.

snit A fit of weeping; a tantrum.

snollygoster "A Georgia editor kindly explains that a snollygoster is 'a fellow who wants office, regardless of party, platform or principles, and who, whenever he wins, gets there by the sheer force of monumental talknophical assummacy.'" [*Colum-*

bus Dispatch, Oct. 28, 1895] President Truman, however, from Missouri and famous for his use of such terms, defined a snollygoster as a "man born out of wedlock."

Snopesism A word coined by Faulkner for the taking over of the South by a grasping, greedy, money-grubbing middle class without any real culture, the word of course deriving from the Snopes family depicted in his novels of fictitious Yoknapatawpha County, Mississippi. "He had to be the sole one masculine feller within her entire possible circumarnbience, not jist to recognize she had a soul still capable of being saved from what he called Snopesism . . ." [William Faulkner, *The Mansion,* 1959]

snot-flyin' drunk Used in Peter Matthiessen's *Killing Mr. Watson,* (1990), which is very accurate in its use of South Florida dialect ca. 1900.

snuff dipping Using snuff by dipping a snuff brush or snuff stick into the snuffbox and then putting the snuff in the mouth; in earlier times the South was jocularly called "the land of snuff dipping."

snuff stick Usually a twig of the blackgum tree, its end chewed until it resembles a brush, that is used for dipping snuff.

so (1) A command intended to make a cow stand still during its milking; also *soo* and *saw.* (2) An old term meaning "straight"; used mainly in the South. "I like my coffee so." Can

also mean "the way I have it," "this way."

sock-dodger; soxdologer An old term for a very large thing.

soda pop Any carbonated soft drink.

sody Soda. See usage example at UNTECHED.

sody pop SODA POP. " 'Wouldn't you like for Mrs. Tubbs to bring you up a cup of coffee or maybe a Coca-Cola? She's usually got a bottle or two of sody pop in the icebox.' " [William Faulkner, *Requiem for a Nun,* 1951]

so far back in jail you can't shoot peas to him A saying made popular by Georgia Governor Marvin Griffin when he addressed civil rights protestors some years ago: "We'll put him so far back in jail you can't shoot peas to him."

so far south they call people from Georgia Yankees Deep in the Deep South. "I'm from so far South we call people from Georgia Yankees."

so fat he's (she's) in his (her) own way A very obese person.

soft berm A soft shoulder on the road; the term, although commonly Southern, is also encountered on road signs in other parts of the country. It could be argued that *berm* is not a regional dialect term, but a word dating back to the days of knightly chivalry, when in Norman times it meant "the ridge between the edge of the moat around a castle" and the castle.

softshell Baptist A Baptist more liberal than his HARDSHELL BAPTIST counterpart.

soft-shelled cooter See FLORIDA COOTER.

so hungry my belly thinks my throat is cut Very hungry, starving. "Jody said, 'I'm so hungry my belly thinks my throat is cut.' " [Marjorie Kinnan Rawlings, *The Yearling*, 1938]

Solid South A term much used in times past when the South's electoral votes could be counted upon by the Democratic party.

something on a stick Something very special. "He really thinks she's something on a stick." The "stick" here probably refers to an ice-cream bar stick.

someway Somehow; also *someways*. "I didn't someway even mind." [Marjorie Kinnan Rawlings, *The Yearling*, 1938]

sommers; some'eres Somewhere (somewheres).

sommumabitch Southern dialect for *son of a bitch*.

son Euphemism for *son of a bitch*. " 'Tell them, by God!' McLendon said. 'Tell every one of the sons . . .' " [William Faulkner, "Dry September," 1931]

son of a biscuit eater A euphemism for *son of a bitch*.

son of a bitch's son of a bitch The absolute worst of people. "All right, that's what we'll do: every Snopes he'll make it his private and personal aim to have the whole world recognize him as THE son of a bitch's son of a bitch." [William Faulkner, *The Mansion*, 1959]

Son of ebony An obsolete term for a black man, often shortened to *ebony*. Harriet Beecher Stowe used the term in *Uncle Tom's Cabin* (1852).

Sons of the South A secret organization, also known as the *Blue Lodge*, formed in Missouri in 1854 for the purpose of introducing slavery into Kansas and other areas of the United States.

soo See SO.

sop Gravy; bread dipped in gravy.

sora The common name of the Carolina rail, *Porzana carolina*, probably from an Indian name for the bird.

sorry Poor, worthless, contemptible. "That's one sorry fellow."

sorry girl A prostitute; mostly a term from the Southern mountains.

soul driver A person who took slaves to market to sell them; an overseer. The expression is recorded as early as 1774.

soul shark A disreputable, often itinerant, preacher.

sour dean A pronunciation of *sardine*. " 'It was a sour dean,' Ned said quietly. 'Don't lie to me,' grandfather said. 'Horses don't eat sardines.' 'This one do,' Ned said." [William Faulkner, *The Reivers,* 1962]

soured To have grown mean and nasty. " 'Old man Ab ain't naturally mean. He's just soured.' " William Faulkner, *The Hamlet,* 1940]

souse An old term meaning "to stick into." "Souse a pin into him, and he'll wake up all right."

South As a designation for the Southern states (states below the MASON-DIXON LINE), South was first recorded in 1781; the *North* as a term for the Northern states is first recorded in 1791.

South Carolina The eighth state admitted to the Union (May 23, 1788); nicknamed the Palmetto State. See also NORTH CAROLINA; SOUTH CAROLINA.

the Southern Chivalry " 'The Southern Chivalry' was a common phrase before and during the Civil War. It was claimed as a proud title by Southerners and their friends, but has always been heard and used by the North with a shade of contempt." [*Magazine of American History,* volume 13, 1885]

Southern brigadier See CONFEDERATE BRIGADIER.

Southern coffee Coffee mixed with chicory as opposed to pure coffee (Northern coffee).

Southern Confederacy This is a more recent term than CONFEDERACY. It wasn't coined at the time of the Civil War but is first mentioned in the writings of James Madison in about 1788.

Southerner This word for a resident of the South may have been first coined between 1820 and 1830. The term appeared first in *Western Monthly Magazine* in 1828.

Southern fried chicken Originally chicken fried in bacon grease, Southern fried chicken has been popular in the American South since before 1711, when the term *fried chicken* is first recorded there. It became popular throughout the country in the 1930s, when it was first widely sold at roadside restaurants.

Southern fringe tree See GRANDFATHER GRAYBEARD.

Southern gentleman This term for a courtly, well-bred Southerner dates back at least to the late 18th century. Clare Booth Luce, in *Kiss the Boys Goodbye,* offered this definition: "If you can shoot like a South Carolinian, ride like a Virginian, make love like a Georgian, and be proud of it as an Episcopalian, you're a Southern gentleman." But an anonymous infidel Yankee defined the chivalrous species as "one who rises to his feet when his wife comes in bearing the firewood."

Southern hospitality The words "Southern hospitality," the hospitality characteristic of Southern people and sometimes considered the epitome of sectional hospitality, have been traced back to 1819, when a traveler from the North wrote in his journal, "The mistress . . . treated us to milk in the true spirit of Southern hospitality." But the South was famous for its hospitality long before this, as it still is today, and the much-used phrase is surely older.

Southern names According to Mario Pei's *What's in a Word* (1968), in the South a greater number of first names can be both female and male than in any other area of the country. Such names include Pearl, Marion, Leslie, Beverly, Kim and Dana. Although these are all used as both male and female names in other sections as well, they are so used with more frequency in the South.

Southern pine See GEORGIA PITCH PINE.

Southlander An infrequently used synonym for a Southerner.

Southron (1) An old synonym for a Southerner that is based on an English word and dates back to the early 19th century. (2) A pronunciation of Southern. " '. . . two Americans, Americans, southron gentlemen . . .' " [William Faulkner, *Sanctuary,* 1931]

sowbelly Fat salt pork taken from the belly of a hog.

sow's bosom SOWBELLY; mostly a mountain term.

spaded Spayed. "They had their dog spaded."

spang Directly, exactly. " 'Out there in the chaparral,' he said quickly, 'about nine or ten miles from town, more or less.' 'Right spang at Friday River!' Bessie said severely, her whole attitude changing." [Erskine Caldwell, "To the Chaparral," *Gulf Coast Stories,* 1956]

Spanish moss The epiphytic plant *Tillandsia usneoides* of the southern United States, which has narrow, grayish leaves and grows in long festoons that drape the branches of trees.

spark An old term meaning "to court"; not confined to the South. "At first I thought he just never wanted me tagging after him, like he wouldn't leave me go with him when he went sparking them girls of Tull's." [William Faulkner, "Two Soldiers," 1943]

spatterdabs Pancakes.

spere Common pronunciation of *sphere.*

spigot Sometimes used instead of *faucet* in the South.

spit cotton To have difficulty spitting due to thirst or embarrassment. "When one is very thirsty and his mouth dry, the spittle white and sticky, he is said 'to spit cotton.' "

[Bennett Green, *Word-Book of Virginee,* 1899]

spittin' image Exactly alike. The germ of the idea behind this phrase has been traced back to 1400 by Eric Partridge, who cites the following example in *A Dictionary of Slang and Unconventional English* (1950): "He's . . . as like these as they had spit him." Similarly, in England and the southern United States, the expression *he's the very spit of his father* is commonly heard. This may mean "he's as like his father as if he had been spit out of his mouth" but could also be a corruption of "spirit and image." If the last is true, it would explain the use of "and image" in the expression since the middle of the last century. *Spittin' image* would then be derived from "he's the very spirit and image of his father," that is, the child is identical to his parent in both spirit and looks. The phrase is also written *spit and image, spitting image, spitten image* and *spit 'n' image.* See also BREATHING IMAGE.

spizzerinctum A rural Southern term meaning "energy, enthusiasm." "I wish I had his spizzerinctum."

splinters Kindling wood, in Georgia and North Carolina.

split To run away, to leave. The expression is recorded as far back as early 19th century Alabama, long before it is recorded as black musicians' slang in the 1950s.

splitting the log Getting money. "One of the most interesting meth-ods of banking gold and silver was to bore holes in large blocks of wood, fill the holes with coins, and drive tightly fitting pegs into them. Then the pegs were sawed off short. This left no way to remove the money except by splitting the log." [Everett Dick, *The Dixie Frontier,* 1948]

spoon bread A baked batter of pudding consistency made of cornmeal, milk, eggs and shortening, usually served as an accompaniment to meat and served with a spoon.

sporting house A brothel. " '. . . in the Memphis sporting house: don't forget that.' " [William Faulkner, *Requiem for a Nun,* 1951]

spraddle To sprawl out; straddle. "They set flat on the ground . . . with their legs spraddled out on either side of the . . . bolt." [William Faulkner, "Shingles for the Lord," 1943]

sprang A pronunciation of the season *spring.*

sprawly Sprawling. ". . . and we watched her write in the big sprawly hand that still looked like somebody thirteen years old in the ninth grade." [William Faulkner, *The Town,* 1957]

spurrer An old term for a *spurt,* as in "a spurt of water."

square The flower bud of the cotton plant.

squeezins Very powerful moonshine.

squinch To squint or draw together; to pinch or squeeze.

squush To squash, crush or squeeze. "Squush that bug.

stancheous An old term for *substantial*.

standin' in need of A common redundancy or extravagant term used in the South, as in "I'm standin' in need of some moonshine."

stand one up and down To vehemently insist. "She stood me up and down that I was wrong."

star (1) A pronunciation of *stare*. (2) A pronunciation of *stair*, as in "He's upstars."

starling Sterling. A pronunciation bordering on a new word that the South's early aristocrats borrowed from upper-class English speech.

Stars and Bars The official flag of the Confederacy during the Civil War. It had two broad red stripes separated by a wide white stripe commonly called the bars and a blue field in the upper left hand corner bearing a circle of stars (one for each of the seceded states). The Stars and Bars is often erroneously depicted as the RED CROSS BANNER, or Battle Flag, in Civil War illustrations.

starving-hungry As hungry as one can be, very hungry. "I know you must be starving hungry and all tired out . . ." [Erskine Caldwell, *Jenny By Nature,* 1961]

state-rights Democrat A designation for Southern Democrats espousing the doctrine of states rights from Civil War times to the present.

state-rights party The majority faction of the Democratic party in the South in Civil War times.

statriot A term based on "states rights" and "patriot" that was popular in the South during the Civil War period.

stay Reside. " 'Hidy, son,' he said . . . 'Which-a-way from here does Mr. Flem Snopes stay?' " [William Faulkner, *The Mansion,* 1959]

stick Penis. "A poor woman always takes better care of your stick than a rich one knows how! That's the law of the land from Sugar Creek to Park Avenue." [Erskine Caldwell, *The Earnshaw Neighborhood,* 1971]

stickman An old term for a country bumpkin.

stick to your own blood Side with your family, right or wrong. "You got to learn to stick to your own blood or you ain't going to have any blood to stick to you." [William Faulkner, "Barn Burning," 1939]

sticky A sweet bun made in Florida and other parts of the South.

still have some snap left in one's garters Probably a Southern expression dating back to the late 19th century and meaning "still energetic, not yet worn out." "I really think," Senator

Russell B. Long of Louisiana told the press on March 17, 1985, "that it's better to retire on Uncle Earl's terms, when you still have some snap left in your garters." Mr. Long was referring to his legendary uncle, former Louisiana governor Earl Long, who may have used the expression too.

still in the bed Often used for still in bed: "He's still in the bed, and we're ready to go."

stitch A short period of time. "There was a certain stitch of afternoon while the boy waited." [Thomas Wolfe, *The Web and the Rock*, 1939]

stob (1) Stab. "He stobbed a knife clean into his LIGHTS." (2) A stake; a stump; a stub.

stob pole A pole used to pole a boat along.

stoled; stold; stolt Stole, stolen.

stomp a mud hole in one's ass and walk it dry To beat up someone badly. "I wish I had you down here. I'd whip your ass. I'd stomp a mud hole in your ass and walk it dry." [Larry Brown, "92 Days," 1990]

stomp-down Downright. "Spot is a stomp-down good retriever."

stone wall nobody's yet clumb over Something no one has been able to do anything about or remedy. " 'I hate things dyin',' he said . . . 'Well [his father said], hit's a stone wall nobody's yit clumb over.' " [Mar-

jorie Kinnan Rawlings, *The Yearling*, 1938]

story A lie; a liar. "You are an old story."

straight-out Downright. "She's a straight-out liar."

straight up Exactly. "He was ready straight up to the minute."

straight up-and-dicular An old humorous term for *perpendicular*.

streaked meat North Carolina term for bacon.

strollop To wander aimlessly. "I was tired of strolloping around all of Alabama."

strowed Strewn. "There was puppies strowed all over the house and yard." [Marjorie Kinnan Rawlings, "Cocks Must Crow," 1939]

stubborn as a cross-eyed mule Very stubborn.

stubborn coal of conscience Moral principle. Perhaps the phrase is William Faulkner's creation, but it sounds familiar. ". . . he never entered their house again after he and Ellen married. I was young then; I was even young enough to believe that this was due to some stubborn coal of conscience, if not remorse . . ." [William Faulkner, *Absalom, Absalom!*, 1936]

study on To think, ponder, consider. " 'Father says for you to come and get breakfast,' Caddy said . . . 'I ain't studying on breakfast,' Nancy said. 'I going to get my sleep out.' " [William Faulkner, "That Evening Sun," 1931]

stump sucker   See CRIBBER.

submissionest   A Southerner before the Civil War who took the part of the North.

suck-egg   Egg-sucking and thus base, mean, no good; applied to men, dogs and mules. "He's as mean as a suck-egg dog."

suffocate for moisture   To die of thirst. " 'Wake up, Miss Reba [said Mr. Binford], before these folks suffocate for moisture.' Miss Reba poured the whiskey . . ." [William Faulkner, *The Reivers,* 1962]

sugah; sugar   (1) A term of endearment in many parts of the South for a woman, girl, man or boy. (2) A kiss or kisses. "Give me a little sugar, honey." Variations are *sugah candy, sugah doodle, sugah foot, sugah plum,* and *sugah pie.*

Sugar Bowl   (1) A nickname for Louisiana, famous for its output of sugar. (2) A college football end-of-season game held in New Orleans since 1936 and so named because the annual trophy is an antique sugar bowl.

sugar corn   Sweet corn, as opposed to the tough field corn.

sugar-mouthed   Flattering, obsequious. "[He seconded] the nomination of Roosevelt in a regular sugar-mouth speech." [Jonathan Daniels, *Tar Heels,* 1941]

sugar mule   Best mule. ". . . Pa always had a good excuse for not going, usually saying Ida, our sugar mule, had the colic and that he couldn't afford to leave her all alone until she got well . . ." [Erskine Caldwell, *Georgia Boy,* 1943]

sugar-pie   Sweetheart, a term of endearment.

sugar rag   Gullah for a sugar-tit (butter and brown sugar tied in a cloth for a child to suck on).

sug-jist   A pronunciation of *suggest.* "Of course I know it. But can you sug-jist a better way than this for me to learn." [William Faulkner, *The Mansion,* 1959]

sull   To sulk, refuse to talk. "There he is mullin' and sullin' about it."

sull up   Grow sullen, sad. "I didn't know what to do. If I said it was bad, she'd sull up or maybe cry." [Larry Brown, "The Apprentice," 1990]

sum bitch   Southern dialect for *son of a bitch;* sometimes written as one word. "He was a wimpy sumbitch from back yonder." [Larry Brown, "Big Bad Love," 1990]

Sumpter   A frequent pronunciation and misspelling of *Sumter,* as in Fort

Sumter, the opening battle of the Civil War. At the start of the war, many newspapers, including the *New York Times,* spelled it this way. William Faulkner's characters use it in several places.

sun-hot Gullah for the heat of the sun. "Sun-hot does not make people sick."

Sunny South A nickname for the Southern states since the early 19th century.

Sunshine State A nickname for Florida, among other states.

sup Sometimes used for *sip.* " 'I want a sup of water,' she said querulously. 'I been laying here wanting a sup of water a long time, but don't nobody care enough to pay me no mind.' " [William Faulkner, "Wash," 1934]

sup dirt To eat dirt. " '. . . I tried to stay in front but Frank shoved me behind him and held me and father shot him and said, 'Get down there and sup your dirt, whore.' " [William Faulkner, *Sanctuary,* 1931]

suption (1) Substance, nourishment. " 'I wisht they wouldn't give me so many of them celeries [celery]. I just cain't learn to stomach 'um somehow. They don't seem to be much suption in 'em.' " [John Faulkner, *Men Working,* 1941] (2) To suck, probably deriving from *suction.* "I don't rightly know how we got the fish we ate in the Navy. Maybe it was a hole in the ship's bottom and a pump that suptioned 'em in."

sure Often used emphatically instead of "certainly." "I'd sure like to have some of that candy."

sure-God Certainly. "I'm sure-God going to be there."

the surrender For over a century, the surrender of General Robert E. Lee at Appomattox Court House, Virginia on April 9, 1865, ending the Civil War has been known simply as *the surrender.*

survigrous A superlative of vigorous, meaning "fierce, vicious, obstinate, angry, active, great, excessive." "He's a lowdown survigrous cuss."

suspicion Suspect. " 'I thought mebbe he was calling his dog, and I was thinking to myself it was a sorry day that never suspicioned me when I was this close . . .' " [William Faulkner, "The Liar," sketch in the *New Orleans Times-Picayune,* July 26, 1925]

swag To sag. "The house has swagged in the center."

swale Swamp.

swamp angel (1) A disparaging term for someone who lives in the swamps or a backwoods area. (2) (Capitalized) An obsolete term for a member of a Southern anti-black group after the Civil War. "Jim Tiddell was there with his crowd of 'Swamp Angels' (for this badge was worn by them all—a green silk ribbon with 'Swamp Angel' on it)." [*Congressional Record,* December 27, 1876] (3) An old term for the Florida mosquito. "The slapping was well started now, it was getting to that fiercest time of evening. Probably them swamp angels plagued me, too, but I was too tense to pay 'em any mind." [Peter Matthiessen, *Killing Mr. Watson*, 1990] (4) (Capitalized) The nickname Confederate troops gave to the big Union Parrott gun used in the seige of Charleston. "My surroundings were not cheerful and my gloomy thoughts were not dispelled by the bursting of a shell from the historic 'Swamp Angel' and the whirring of its fragments which passed uncomfortable close to me." [James Morgan, *Recollections of a Rebel Reefer*, 1917]

swamp dew   Moonshine liquor.

Swampers   Old name for the settlers who lived in the Okefenokee Swamp of Georgia and Florida.

Swamp Fox   The nickname of General Francis Marion, South Carolina Revolutionary War hero, whose men hid in the swamps after attacks on the British.

swamp-mucker   An old term for a Georgian or a South Carolinian from the low country.

swamp pine   See SLASH PINE.

Swamp trash   A synonym for POOR WHITE TRASH. " 'Look ter me [like] . . . swamp trash." [Margaret Mitchell, *Gone With the Wind*, 1936]

swan   An old term for *swear*. "Well, I swan, don't get all het up about it."

swarved   Crowded. "They're all swarved up together."

swayged down   Deriving from "assuage," this expression is used to describe a swelling such as a boil decreasing in size or disappearing after being lanced or treated with medicine. "He put some salve on that cyst and it swayged down."

sweat and swivit and scrabble   Solve a problem by worrying and working hard. The origin of the word *swivit* (a state of anxiety) is obscure. " 'So maybe we better do like they seem to want, and let them sweat and swivit and scrabble through the best they can by themselves.' " [William Faulkner, *Requiem for a Nun*, 1951]

sweet bubby   The strawberry shrub, *Calycanthus florindus*. "Another shrub that belongs to us and eastern Asia and that tempts one to nibble is what the people here call 'sweet bubbies.' It appears in old-fashioned Northern gardens under the name of sweet-scented or flowering or strawberry shrub." [M. W. Morley, *The Carolina Mountains*, 1913] So called because of its blossoms' supposed resemblance to female breasts.

sweeter than a suck of sugar   Very sweet and appealing. " 'You look sweeter than a suck of sugar, baby,' he shouted to her through the open window." [Erskine Caldwell, "The

Courting of Susie Brown," *The Complete Stories of Erskine Caldwell,* 1953]

sweet gum The gum exuded from the sweet gum tree, which was used as a chewing gum. "Them two gals ain't moved yet, just setting there in their Sunday clothes, chewing sweet gum . . ." [William Faulkner, *The Hamlet,* 1940]

sweet magnolia An abundant Atlantic-coast Southern magnolia, *Magnolia virginiana.*

sweet mouth See SWEET-TALK.

sweet potato bun Buns made with sweet potatoes and following an old Southern recipe.

sweet potato coffee A rare Southern coffee made from the sweet potato.

sweet potato ice cream A dish that appears to be made only down South.

sweet potato pie Quintessential Southern cuisine, the dish dating back to at least the early 19th century.

sweet potato pone An old Southern bread made of sweet potatoes, flavored with spices and baked in a tin pan.

sweet potato pudding One early cookbook called this "a Southern dish fit to grace the table of an epicure."

sweet potato soup Soup made with sweet potatoes.

sweet potato waffle Fanny Farmer listed this recipe in her famous cookbook.

sweet talk; sweet mouth Smooth unctuous flattery designed to win over a person. There is no proof of it, but this Southern Americanism possibly comes from Krio, an English-based Creole of Sierra Leone, specifically from the expression *swit mot,* (sweet mouth) for "flattery." To *sweet mouth* someone is the opposite of to *bad-mouth* him.

sweet tater Sweet potato.

swimmy-headed Dizzy. "I was swimmy-headed all day after I walked into that post."

swinge To singe. "All his hair was swinged off."

swinged Swung. "They swinged on the glider."

swiome Mainly Southern talk meaning a "swinging action around to the side." "The swing came around in a swiome and almost hit me."

Swiss broom An old expression heard among blacks in Louisiana for a whiskbroom.

switch Thin branch of a bush or tree. "I'm gonna take a switch to you."

swole; swoled Swollen, swelled. "He hit his head and was all swoled up."

swurging A pronunciation of *surging*. "And then hyer hit is about midnight and that durn fellow comes swurging outer the woods wild as a skeered deer . . ." [William Faulkner, "A Bear Hunt," 1934]

T

tack An old, perhaps obsolete word for a messy, unfashionable person. See also TACKY.

tacky Once an exclusively Southern expression, used mainly by women, for unfashionable or ugly clothes, *tacky* has in recent times become popular throughout the country.

tadpoles A term for people; heard mainly in Mississippi, whose inhabitants were sometimes called tadpoles.

take and rake An invitation to begin eating. "Everybody take and rake now."

take foot in hand To walk. "Take your foot in hand and come along."

take in To begin. "School takes in at nine o'clock and takes out at three."

take leave of one's senses To become irrational or crazy; to act without any common sense. Widely used in the South and other regions of the United States.

taken; takened Took. "And we all taken off our hats." [William Faulkner, "Shingles for the Lord," 1943] "She cain't fergit the time the Yankees takened her needles and

thread . . ." [Marjorie Kinnan Rawlings, *The Yearling,* 1938]

take out To close. See also TAKE IN.

takes like a hog after persimmons Similar in usage to "takes like a fish to water." "He takes to you like a hog after persimmons."

take the bun To TAKE THE CAKE, win the prize.

take the cake Cakes have been awarded as prizes since classical times, so when slaves on Southern plantations held dance contests to help a needy neighbor, or just for the fun of it, giving a cake to the winning couple was no innovation. But the *cakewalk* inspired by these contests was surely a black contribution to American culture. Dancers tried to outdo each other with fancy steps, struts and ways of walking (perhaps cleverly mocking their owners) while the fiddles played and the chant went up, "Make your steps and show your style!" By 1840 *cakewalk* was recorded as the name of these steps, which became the basis of many tap dance routines still seen today. Whether the expression *that takes the cake* (that wins the highest prize) comes from the cakewalk is another matter. Though the phrase is recorded a century earlier elsewhere, its modern usage almost certainly originated with the cakewalk in America. Today it has taken on a different meaning and is said of something (or someone) that is so unusual as to be almost unbelievable.

take the chute An old term, not in much use any more, for taking a road, as in "The Douglas men are rushing to Lincoln and the Bell men are taking the same chute." *Chute* at one time meant "a road or path" but is now generally confined to a small, often half-silted, sluggish channel. The word is most often heard in *chute-the-chute*, an amusement park water ride, and *shooting the chute*, taking that ride.

take up books To begin school. "It's September and time to take up books."

taking up for Defending, sticking up for. " 'Shut up, William,' she said. 'Stop taking up for your Pa.' " [Erskine Caldwell, *Georgia Boy*, 1943]

tale A malicious lie. "I've heard a tale on him I want to put right."

talkingest The most talkative. "That's the talkingest person I ever heard."

tallywags The penis and testicles; mainly Southern mountain talk.

tap A nut belonging to a screw or bolt. "Get me a tap that fits this bolt."

tar A common pronunciation of *tear* or *tire*.

Tara The famous plantation on which Scarlett O'Hara and her family lived in Margaret Mitchell's *Gone With the Wind* (1936), hence a name for any Southern plantation, even a joking name for any Southern home.

tarheel A nickname for a North Carolinian. "A brigade of North Carolinians . . . failed to hold a certain hill (in a Civil War battle) and were laughed at by Mississippians for having forgotten to tar their heels that morning. Hence originated their cant name, 'Tar-heels.' " [*Overland Monthly*, volume 3, 1869]

Tarheel State A nickname for North Carolina. See also TARHEEL.

tarnation An old expression used in the South and other regions meaning "damnation" and formed from *eternal (tarnal)* and *damnation*.

tarpollyon Pronunciation of *tarpulin*. " 'All right, all right,' Boon said. 'What I'm talking about, you laid there under that tarpollyon all the time and let me get out in the mud and lift this whole car out single-handed by main strength.' " [William Faulkner, *The Reivers*, 1962]

Tar State A nickname for North Carolina. See also TARHEEL.

tasted Tasting. "It was a good-tasted apple."

ta ta's Slang for female breasts, used recently in a few works by Southern authors and in the movie *An Officer and a Gentleman*.

tater A common pronunciation of *potato*.

Taxas A frequent pronunciation of *Texas* in Texas.

tearing up the pea patch Red Barber popularized this Southern U.S. expression that means "going on a rampage" when he broadcast Brooklyn Dodger baseball games from 1945 to 55, using it often to describe fights on the field between players. Barber hails from the South, where the expression is an old one, referring to the prized patch of black-eyed peas, which stray animals sometimes ruined.

tear up Jack To raise a commotion, cut up. "Watch out or he'll tear up Jack. He's a real troublemaker."

tech A pronunciation of *touch*. "I wouldn't tech it with a 10-foot pole." See also UNTECHED.

tell Gullah for *told*. "He tell me to come here."

tell for Told; heard in Cajun speech. "He tell for me to go."

telling Anything told, a statement. "There's a lot of tellings about the South in that book."

tell it on To tell or inform on someone. "If you stop driving fast, I won't tell it on you."

tell the truth and shame the devil Apparently a Southern saying. " 'Tell the truth Jody,' he said, 'and shame the devil.' " [Marjorie Kinnan Rawlings, *The Yearling*, 1938]

Texas T-shirt William Safire's "On Language" column in the *New York Times* (March 27, 1991) defined this as a humorous derogatory term for "one of those disposable [toilet] seat bibs that are found in interstate roadside bathrooms."

Texas yell See REBEL YELL; REBEL YALE.

thang Common pronunciation of *thing*.

thankee Thank you; sometimes heard in rural areas; recorded in Peter Matthiesson's *Killing Mr. Watson*, 1990.

thar A pronunciation of *there*.

that (1) Sometimes omitted in speech, as in "You'll see a heap more things is strange." [Marjorie Kinnan Rawlings, *The Yearling*, 1938] (2) Frequently used in Cajun speech, as in "That time they go to that bayou" ("Then, they went to the bayou").

thataway That way, a shortening of *that there way*. "A deer'll sink in thataway." [Marjorie Kinnan Rawlings, *The Yearling*, 1938]

that dog don't hunt That idea or theory isn't logical, doesn't wash; popularized in the movie *J.F.K.* (1991), set in New Orleans and Texas.

that's how the cow ate the cabbage. An expression to indicate the speaker is laying it on the line, telling it like it is, getting down to brass tacks—with the connotation of telling someone what he or she needs to know but probably doesn't want to hear. According to Little Rock attorney Alston Jennings, who submitted this Southernism to Richard Allen's February 2, 1991, "Our Town" column in the *Arkansas Gazette,* the expression has its roots in a story about an elephant that escaped from the zoo and wandered into a woman's cabbage patch. The woman observed the elephant pulling up her cabbages with its trunk and eating them. She called the police to report that there was a cow in her cabbage patch pulling up cabbages with its tail. When the surprised police officer inquired as to what the cow was doing with the cabbages, the woman replied, "You wouldn't believe me if I told you!" A good story, regardless.

that's two different buckets of possums! Two different stories. "That's two different buckets of possums! You tell me one thing, and he tells me another."

that takes the rag off the bush That beats everything, takes first place, etc; may have originated with hunters, possibly in the West, who fired at rags that were targets hung on bushes.

the (1) Often omitted in Cajun speech. "I make whole place clean." (2) Often used for "a" in Cajun speech. "I'm the fool, I reckon."

theirin; theirn There's. ". . . even Miz Snopes had to admit that that was a good swap from anything that could get up and walk from Beasley's lot to theirin by itself . . ." [William Faulkner, *The Hamlet,* 1940]

theirselves Themselves.

them there Those. "I'll have some of them there apples."

them-uns Infrequently used for *them, those.*

there Often used superfluously, as in "That there girl's mine." See HERE.

there's more ways of killing a cat than choking him to death with butter There are many better, easier ways to do something than the difficult way someone is doing it presently.

these here These. "Let these here ripen a while."

they It often appears that *they* is substituted for *there* by Southerners, as in "They's no time left," but such "theys" are usually a rapid pronunciation of *there* (THAY-uh) *is.*

they-all They.

they-uns They.

things Gullah for animals, especially farm animals. "He left her with all the things to feed."

thisaway This way, a shortening of *this here way.*

this child A humorous term used by a speaker in reference to himself. "This child is too smart for that."

thole To endure; an archaic term. "Sweet ladies, long may ye bloom,/ and toughly I hope ye may thole." [John Crowe Ransom, "Here Lies a Lady," 1924]

thorough Thoroughly. "I want you to thorough clean the house."

those Often used in Cajun for *this* or *these:* "Those man is right."

thoughty Thoughtful. "Well, that's mighty thoughty of you." [John Faulkner, *Men Working,* 1941]

thout Without; unless; an expression heard mainly in East Texas. "I couldn't go thout I had my good saddle."

th'ow A pronunciation of *throw* common among blacks and with some use among whites.

thriblets Triplets. "If old Anse had been about seventy-five years younger, the three of them might have been thriblets." [William Faulkner, "The Tall Men," 1943]

three bricks shy of a load Not very bright, dull-witted. "He's three bricks shy of a load."

thribble; tribble Triple.

throw a double duck fit To be in an extreme state of anger or agitation.

"She got him so riled up he threw a double duck fit."

throwed it out Threw it out.

throw off on To make fun of. "Now you're throwin' off on my sister." [Marjorie Kinnan Rawlings, *Cross Creek,* 1942]

Thump 'em and see if they talk back Said when testing a melon to see whether it's ripe.

thundering herd A colorfully descriptive Texas term for baked beans.

thuse An old term for a college pep rally; from *enthusiastic.*

tie a knot in his (her) tail To impede someone from doing something by placing an obstacle in his path or making life difficult for him. "We'll serve him with a restraining order. That'll tie a knot in his tail." Also *put a knot in his (her) tail.*

tie-tongued Tongue-tied. "He is what we call tie-tongued." [Marjorie Kinnan Rawlings, *Cross Creek,* 1942]

tight A difficult or dangerous position, a bind, a quandary; deriving from a tight place. "Any time you get in a tight, us is here to do what we can." [Marjorie Kinnan Rawlings, *Cross Creek,* 1942]

tight as Dick's hatband Stingy, an old English phrase. "He's tight as Dick's hatband." Historically the expression refers to the fact that the crown was too tight or dangerous to be worn by a certain king of England. The particular king's identity is unknown, but one popular theory suggests Oliver Cromwell's son Richard, often called Tumbledown Dick, who was nominated by his father to succeed him but served for only seven months because he received no support from the army. Another candidate is King Richard III, this Richard said to have been uncomfortable wearing a crown bought with blood. Because "tight" is a synonym for "stingy," the phrase came to mean stingy in the South.

tighter than skin on a sausage Very cheap. "He has the first cent he ever earned; he's tighter than the skin on a sausage."

till the last pea's out of the dish To the very end, for a long time. "The governor's going to stay in the race till the last pea's out of the dish."

time When; a shortening of "by the time." "You'll not be so merry, time the day be done." [Marjorie Kinnan Rawlings, *The Yearling*, 1938]

tin A common pronunciation of *ten*. "I wouldn't give tin cents for it."

Tinnissee A pronunciation of *Tennessee*. See also MIMPHIS.

tippy-toed On tiptoe. "A yearlin' 'll walk tippy-toed." [Marjorie Kinnan Rawlings, *The Yearling*, 1938]

tipsy cake A cake soaked in wine.

tipsy parson An old name for the indigo bunting in the Carolinas.

titi A large Gulf State shrub of the Cyrilla family; its name possibly derives from an American Indian language.

to Often omitted from the infinitive in Cajun speech. "I'm going make myself a drink." (2) Sometimes used superfluously in infinitives. "We'd best to go." [Marjorie Kinnan Rawlings, *The Yearling*, 1938] (3) In. "I don't reckon there's nothin' open to town this time of evening." [John Faulkner, *Men Working*, 1941] (4) The. " 'What to hell are you doing here?' " [William Alexander Percy, *Lanterns on the Levee*, 1941] (5) At. "He lives to John's place." (6) Often used to make explicit that a verb is an infinitive. "She made us all to eat every bit on our plates." (7) Often inserted by Southerners shortly after "have" when asking a question. "Shall I have him to call you?"

toadfrog A toad; rarely means a frog.

toad-strangler A very heavy rain. " 'Hit's a toad-strangler of a rain,' he said." [Marjorie Kinnan Rawlings, *The Yearling*, 1938]

tobacco road See quote for definition. "The road on which Jeeter lived was the original tobacco road his grandfather had made. It was about fifteen miles long and extended in a southeasterly direction from the foothills of the Piedmont, where the sand started, and ended on the bluffs at the river. The road had been used for the rolling of tobacco casks, large hogsheads in which the leaf has been packed after being cured and seasoned in the clay-chinked barns; thousands of hogsheads had been rolled along the crest of the ridge which connected the chain of sand hills, and they had made a smooth firm road the entire distance of fifteen miles . . . After seventy-five years the tobacco road still remained, and while in many places it was beginning to show signs of washing away, its depressions and hollows had made a permanent contour that could remain as long as the sand hills. There were scores of tobacco roads on the western side of the Savannah Valley, some only a mile or so long, others extending as far back as twenty-five or thirty miles into the foothills of the Piedmont. Anyone walking cross-country would more than likely find as many as six or eight in a day's hike. The region, topographically, was like a palm leaf; the Savannah was the stem, large at the bottom and gradually spreading out into the veins at the top. On the side of the valley the creeks ran down like the depressions in the palm leaf, while between them lay the ridges of sand hills, like seams, and on the crests of the ridges were the tobacco roads." [Erskine Caldwell, *Tobacco Road,* 1932]

to get it Get it. "I'll have him to get it for you."

tol-able (tolderable) well Heard in Texas for fair, pretty good. "I'm feeling tol-able well."

tole Pronunciation of *told.*

tolerable In fairly good health. "I'm feelin' jus' tolerable."

toll To lure, entice, lead on. "That widow had tolled my Will into her clutches." [Marjorie Kinnan Rawlings, "Cocks Must Crow," 1939]

toll away To send away with a warning; probably from the sound of a tolling bell used to dismiss as well as to summon. "They said I didn't run away from home but that I was tolled away by a crazy man who, if I hadn't killed him first, would have killed me inside another week." [William Faulkner, "Uncle Willy," 1936]

tolt Told.

tomatoeses A plural of *tomatoe.*

tomcat A wild, sexually active man. " 'Do what?' Varner said. 'To who? Don't you know them damn tomcats are halfway to Texas now?' " [William Faulkner, *The Hamlet,* 1940]

tomorrow is another day: "After all, tomorrow is another day!" is the last sentence in *Gone With the Wind* (1939), Scarlett O'Hara speaking these words as she plans on going home to Tara and winning back Rhett Butler. The expression, however, dates to at least the early 16th century.

tom-walkers Stilts.

too Gullah for *very.* "I too glad you came."

too big for his (her) britches A conceited person with too high an opinion of himself; heard in other regions as well.

too high for picking cotton An old term describing someone who is a little drunk; first recorded in Parson Weem's *The Drunkard's Looking Glass* (1818).

took To have taken. " 'Then I taken my slingshot and I would have liked to took all my bird eggs, too . . .' " [William Faulkner, "Two Soldiers," 1943]

took down with Came down with. "He took down with pneumonia."

tooken Taken. "A lot of these mill hands used to be tooken back home for burial." [Jonathan Daniels, *Tar Heels*, 1941]

too poor to paint and too proud to whitewash A term describing any impoverished Southern gentleman or lady. Whitewash is much cheaper than paint.

too slow to catch the itch Extremely slow. "He's too slow to catch the itch."

too sorry to hit a lick at a snake Extremely lazy.

tooth doctor An old-fashioned, perhaps obsolete, term for a dentist.

tootle An old term for nonsense. " 'It all sounds like tootle to me.' "

[Margaret Mitchell, *Gone With the Wind*, 1936]

tootling Kidding, fooling. "You jist tootlin' me." [Marjorie Kinnan Rawlings, *The Yearling*, 1938]

torn-down Tough, violent, good for nothing. "He's a torn-down scoundrel, the torn downedest I ever seen."

tossel The tassle on a corn plant.

tote *Tote* is of uncertain origin but possibly comes from the African Konga and Kikonga language *tota* (to carry). The word may have passed into English through the Gullah dialect in the Southern United States and is now widely used throughout the United States. "I'll be toted in dead." [Marjorie Kinnan Rawlings, "Cocks Must Crow," 1939]

tote the mail A Southern black expression meaning "to run away fast." "I toted the mail when I saw him coming."

touch-me-not A very haughty or ill-tempered person.

touchous Highly sensitive or touchy. "You're getting might touchous."

tough as puttin' socks on a rooster Very difficult and time-consuming.

town trash See TRASH.

tow sack See CROCUS SACK.

towser An energetic, personable man.

trash (1) An old term for candy or sweets, what might be called junk food today. "Don't eat trash before dinner." (2) Low-class people, low-life. "Then she said quietly, aloud, without rancor, without heat: 'Trash. Town trash.'" [William Faulkner, "There Was a Queen," 1933] See also POOR WHITE TRASH.

trashy poor and no 'count Someone with no breeding at all.

trashy wench A prostitute, a woman of low reputation. "'Get off those steps, you trashy wench!' she cried. 'Get off this land! Get out!'" [Margaret Mitchell, *Gone With the Wind,* 1936]

treadsalve; treadsaft Spurge nettle, a very prickly plant of the nightshade family.

trill "'Ain't you ever trilled a bell in your life?' Preacher Hawshaw asked . . . 'It goes ding-a-ling . . . stop tolling it and begin trilling it!'" [Erskine Caldwell, *Georgia Boy,* 1943]

tremblish Gullah meaning "trembly." "His hands acted tremblish."

trembly Trembling.

tremenjus Tremendous.

trick Any article, but especially a toy.

trimble Tremble.

troll An old term meaning "to ramble, to walk around." "There he was trolling along without a care in the world."

tromp To walk, stamp, tramp on. "If I thought enough of a rug to have to git it all the way from France I wouldn't keep hit where folks coming in would have to tromp on hit." [William Faulkner, "Barn Burning," 1939]

tromple Trample. "Watch out or you'll get trompled on."

truck Stuff, nonsense. "'Hush, white man,' the Negro said. 'Hush. Don't be telling us no truck like that.'" [William Faulkner, *The Hamlet,* 1940]

truth to tell To tell the truth. "Truth to tell, I like the Florida heat."

tuckahoe Any Virginian living east of Virginia's Blue Ridge Mountains; can also mean "one who speaks with a Southern accent." See also COHEE.

tump To knock over, overturn; rarely recorded but still in use. "Don't tump over my bucket of paint."

turkey-and-hog dinner A dinner of turkey and ham traditionally eaten on New Year's Day. "The New Year's Day turkey-and-hog dinner had made the woman droopy and dull-eyed." [Erskine Caldwell, "Blue Boy," *The Complete Stories of Erskine Caldwell,* 1953]

turn A load or armful of something. "He brought in a turn of wood."

turn him in the cold Said in Kentucky of a woman who turns down a man's marriage proposal: "She turned him in the cold."

turn loose; turn aloose To let go, free, get rid of. "Will turned him aloose." [Marjorie Kinnan Rawlings, "Cocks Must Crow," 1939]

turn one every way but loose A threat to beat someone up badly in a fight. "I'll turn you every way but loose."

turn-row A deep furrow in the center of a field that is formed by reversing the direction in which the furrows fall; land situated at the end of a field that is used for turning a plow at the end of a row.

Turpentine State A nickname for North Carolina because of its large production of turpentine.

twict Twice. "Think twict before you speak."

twistification An old term for a country dance.

twouble Common pronunciation of *terrible*.

U

ugly (1) Ugliness. "It was ugly, and God don't love ugly." (2) An old term for sexual intercourse. "He was in for thirty days for throwing bricks at a woman at a church social because she wouldn't do ugly for forty cents." [*Atlantic Monthly,* September 1938] (3) Disagreeable, mean. "Don't be so ugly now." (4) A historical colloquial Southernism for the quality of ugliness. In 1835 a Georgia writer noted, "I want to get in the bread of them sort o' men to drive ugly out of my kin folks."

ujinctum An old term, mostly confined to the southeastern Kentucky mountains, for hell.

unaker A famous porcelain clay found in western North Carolina.

unbalm The opposite of *embalm*. It is possibly a Faulkner invention: " 'Why don't you,' Father said, 'if you could just kind of unbalm Jabbo a little—you know; so he wouldn't get cold or hungry—tie him on the back of the car like he was an extra wheel or engine, then every time you had a puncture or it wouldn't start, all you'd have to do would be to untie Jabbo and stand him up and unbalm him—is that the word? Unbalm.' " [William Faulkner, *The Town,* 1957]

unbleached Americans A friendly white slang term for American blacks, used from before the Civil War to the end of the 19th century.

unbreathing Breathless. "We waited unbreathing." [William Alexander Percy, *Lanterns on the Levee,* 1941]

unbutton the collar of An obsolete slang term meaning "to kill." A 19th century newspaper observed: "This Kentuckian would think no more of taking his jack-knife and unbuttoning that Creek's collar than he would of taking off his coat."

Uncle A form of address, little-used anymore, for an elderly male black, once considered a pleasant, friendly salutation by whites, as was its variation, *Unkey.* Today the term is considered derogatory by blacks. See usage example at AUNTIE.

Uncle Bud A Southern term for beer; derives from the popular Budweiser brand of beer. "I did that a lot. Usually while I was under the influence of Uncle Bud." [Larry Brown, "92 Days," 1990]

undecent An old, perhaps obsolete term for *indecent.*

underminded Undermined. "He underminded the building."

under the hack Dispirited. "Being fired got me under the hack." See also HACK.

unfinancial Without money.

unhealth Sickness, decline, decay, etc. " 'This is the penetentiary. I can't imagine no more unhealth a man can have than to be locked up inside a bobwire pen for twenty or twenty-five years.' " [William Faulkner, *The Mansion*, 1959]

Union League A society organized in the North during the Civil War to inspire loyalty toward the Union; after the war it also became a secret political society among blacks in the South.

United Daughters of the Confederacy A patriotic, benevolent and social organization of Southern women descended from those who fought for the Southern cause, or gave aid to it, during the Civil War; founded in Nashville, Tennessee in 1894.

Unity States United States. "And now me and Pete expected Pap to say something else foolish, like he done before, about how Uncle Marsh getting wounded in France and that trip to Texas Pap taken in 1918 ought to be enough to save the Unity States in 1942, but he never." [William Faulkner, "Two Soldiers," 1943]

Unkey See UNCLE.

unlessen Unless. " 'We just sent for his jockey,' Ned said. 'Then you can see him work . . . Unlessen you in

a hurry to get back to yourn.' " [William Faulkner, *The Reivers*, 1962]

unmorals Immoral behavior. " 'Women are not interested in morals [Mother said]. They aren't even interested in unmorals.' " [William Faulkner, *The Town*, 1957]

unnatural Unnaturally. "It's so unnatural quiet."

unpleasantness The Civil War; a term used in the South and other regions after the war was over, often in the form *The Late Unpleasantness,* less often in the form *The Little Unpleasantness.*

unreconstructed rebel See UNRECONSTRUCTED SOUTHERNER.

unreconstructed Southerner A term applied to a Southerner not reconciled to the results of the Civil War; first recorded in 1867, it is still used today. *Unreconstructed rebel* is a later variation. Following is a stanza of "A Good Old Rebel (Unreconstructed)" by Innes Randolph (1837–87):

I am a good old rebel—
　Yes; that's just what I am—
And for this land of freedom
　I do not give a damn.
I'm glad I fit agin 'em,
　And I only wish we'd won;
And I don't ax no pardon
　For anything I've done.

unteched Untouched. ". . . while she et an ice-cream sody . . . and the ice melted into the unteched Coca-

Cola in front of him." [William
Faulkner, *The Mansion*, 1959]

Unterrified Democrat An unswerv-
ingly loyal Democrat, generally from
the South. The obsolete term is first
recorded in 1832 in reference to supporters of Andrew Jackson, and the
name was often shortened to simply
the Unterrified.

unthoughted Thoughtless, badly
thought out. "You keep saying unthoughted things."

upchuck To regurgitate, vomit.

upon the top (side) of the earth On
the face of the earth. "Asheville was
the greatest place upon the top of
the earth to live." [Thomas Wolfe,
Letters, 1924]

upped and To have acted suddenly,
impulsively; also *up and*. "He upped
and left."

uppowoc An obsolete Indian word
for tobacco, first recorded in the South
in 1588.

**up shit creek without even a piss pad-
dle** In a totally hopeless situation.
". . . 'how's that for an old Southern boy once up shit creek without

even a piss paddle.' " [Calder Willingham, *Rambling Rose*, 1972]

up the road a piece An undeter-
mined distance away. "He never told
anybody where he had been. Just up
the road a piece." [William Faulkner,
"Hair," 1931]

us We. "Any time you get in a tight,
us is here to do what we can." [Mar-
jorie Kinnan Rawlings, *Cross Creek*,
1942] A common redundancy in Cajun speech, as in "Us, we believe you
right."

used-to-be A Southern term for a
has-been. "He's an old washed-out
used-to-be."

used to could Used to be able to.
"She used to could milk the cows."

used to couldn't see that Couldn't see
or understand something in the past.
"I used to couldn't see that, but now
I understand."

use to couldn't A phrase often used
in Cajun speech to mean "was at one
time unable to." "I use to couldn't
run" ("I wasn't able to run").

useless as tits on a boar hog About
as useless as one can get.

us-ums Us; rarely heard anymore.

V

V Formerly used in the South and other regions to mean a five-dollar bill. See also X.

Vallandinghamers See COPPER-HEAD.

vanity cake A Mississippi dessert often served at tea time.

vapors An old-fashioned term used in the South and elsewhere for an hysterical nervous state, often a feigned illness.

various At odds or variance. "They never agree, they're various with each other."

varmint Vermin; an undesirable animal; an obnoxious person. A pronunciation bordering on a new word that the South's early aristocrats borrowed from upper-class English speech. " 'I think you like me because I am a varmint. You've known so few dyed-in-the-wool varmints in your sheltered life that my very difference holds a quaint charm for you.' " [Margaret Mitchell, *Gone With the Wind*, 1936]

varsity University. Another pronunciation bordering on a new word that the South's early aristocrats borrowed from upper-class English speech.

venture An adventure.

veranda A large porch, which is also called a *piazza* and a *gallery* in the South.

very spit of The spitting image of, very close in appearance to. "He's the very spit of his father. The pure spit of him." See also SPITTIN' IMAGE.

veto This was the name of an old New Orleans alcoholic drink, so named, probably, in honor of President Andrew Jackson's vetoes of congressional bills.

vigilance committee A pre-Civil War and Civil War organization using extralegal means to intimidate blacks and abolitionists.

vigintial crop This old term, referring to a crop produced in 20 years, was used in reference to slave-breeding, as is witnessed by these words from a speech by C. J. Faulkner to the Virginia legislature in 1832: "Shall society suffer that the slaveholder may continue to gather his vigintial crop of human flesh?"

Virginia Sir Walter Raleigh suggested that Virginia be named after England's Elizabeth I, the Virgin Queen, when in 1584 he founded his colony, probably on what is now Roanoke Island. (The island, which is off North Carolina, was originally part of the great area from Florida to Newfoundland that Virginia encompassed.) Virginia, the Old Dominion State, was the site of the first permanent English settlement, at Jamestown in 1607. Often called the "Mother of Presidents," the state sent Washington, Jefferson, Monroe, Tyler, William Henry Harrison and Wilson to the White House. As to the state's exact naming, one writer tells us that Queen Elizabeth graciously accorded the privileges proposed by Raleigh, giving to this new land a name in honor of her maiden state, and it was called Virginia. Raleigh was knighted for his service and given the title of Lord and Governor of Virginia.

Virginia Tobacco grown in Virginia.

Virginia breakdown See BREAKDOWN.

Virginia fence An obsolete expression alluding to the uncertain course of one who is drunk by referring to the zigzag Virginia rail fences.

Virginia gouger A term once used to describe a man from Virginia who gouged an opponent's eyes out in fighting. The term *Carolina gouger* was also common, and some North-

erners thought all "Southlanders" fought this way. "When the trader got home, he would tell terrible stories of the Southlanders being gougers." [James Paulding, *The Diverting History of John Bull and Brother Jonathan,* 1813]

Virginial A festival held every five years in 19th century Jamestown.

Virginianism A Virginia Americanism.

Virginia truffle The subterranean fungus *Poria cocos* found in the Southern states. Also called *Indian bread, Indian loaf* and *tuckahoe*.

Virginia weed Tobacco.

vittles Victuals, food. This backcountry Southern word is actually a very old, proper English one, and *victuals* is a pedantic misspelling of it.

volunteer A bastard, an analogy with a "volunteer plant" in the garden (one not planted by design).

vow and bedamn Strongly swear to something. " 'Now you go ahead and do what the country records is supposed to do. I'll vow and bedamn if I'm going to be cheated out of legal marriage to Nellie after all this time has gone by.' " [Erskine Caldwell, "Momento," *Gulf Coast Stories,* 1956]

W

wagpole Tail. " 'He's a mighty playful dog, Lonnie,' Arch said, catching up a shorter grip on the tail, 'but his wagpole is way too long for a dog his size . . .' " [Erskine Caldwell, "Kneel to the Rising Sun," *The Complete Stories of Erskine Caldwell*, 1953]

waiter Gullah for a best man or bridesmaid. See also CONJURE BAG.

wait on To wait for. "I can't be waiting on you all morning."

walkalong Joe A dance of black origin in which dancers move in a large circle; also called *walkaround*.

walking off with the persimmons See EATIN' A GREEN SIMMON.

wall To roll one's eyes in an exaggerated fashion, emphasizing the whites. "If fish could bat their eyes, or wall them like El Greco's saints . . ." [William Alexander Percy, *Lanterns on the Levee*, 1941]

waller To wallow, roll about. "Stop wallern' about in that bed, boy!"

walloper A hard, heavy blow. "He must have taken some wallopers." [Jonathan Daniels, *Tar Heels*, 1941]

Wallstreet Panic Faulkner created or recorded the most unusual of Southern names in *The Hamlet* (1940). As Ech Snopes explains: ". . . [We] figured if we named him Wallstreet Panic it might make him get rich like the folks that run that Wallstreet panic [in 1928]."

wampus See CATAWAMPUS (second definition).

wanted up Wanted to get up; an East Texas expression. "He wanted up and howled like all get out."

wants up Wants to get up. "He's tired of being in bed. He wants up."

the War The Civil War. "In the South, the War is what A.D. is elsewhere; they date from it. All day long you hear things 'placed' as having happened since the War; or 'du'in' the War, or 'befo' the War." [Mark Twain, *Life on the Mississippi*, 1883]

War Between the States The Civil War.

War for Constitutional Liberty The Civil War.

War for Nationality The Civil War.

War for Separation The Civil War.

War for Southern Freedom The Civil War.

War for Southern Independence The Civil War.

War for Southern Nationality The Civil War.

War for Southern Rights The Civil War.

War for States' Rights The Civil War.

War of Secession The Civil War.

War of the North and South The Civil War.

War of the Sixties The Civil War.

War to Suppress Yankee Arrogance The Civil War.

was Often used in Cajun speech with a present tense verb to indicate past tense: "We was walk back soon" ("We walked back soon").

was a year; was a week; etc. A year, week, etc., ago. "I saw him was a week."

wash Either a bump or a depression in a road.

wash-hole An old term for a swimming hole.

washing Swimming. "Let's go in washing."

washline A clothesline.

wasp's nest White bread (from its texture). "I made some wasp's nest bread." [Marjorie Kinnan Rawlings, *Cross Creek,* 1942]

watch the night fully accomplish To watch darkness fall completely. "They ate supper by lamplight, then, sitting on the doorstep, the boy watched the night fully accomplish . . ." [William Faulkner, "Barn Burning," 1939]

water Gullah for a tear. "Not a water drained out my eye."

wave the bloody shirt Used in both the North and the South from after the Civil War until the present to indicate any means employed to stir up hostility between the North and the South. "The G.A.R. (Grand Army of the Republic) waved the Bloody Shirt in many a political campaign, advising its boys in blue to 'vote as you shoot!' " [Jerome Kerwin, *Civil-Military Relationships in American Life,* 1948]

wawnchalla A pronunciation of *want you all to.*

wax An old term for chewing gum.

ways Distance, way. "It's a long ways from here."

way yonder Very much, a great distance. "He's a way yonder ahead of me."

we Gullah for *our.* "He sent dat rat to kill we joy."

We ain't what we want to be, and we ain't what we're goin' to be, but we

ain't what we was An old optimistic saying that originated in South Carolina.

weakified Weak or tired. "I feel weakified." [Marjorie Kinnan Rawlings, *The Yearling*, 1938]

weak jerks A case of nerves, jumpiness. " 'I git the weak jerks thinkin' about 'em [wolves].' " [Marjorie Kinnan Rawlings, *The Yearling*, 1938]

we-all We. "[A corporation] lapsed into Southern mountain talk. Thomas J. Watson, president of I.B.M., took full-page ads in the press to proclaim: ' "I" represents only one person. "We" may mean only two or a few persons. Our slogan now is WE-ALL . . . President Roosevelt, our Commander-in-Chief, can be certain that WE-ALL are back of him.' " [*Time*, January 12, 1943]

we-all's Our, ours. "This property is we-all's."

wear out To beat or whip thoroughly, to spank a child. "I hope she wears him out." [John Faulkner, *Men Working*, 1941]

wear the britches To be the real authority; used especially of a wife in a family. "She wears the britches in that house."

wear the green willow To be sad or disappointed in love. "She's wearing the green willow since he left her."

wear to a frazzle To wear out, wear thin. See usage example at WHY IN PLUPERFECT HELL.

wear to a nub To wear down. "It drove me crazy and wore me to a nub." [Calder Willingham, *Rambling Rose*, 1972]

webfooter A term for a Southern infantryman during the Civil War.

weedmonkey A mostly Southern mountain term meaning "to be a prostitute or loose woman." "Let's go weedmonkeying tonight."

well, I'll be A shortening of all the other *well, I'll be . . .* expressions, such as *well, I'll be damned*.

well, I'll be a suck-egg mule! Common exclamation. " 'Well I'll be a suck-egg mule!' Ty Ty said. 'I wasn't doing a thing but standing there.' " [Erskine Caldwell, *God's Little Acre*, 1933]

well, I'll be black-dogged! Euphemism for *I'll be damned*.

well-knowed Well-known. "He were a well-knowed person."

well, shoot a bug! Well I'll be damned, if that don't take the cake.

well slap the dog (or **cat**) **an spit in the fire!** An old rural exclamation of surprise.

wench A derogatory term for a black female slave in slavery times or for a black female servant.

went Sometimes used for gone, as in "She's went to the store, I reckon."

West-by-God-Virginia A humorous name for West Virginia said to have been coined by an irate native when it was said he came from Virginia. Replied the man: "Not Virginia, but WEST, by God!, Virginia!"

West Virginia West Virginia is composed of 40 western mountain counties that seceded from Virginia at the outbreak of the Civil War, these counties voting not to secede from the Union and forming their own state government. After rejecting New Virginia, Kanawha and Alleghany, the new state settled on West Virginia for a name, an ironic choice since Virginia extends 95 miles farther west than West Virginia does. West Virginia had considered seceding from Virginia several times due to unequal taxation and representation, and the Civil War provided an excellent excuse. Its constitution was amended to abolish slavery, and President Lincoln proclaimed West Virginia the 35th state in 1862, justifying his action as a war measure. Nicknamed the "Mountain State" and often called the "Panhandle State," it has an odd outline, leading to the saying that it's "a good state for the shape it's in."

West Virginny West Virginia. "He's from West Virginny." [Marjorie Kinnan Rawlings, *South Moon Under,* 1933]

we-uns We or us. " 'What for you uns,' said they, in their barbaric dialect, 'come down her to fight we uns?' " [*Harper's Magazine,* December 16, 1864]

we've howdied, but we ain't shook Said of somebody one knows but doesn't know well.

wha Who. An early Southern pronunciation of *who,* deriving from the Scotch-Irish schoolteachers of the South, who were often indentured servants.

whang-doodle An extraordinary person or thing. "Down in Mississippi we'd call her a whang-doodle!"

whapper-jawed WHOPPER-JAWED.

whar A pronunciation of *where.*

what That; which; who. Often heard in Cajun speech. "This is the man what owns the store." "He is the man what knows."

what for? Why?; heard in Cajun speech. "What for you come here?"

what the world's going to The Southern version of what is usually *what the world's coming to* in other regions of the country. "It's pitiful what the world's going to now." [Larry Brown, "Old Soldiers," 1990]

wheel baw A wheelbarrow; used in North Carolina.

whelp Welt. "He had great whelps all over his body."

when elephants roost in trees Never. " 'You'll get a dollar a pound [for cotton] when elephants roost in trees!' " [Margaret Mitchell, *Gone With the Wind*, 1936]

when the cheese begun to bind When everything came together, when the plot unfolded. ". . . Uncle Mink never seemed to have any trouble reconciling Jack Houston up in front of that shotgun when the cheese begun to bind." [William Faulkner, *The Mansion*, 1959]

where's at Often used for "where is" in Cajun speech. "Where's at the place?"

wheresomever Wherever. " 'Clare to wheresomever the hogs be.' " [Marjorie Kinnan Rawlings, *The Yearling*, 1938]

where yat? A common greeting used instead of hello and similar greetings in the Irish Channel section of New Orleans.

whet A long time. "He stayed quite a whet."

which (1) Who or that. "That same air Jones, which lived in Jones,/ He had this pint about him." [Sidney Lanier, "Jones's Private Argument," 1870] (2) Often used as a conjunctive in a confusing way, as in: "The President was not happy with the results of the election, which I couldn't be happier about that." (3) Often used for what. " 'I shot it,' she said. 'You which?' old Het said." [William Faulkner, *The Town*, 1957]

which-a-way Which way. "Which-a-way did he come from?" [Marjorie Kinnan Rawlings, *The Yearling*, 1938]

whiles A while. "Now we'll set awhiles." [Marjorie Kinnan Rawlings, *The Yearling*, 1938]

whilst While. "Whilst I was asleep." [Marjorie Kinnan Rawlings, *The Yearling*, 1938]

whimpery Sad and whimpering. "He became whimpery."

whistlin' Dixie See YOU AIN'T JUST WHISTLIN' DIXIE.

white bacon Salt pork.

white buckra See BUCKRA.

White Camellias See KNIGHTS OF THE WHITE CAMELLIA.

white captain A title of respect, sometimes obsequious, used by a black man to a white man. " 'I wouldn't eat up your mule, boss. I never thought of anything like that. But, please, sir, white captain, don't bring no conjure-man around here.' " [Erskine Caldwell, *God's Little Acre*, 1933]

whitefolks Form of address, often disparaging, by blacks to white people. "We just stood there, facing Butch and the other man, who now held Lightning. 'What's it for, Whitefolks?' Ned said." [William Faulkner, *The Reivers*, 1962]

white folk's nigger (negro) A reproachful term among blacks for a black person who toadies to white people.

White League An organization formed in the South after the Civil War to maintain white supremacy.

White Line A secret political organization formed in about 1875 and devoted to white supremacy.

white man A term once used by white Southerners to distinguish themselves from Yankees or Northerners. "Yonder's the Yankees on one side, and here's the blamed niggers on t'other, and betwixt or betweenst 'em a white man's got mighty little chance." [*Century Magazine,* August 1887]

white marsh An old name in Louisiana and South Carolina for Southern wild rice.

white mule Potent moonshine. ". . . he hadn't spent no twenty-five or thirty dollars worth of white mule whiskey jist to purify the Snope's name outen Atlanta, Georgia." [William Faulkner, *The Mansion,* 1959]

white nigger (negro) An offensive term for a black person of very light color, sometimes an albino; a white person who does hard manual labor.

white Republican An old post-Civil War term for a white member of the Republican party.

white trash See POOR WHITE TRASH.

whittlety-whet When two people were running a close race, oldtimers in Kentucky said, "It is whittlety-whet who will get there first."

whit up To sharpen. "I could whit up one of Jackson's butcher knives and finish it myself, with another drink or two." [William Faulkner, "The Tall Men," 1941]

who laid the chuck (laid a chuck; laid the rails; tied the pup) With authority; to perfection. "They could raise hogs to who-laid-a-chuck, but they couldn't raise children." "She can sing from who laid the chuck."

whole enduring day The entire, whole day; long period of time. "He's done nothing the whole enduring day."

whomper-jawed WHOPPER-JAWED.

whoo-ee Wow. "Whoo-ee, she's pretty as a picture."

whop Whip. " 'He'll whop any dog.' " [Marjorie Kinnan Rawlings, *The Yearling,* 1938]

whopper-jawed Large or crooked protruding jaws.

whoses Whose, in the speech of some blacks and whites. " 'Whoses house?' Jimson asked, his mouth hanging open. 'Whoses house did you say?' " [Erskine Caldwell, "Big Buck," *The Complete Stories of Erskine Caldwell,* 1953]

who tied the pup See WHO LAID THE CHUCK.

whupped A pronunciation of *whipped*.

why in pluperfect hell An exclamation of exasperation. " 'Why in pluperfect hell can't he leave the woman alone? There ain't no sense in a man going rutting every day in the whole year. The woman will wear Shaw to a frazzle.' " [Erskine Caldwell, *God's Little Acre*, 1933]

widder Widow. A pronunciation bordering on a new word that the South's early aristocrats borrowed from upper-class English speech.

widder woman; widow woman A widow.

wild as an acre of snakes Very wild. "He's the wildest man in Texas, wild as an acre of snakes."

wild as spikehorn bucks Very wild. "I remember them—two little critters exactly alike, and wild as spikehorn bucks, running around here day and night . . ." [William Faulkner, "The Tall Men," 1941]

will Often dropped as an auxiliary verb in Cajun speech. "What you do now?"

willipus-wollopus A huge, fabulous creature. "The [Southern] newspapers showed cartoons of Northern corporations as tigers, money bags, willipus-wollopuses, rolling over

helpless little men." [*Saturday Evening Post*, January 3, 1942]

winder Window. A pronunciation bordering on a new word that the South's early aristocrats borrowed from upper-class English speech.

windowlight (pronounced wenderlight) Window.

wine book According to an October 31, 1989, article in the *New York Times*, a wine book is a ledger in which the crew leaders or bosses of migrant workers in Southern states "record the claims that they make on the worker's wages, beyond the $40 or $50 per week that they charge for their meals. The name of a worker is written at the top of each page, which, except for the occasional date and odd notation is nothing but a list of numbers showing dollars and cents. But the crew leaders know what transaction each charge represents." Transactions often include wine, of course, and also cocaine and crack, the crew leaders rarely telling a worker the high price of the drugs until the money is deducted from his salary. Such are the more subtle ways of debt servitude today. The expression *wine book* has been around at least two or three decades but is not often recorded.

wiry as hog-bristles Said of hair that is very stiff and unmanageable. "Sometimes he could manage to make it [his hair] lie down for a few minutes by sousing his head in a pan o water and then combing it hurried but as soon as the water began to dry, the hair would stand up straight as if it were attached to springs. Dude's hair was as wiry as hog-bristles." [Erskine Caldwell, *Tobacco Road,* 1932]

witch woman   A witch. "She was known far and wide as a witch woman."

with a penny to bless him (her)   With a penny to his (her) name. " 'Oh, Captain Butler, I haven't a relative with a penny to bless him!' " [Margaret Mitchell, *Gone With the Wind,* 1936]

without   Unless. "Can't you come without I have to carry you?"

wobble   Shake. "Sheena Baby was getting smaller in the distance with each step, and I could see that fine ass she has wobbling. I knew she'd wobble it harder when she heard something [a car] coming down the road." [Larry Brown, "Falling Out of Love," 1990]

womens   Women. "Some Negro womens come by." [Marjorie Kinnan Rawlings, *Cross Creek,* 1942]

wonderment   A curiosity or cause of wonder. "It was a wonderment how fast they growed."

won't   Heard in North Carolina for "wasn't." "It won't me that did it."

woods colt   An illegitimate child. ". . . everybody else in ten miles of
e Bend knew that old Will Warner

was going to have to marry her off to somebody, and that quick, if he didn't want a wood's colt in his back yard next grass." [William Faulkner, *The Mansion,* 1959]

wool-hat boys   Small farmers, tenant farmers, sharecroppers.

woolyhead   An offensive term for a black person dating back to the early 19th century.

woon't   Won't. See also PAAMS.

wopple-jawed   WHOPPER-JAWED.

words and trickery and flummery   Euphemistic pretense. " 'It sounds like a farm to me,' said Mother. 'Calling it a dairy establishment that's just words and trickery and flummery.' " [Calder Willingham, *Rambling Rose,* 1972]

wore out   Tired. "I'm all wore out."

working without a full set of lights   Stupid. "He's working without a full set of lights."

work like hell-on-fire   To work to the utmost of one's capacity. "That's when he said he made up his mind to work like hell-on-fire and never be poor like that again." [Erskine Caldwell, *The Earnshaw Neighborhood,* 1971]

worried up   Worried. "There she was, all worried up about every little thing."

worrisome   Wearisome. "It was a worrisome place to work."

worryation Gullah for *worry*. "I done had enough worryation."

worth doodley squat Worth nothing, of no value; sometimes shortened to *worth doodley*. "He ain't worth doodley squat."

worser Worse. "Mrs. Killigrew was worser deaf than even Killigrew." [William Faulkner, "Shingles for the Lord," 1943]

worse than the plagues of Egypt! A terrible pest, a very bothersome person. " 'In Heaven's name, what are you doing home again? You're worse than the plagues of Egypt!' " [Margaret Mitchell, *Gone With the Wind*, 1936]

worstest Worst.

would use to Would. "I would use to watch it all the time . . ." [William Faulkner, "Shingles for the Lord," 1943]

W.P.&A. The Depression-era W.P.A. (Works Progress Administration).

wrastle Wrestle. ". . . I was the one Father had to grab and hold, trying to hold me, having to wrastle with me like I was another man instead of just nine." [William Faulkner, "Shall Not Perish," 1943]

wrenching out Heavy cleaning. " 'Now I get all that wrenching out to do over.' " [Eudora Welty, *The Optimist's Daughter*, 1972]

wring-jaw An old term for especially potent hard cider. There was an expression *wring-jawed* for drunk as well.

write Wrote; heard in Cajun speech. "He write me many letters."

writhen Twisted. "He was writhen by shame." [Thomas Wolfe, *Look Homeward, Angel*, 1929]

wusser See WORSER.

X

X Formerly used in the South and other regions to mean a ten-dollar bill. "Is there not . . . an X left to redeem the MSS?" [*Louisville* (Ky.) *Public Advertiser*, August 21, 1840]

Y

yager A long-barreled rifle with a large bore popular in the South from about 1777 until the late 19th century and often called the *Mississippi jager*.

yahoo A rural resident.

y'all See YOU-ALL.

yam *Yam* can be traced back to the Senegal *nyami* (to eat) and was introduced to America in the South, via the Gullah dialect *njam*, meaning the same, in 1676. The word, however, had come into European use long before this. *Yam* is often used interchangeably with sweet potato.

Yamassee The name of a tribe of Carolina Indians important in early Carolina history.

Yank A Northerner, once more scurrilous than *Yankee*.

Yankee See DAMN YANKEE.

Yankee bummer A Civil War term for deserting Northern soldiers who looted and burned without restraint, the most infamous among them being *Sherman's bummers,* who rode on the flanks of General Sherman's army.

Yankee bump A bump or depression in a road; heard in West Virginia and other areas.

Yankee catchers A company of Confederate soldiers organized in Virginia in 1861.

Yankee cheesebox on a raft A widespread derisive Southern description of the U.S. armored warship the *Monitor,* which fought the famous Civil War battle against the Confederate *Merrimac;* also *cheesebox upon a plank.*

Yankee dime An old expression meaning "a kiss."

Yankeedom Occasionally used as a Southern term for the North during the Civil War.

Yankee Invasion The Civil War.

Yankeeland A chiefly Southern expression for the northern U.S. states.

the Yankees are coming! A common expression that struck fear in the hearts of Southerners in many towns toward the end of the Civil War. "She gathered up her skirts and ran down the street, and the rhythm of her feet was 'The Yankees are coming! The Yankees are coming!'"

. . . This was an inferno of pain and smell and noise and hurry-hurry-hurry! 'The Yankees are coming! The Yankees are coming!' " [Margaret Mitchell, *Gone With the Wind,* 1936]

Yankee shot The navel or belly button. "That's your Yankeeshot, child. That's where the Yankees shot you."

Yankee tea Urine; a term used by Southern soldiers during the Civil War.

Yankee vegetables Undercooked greens, which in true Southern cooking should simmer as long as half a day.

yapped up Marked up, messed up. "Hit wouldn't do to have the earth all yapped up with the tracks o' the dead." [Marjorie Kinnan Rawlings, *South Moon Under,* 1933]

yarb See HERB.

Yazoo Fraud (Claims, Purchase) Expressions pertaining to Georgia's 1795 sale of lands near the Yazoo River to four crooked companies who profited immensely from their resale to the U.S. government.

year Often the pronunciation for *ear.* "I ate a year of corn."

yearling Often applied indiscriminately to a calf of any age.

yearth Earth. " 'Ye kin dig and ye kin dig, young man,' the reedy voice said. 'For what's rendered to the yearth, the yearth will keep until hit's

ready to reveal it.' " [William Faulkner, *The Hamlet,* 1940]

ye gods and little fishes! Common exclamation. "We heard a noise at the back door and then an astonished exclamation: 'Ye gods and little fishes!' It was Daddy, hunched forward and staring through the curtains of the back kitchen door." [Calder Willingham, *Rambling Rose,* 1972]

yell See REBEL YELL.

yellow jasmine The Carolina jasmine.

yellow jessamine The Carolina jasmine.

yellow leg A rare Union term for a Confederate soldier during the Civil War.

yellow; yeller Since at least the early 19th century Southern blacks of a brown or mulatto color have been called by such contemptuous terms as *yellow* or *yeller boy, yellow darky, yellow girl, yellow woman, yellow bitch, yellow skin* and *high yellow.*

yellow plug A cheap plug of chewing tobacco. "He took a fresh chew of yellow plug. There was nothing else he could do." [Erskine Caldwell, *God's Little Acre,* 1933]

yellow rose of Texas The yellow rose of Texas, which is part of that state's folklore and even has a famous song written about it, actually originated in the 1830s on a farm in New York City near the present-day Pennsylvania Station. There a lawyer named George Harison found it as a seedling growing among the other roses on his property and began cultivating it. Settlers soon took the yellow rose west with them and legend has it that Texans finally claimed it as their own when Mexican General Santa Anna, the villain of the Alamo, "was distracted by a beautiful woman with yellow roses in her hair." We have this nice story on the authority of Stephen Scanniello, rosarian of the Cranford Rose Garden in the New York Botanical Garden who told it to garden columnist Anne Raver of the *New York Times* (6/18/92).

yerb   See HERB.

yessum   A pronunciation, both black and white, of *yes ma'am*. " 'Yessum,' Quentin said. 'Yes,' the grim quiet voice said from beyond the unmoving triangle of dim lace . . ." [William Faulkner, *Absalom, Absalom!,* 1936]

yester   Yesterday; mainly a Southern mountain term.

ye-uns   An old term for the plural *you*.

y'heah   You hear; a common Southern redundancy added to the end of sentences in the form of a question. "Y'all call us soon, y'heah?"

yit   A pronunciation of *yet*. " 'Well, Kernel, they kilt us but they ain't whipped us yit, air they?' " [William Faulkner, *Absalom, Absalom!,* 1936]

yo   An eye; a country term once common among small farmers. Also a pronunciation of "your."

Yoknapatawpha   The fictional county William Faulkner created in Mississippi, based loosely on the area where he lived around Oxford, Mississippi.

yon   Yonder, over there. "The second time he said: 'Yon's yo wife wantin something.' " [William Faulkner, *Sanctuary,* 1931]

york   An old, probably obsolete term meaning "to vomit."

you ain't just whistlin' Dixie   You're not just talking or making small talk, you're saying something important, worthwhile. DIXIE refers to the popular song.

you-all   The plural of you. *You-all* (often pronounced *y'all*) is widely considered the *ne plus ultra* of Southern dialect, but this expression, used throughout the South, is much misunderstood. Mainly applied to two or more people, *you-all* can be used when the speaker is addressing one person, but only when the sentence implies plurality. Except for some speakers in the Ozarks and rural Texas, only a ham of a stage Southerner would use *you-all* so undiscriminately as to say "That's a pretty dress you-all are wearing." But a Southerner might well say "How you-all?"—the question intended to inquire of the health of you and your entire family or group. Further, the inflection of the phrase is all important. When th *you* in *you-all* is accented, as in "Yo all must come," this means that the group near the speaker is invited. The contraction of *you-all, y'all,* is always used in this plural sense. Recently the American Southernism *y'all* (or *yawl*) has been explained, though hardly to the satisfaction of everyone, as a calque (a filling in of an African structure with English material) from the West African second person plural *unu,* which is also used in the American black Gullah dialect. This interesting theory is advanced in a study by Jay Edwards in Hancock and Decamp's *Pidgins and Creoles* (1972): "In the white plantation English of Louisiana the form *y'all* (semantically *unu*) was probably learned by white children from black mammies and children in familiar domestic situations." In any case, the closest thing that has been found in English to the collective second person plurals *you-all* and *you-uns* is the collective second person *you-together* that is sometimes heard in England's East Anglia dialect today. (See also INTRODUCTION.)

you-all (y'all) come! Come back again; said in leave-taking.

you-all's The possesive plural you. "We were just coming over to you-all's." See YOU-ALL.

you come! Come back again; said in leave-taking.

youngling Gullah meaning "a child."

young sapling A young man, usually in his teens. " 'I never seen a woman preacher carry-on over a young sapling like that before,' Jeeter said." [Erskine Caldwell, *Tobacco Road,* 1932]

young'un A child; a shortening of "young one." "It's for the young'un."

your cotton is low Your slip is showing.

your druthers is my ruthers A mostly black phrase meaning "Your preference is mine."

yourn Yours. "Them bloodhounds of yourn . . ." [Marjorie Kinnan Rawlings, *The Yearling,* 1938]

you'uns You people. "You'uns come right on over."

yuther Other. "Any yuther folks comin'?"

Z

zebra The obsolete term *zebra* for a convict (suggested by the striped suits prisoners wore) appears to have originated in the South in the late 19th century.

Zephyrinas An old Charleston biscuit recipe, named after Zephyras, Greek god of the west wind, because the biscuits are so light.

zink The kitchen sink, in Texas.

zombie Though widely used today for one of the "walking dead" or for any unresponsive, oafish "dummy" with a vacant corpse-like manner, *zombie* came into national use from the South. *Zombie* may have originally been the snake god (called a *nzambi*) worshiped in West Indian voodoo ceremonies based upon the python god in West Africa—since dead people were said to be brought to life in these ceremonies, such imagined corpses shuffling along half-dead and half-alive were called *zombies*. African slaves shipped to the South may well have brought the term with them. Another explanation is that *zombie* comes from the Louisiana Creole word for phantom or ghost, which in turn derives from the Spanish *sombra* (ghost).

zondike The zodiac. "Zondike signs." [Marjorie Kinnan Rawlings, *South Moon Under,* 1933]

zoon To go fast, run fast, often with a hum or buzz; also *june*. "He went zooning across the meadow."

Zouave A soldier serving in any of certain Southern volunteer units in the Civil War. "[He] stood out in the crowd like a tropical bird—a Louisiana Zouave, with baggy blue and white striped pants, cream gaiters and tight little red jacket . . ." [Margaret Mitchell, *Gone With the Wind,* 1936]